PENGUIN CLASSICS

THE NEED FOR ROOTS

Simone Weil (1909–43) was a French political activist, mystic and a singular figure in French philosophy. She studied at the elite École Normale Supérieure de jeunes filles, obtained her *agrégation* (a highly competitive national teaching qualification) in philosophy in 1931, worked at Renault from 1934 to 1935, enlisted in the International Brigades in 1936 and worked as a farm labourer in 1941. She left France in 1942 for New York and then London, where she worked for General de Gaulle's Free French movement. Many of her works were published posthumously, consisting of some notebooks and a collection of religious essays. They include, in English, *Waiting for God* (1951), *Gravity and Grace* (1952), *The Need for Roots* (1952), *Notebooks* (two volumes, 1956), *Oppression and Liberty* (1958) and *Selected Essays, 1934–1943* (1962).

Ros Schwartz is an award-winning translator from French. Acclaimed for her new version of Antoine de Saint-Exupéry's *The Little Prince*, published in 2010, she has over 100 fiction and non-fiction titles to her name. Ros contributed a chapter to the academic publication *The Translator as Writer* (Continuum, 2007), and regularly writes for professional journals as well as giving talks and translation workshops around the world, and mentoring. The French government made Ros a Chevalier de l'Ordre des Arts et des Lettres in 2009, and in 2017 she was awarded the Institute of Translation and Interpreting's John Sykes Memorial Prize for Excellence.

Kate Kirkpatrick is Fellow in Philosophy at Regent's Park College, University of Oxford. She is the author of several books and articles on twentieth-century French philosophy, including *Sartre on Sin: Between Being and Nothingness* (Oxford University Press, 2017), *Sartre and Theology* (Bloomsbury, 2017), and the internationally acclaimed biography of Simone de Beauvoir, *Becoming Beauvoir: A Life* (Bloomsbury, 2019).

SIMONE WEIL

The Need for Roots

Prelude to a Declaration of Obligations towards the Human Being

Translated by
ROS SCHWARTZ
With an Introduction by
KATE KIRKPATRICK

PENGUIN BOOKS

PENGUIN CLASSICS

UK | USA | Canada | Ireland | Australia
India | New Zealand | South Africa

Penguin Books is part of the Penguin Random House group of companies
whose addresses can be found at global.penguinrandomhouse.com

First published in French as *L'Enracinement* by Gallimard 1949
First published in English 1952
This edition published by Penguin Classics 2023
002

Translation copyright © Ros Schwartz, 2023
Introduction copyright © Kate Kirkpatrick, 2023
Notes copyright © Ros Schwartz, Kate Kirkpatrick, 2023

This book is supported by the Institut Français (Royaume-Uni) as part of the Burgess programme.

The moral rights of the translator have been asserted

Set in 10.25/12.25pt Sabon LT Std
Typeset by Jouve (UK), Milton Keynes
Printed and bound in Great Britain by Clays Ltd, Elcograf S.p.A.

The authorized representative in the EEA is Penguin Random House Ireland,
Morrison Chambers, 32 Nassau Street, Dublin D02 YH68

A CIP catalogue record for this book is available from the British Library

ISBN: 978-0-241-46797-8

www.greenpenguin.co.uk

MIX
Paper | Supporting
responsible forestry
FSC® C018179

Penguin Random House is committed to a
sustainable future for our business, our readers
and our planet. This book is made from Forest
Stewardship Council® certified paper.

Contents

Introduction

What do I love when I love my country? What do we need when we need to be free, or to belong? How does this love – how do these needs – go wrong? Such questions often go unasked – and when they are asked, it is not always with equal urgency. In early 1943, however, when France was occupied by Nazi Germany and Simone Weil was exiled in London, they weighed heavily on her heart. 'France,' she wrote, 'has no reality today other than memories and hope.'*

Like its author, the book before you defies classification. Originally written in the offices of the Fighting France movement (more commonly known by its previous name, the Free France), *The Need for Roots* responds to questions raised by war and resistance, and to visions of political reconstruction after liberation.† What must the Free France be and do? What conditions would be needed to establish a country that could legitimately demand devotion? Weil begins, famously, with a rejection of the primacy and efficacy of rights. The people of 1789 – the people of the French Revolution, who drafted and fêted the *Declaration of the Rights of Man and of the Citizen*, whose title Weil acknowledges and contests in her own – declared certain

---

* See p. 77.
† Following the defeat of the French Third Republic and the formation of the German puppet state of Vichy France under the leadership of Marshal Pétain, Charles de Gaulle fled to Britain. Free France (*France Libre*) was the government in exile established under his leadership in London after the Fall of France in June 1940. It was officially renamed 'Fighting France' (*France Combattante*) in July 1942, but much Weil scholarship refers to this government by the better-known 'Free France' even when referring to its activities after this date.

rights universal. We are born free, they said, and remain equal in rights. The only permissible forms of social distinction – of hierarchy between equals – must be founded on the common good. Needless to say, it did not take a century and a half or the atrocities of Nazism to reveal the rift between this rhetoric and reality.

At the time of their declaration, only 'active citizens' of France – male property owners aged over twenty-five – were entitled to the rights called 'universal'. In 1791 Olympe de Gouges published the *Declaration of the Rights of Woman and of the Female Citizen*, decrying the hypocrisy of a government that proclaimed universal rights of man and denied the 'natural, inalienable, and sacred' rights of woman. In the nineteenth and early twentieth centuries, French colonial expansion relied on violence and coercion, violated its own democratic values, and designated colonized persons 'subjects', not citizens. No number of proclamations would overcome the simple fact, as Weil saw it, that without recognition rights do not amount to much. A right, she claims, 'is not effective on its own, but solely in relation to the obligation to which it corresponds'.*

After the Fall of France in June 1940, the grief of the occupied and the exiled found a common outlet in wondering: How did this happen? Military strategy could only explain so much. What had caused the moral deterioration that led not only to defeat, but to capitulation to and collaboration with the Nazis in the Vichy government? Even if the territory of France could be re-won, how could the spirits of its people recover from this degradation? By the time Weil wrote *The Need for Roots*, she and many interlocutors had been debating these questions for years. Her classical and philosophical education did not leave her ignorant of the myriad nations and peoples who had suffered military and moral downfall. But this was different, she thought, because the first half of the twentieth century was characterized by a strikingly new

* See p. 3.

phenomenon: 'the weakening and near disappearance of the concept of value.'*

Since May of 1942 Weil had been travelling with the aim of returning to occupied territory – first leaving the then-unoccupied Marseille for New York. She had an idea to take nurses to the front line, but it wasn't gaining much traction.† Through an old classmate – Maurice Schumann, a fellow student of the philosopher Émile-Auguste Chartier ('Alain') – she was recommended to André Philip, the Minister of the Interior in General de Gaulle's government in exile in London. In a letter to Weil dated 14 September, Philip wrote to introduce himself, writing that he had known of her for a long time, 'having read many of her articles with admiration before the war'.‡ He was coming to New York, and he hoped to see her.

Two things happened during his visit that played a significant role in the origins of this work. First, Weil attended a lecture given by Philip, in which he called for the moral and spiritual renovation of France. The Free France, he claimed, had different and superior values to those of Vichy – Free French values were universal, and 'centred on the fundamental

---

* Simone Weil, 'The Responsibilities of Literature' in *Simone Weil: Late Philosophical Writings*, ed. Eric O. Springsted, Notre Dame: University of Notre Dame Press, 2015, p. 152. According to Weil, the concept of value is 'at the center of philosophy', and knowingly or not it is present to our minds every day – our thoughts and actions are directed towards things we consider good. But we rarely direct our thoughts to reflect on the values we live by, or the hierarchy of things we consider good. Why? One reason, Weil surmised, is that we do not believe 'we have reason enough' for holding the values we do. (See 'The Concept of Value' in *Simone Weil: Late Philosophical Writings*, p. 30.)

† See Simone Weil, *Œuvres complètes, IV 1: Écrits de Marseille (1940–1942). Philosophie, science, religion, questions politiques et sociales*, Paris, Gallimard, 2008, pp. 402–4. Subsequent references to Weil's *Œuvres completes* in this series will be given with the abbreviation OC and the volume numbers.

‡ Cited by Florence de Lussy, 'Présentation', *L'Enracinement ou Prélude à une déclaration des devoirs envers l'être humain*, Paris: Flammarion, 2014, p. 16. Subsequent references to this edition of *L'enracinement* are given with the abbreviation ENR and the page number.

idea of the sacred character of the human person.'* He called
for a new declaration of human rights, which he said would be
'a profession of faith.'†

Second, Philip interviewed Weil for a position in the Com-
missariat for the Interior in London. She was hired to work in
his cabinet under the joint leadership of Philip and Francis-
Louis Closon, although what exactly she would be doing there
was not clear to her when she accepted the post and crossed the
Atlantic.‡ When she arrived in London on 14 December 1942,
she hoped she would not be doing desk work for long. She
wanted to be sent on her mission, on the ground, on the continent. As Closon put it: 'She wanted to rejoin the French, share
their misery, commune with them in their misfortune.'§ When
de Gaulle read Weil's plan to parachute nurses onto battlefields
to minister to the wounded, armed only with their own compassion, he put it down and exclaimed: 'she's crazy!'¶

Instead, Weil would spend her days in Mayfair, in an office
at 19 Hill Street near Berkeley Square, where she received
reports from France, edited them, and wrote. She wrote so
much in this period – the final chapter of her life – that her
friend and biographer Simone Pétrement describes her prod-
uctivity as 'almost beyond belief'.** The titles and sheer
number of her labours in London show the range and intensity
of her preoccupations: in addition to fragments and letters she

---

* ENR 429. Philip's lecture, 'Les fondements juridiques et moraux de la resistance française', was delivered on 7 November 1942 and is available in French
in ENR and in English in Eric O. Springsted and Ronald Collins (ed.), *A Declaration of Duties Toward Humankind: A Critical Companion to Simone
Weil's The Need for Roots*, Durham, NC: Carolina Academic Press, 2022,
Appendix II, 'The Legal and Moral Foundations of the Resistance'. See the
introduction to this work for more information on Weil's time in New York. I
am grateful to the authors for their correspondence and for sharing their work
with me in advance of its publication.

† ENR 432.

‡ Simone Pétrement, *Simone Weil: A Life*, trans. Raymond Rosenthal, New
York : Pantheon Books, 1976, p. 491.

§ See Francis-Louis Closon, *Le Temps des passions. De Jean Moulin à La
Libération (1943–1944)*, Paris: Presses de la Cité, 1974, pp. 32–5.

¶ Pétrement, *Simone Weil*, p. 514. In French: 'elle est folle!'

** Pétrement, *Simone Weil*, p. 492.

wrote essays, notebook entries and reports on topics including 'What Is Sacred in Every Human Being?', 'Are We Fighting for Justice?', 'The Legitimacy of the Provisional Government', 'Draft for a Statement of Obligations', 'Remarks on the New Constitutional Project', 'Essential Ideas for a New Constitution', 'This War is a War of Religions', 'Reflections on Revolt', 'On the Abolition of All Political Parties', 'Is there a Marxist Doctrine?', 'Concerning the Colonial Problem in its Relation to the Destiny of the French People', 'Notes on Cleanthes, Pherecydes, Anaximander, and Philolaus', translations of extracts from the Upanishads and more – as well as, of course, *The Need for Roots* itself.

Did she sleep? We do not know how often or how much – she is reputed to have locked herself in her office overnight more than once to keep working.* Nor do we know to what extent these habits contributed to her decline and death less than ten months after her arrival in London, on 24 August 1943. We do know, however, that several Resistance committees had developed projects for the reorganization of the country after the war, and after the Allied victories in North Africa, by the end of 1942, those words – 'after the war' – had begun to seem less dreamlike and more like heralds of a nascent reality. New constitutions were discussed, and codes were drafted that included 'the duties of man and the citizen'.† It was a moment of utopian reflection, and some parts of the Resistance, as Weil saw it, wanted France to be reborn only to resurrect the old mistakes of 1789: they wanted, again, to make rights the founding basis of society. André Philip was among them: his New York lecture cited Jacques Maritain, a prominent personalist thinker who claimed that what is sacred in each human being is the 'person' or 'personality' (Fr: *la personne*).‡

---

* Pétrement, *Simone Weil*, p. 492.
† Paul Maisonneuve proposed on 25 November 1942 a fifteen-point list of 'Duties of the man and the citizen'. See Lussy, 'Présentation', ENR, p. 15.
‡ Politically, personalists claimed to offer a middle way between individualism and socialism. See Emmanuel Mounier, *Manifeste au service du personnalisme*, Paris: Éditions Ésprit, 1936; *A Personalist Manifesto*, trans. the monks of St John's Abbey, New York: Longmans, Green and Co., 1938.

Maritain, and the current of personalist thinking of which he was a part, regarded 'personality' or personhood as the fundamental concept of philosophy – it is what gives meaning to all of reality and its supreme value. Drawing on the natural law tradition, in his 1942 work *The Rights of Man and Natural Law*, Maritain argued that justice involved rendering to each their due – and that what was due each person were inalienable natural rights.* It was no secret that de Gaulle wanted a new declaration, or that Maritain's views were gaining ground, and in January 1943 Philip's New York lecture was published in the London monthly *Volontaire pour la cité chrétienne* as 'A new declaration of the rights of man'.†

Although it is important not to overstate their differences, Weil thought the approach taken by Philip and Maritain was a mistake – in fact, it made more than one mistake. When Maritain spoke of 'the rights of the human person', she objected, he combined 'two insufficient notions'.‡ Instead, she believed, the language of rights and persons should be replaced by the more 'concrete and supple' concepts of obligation and need.§

What she means by this, and the moral vision sustaining her critique of rights in *The Need for Roots*, is illuminated through the prism of another of her London writings, 'What Is Sacred in Every Human Being?'.¶ In it Weil writes that what the French called democracy 'wasn't working' so it was 'necessary to invent something else', something that better acknowledged the different senses of the word 'justice' and the domains to which they apply.** Weil agreed with Maritain that there is something

* Maritain's *Les Droits de l'homme et la loi naturelle* was first published in French in New York in 1942 by the Éditions de la Maison française.
† See ENR, p. 425.
‡ Simone Weil, 'What Is Sacred in Every Human Being?', trans. Eric O. Springsted, in *Simone Weil: Late Philosophical Writings*, p. 104; Simone Weil, *Écrits de Londres et dernières lettres*, Paris: Gallimard, coll. "Espoir", 1957, p. 27.
§ 'Fragment', in Simone Weil, *Écrits de Londres et New York*, Paris: Gallimard, coll. 'nrf', 2013, p. 377. References to this work will subsequently be given by the abbreviation ELN.
¶ The title in French is *'La personne et le sacré'*, a literal translation of which would be 'The Person and the Sacred'.
** Weil, 'What Is Sacred?' p. 107.

sacred about each human being. But it is not their particular 'personality': it is the impersonal fact that they are human. 'It is him, this man, wholly and simply.'* Each human being, she claims, carries the childlike expectation 'that good and not evil will be done to us, despite the experience of crimes committed, suffered, and observed.'† It is this impersonal expectation – and the surprised cry of the heart when it sees or suffers evil – that is sacred.

This sacred part of the human is not the part that lays claim to rights, which belong to a lower domain. To illustrate this lower region, Weil gives the example of a child who watches with eager entitlement to make sure he will get an equal slice of cake. The word 'justice' is used to refer to both parts of the human soul: the part that cries out in the face of evil, and the part that wants equal cake.

Maritain claimed that the value of the person, his freedom, and his rights, came under the order of things that were naturally sacred. But this was to make the penultimate ultimate, Weil objected: the person, and freedom, and rights, are all subordinate and relative to the sacred, and to the obligations we have towards other human beings. Her concern was partly that the language of rights too easily gives way to a 'spirit of haggling' and a failure to recognize what is truly valuable:

> The concept of rights is linked to that of sharing out, of exchange, of quantity. It has something of the commercial to it. It evokes legal proceedings and pleadings. Rights are always asserted in a tone of contention; and when this tone is adopted, force is not far behind to back it up, otherwise, it would be ridiculous.‡

At this level, it is impossible to keep one's eyes on the real problem. In a market stall a vendor can refuse to sell his goods if someone asks for a cheaper price – he can say 'no, I have the right not to sell for that price'. But consider a girl being forced

---

* Weil, 'What Is Sacred?' p. 104.
† Weil, 'What Is Sacred?' p. 105.
‡ Weil, 'What Is Sacred?' p. 113.

into a brothel. Are the words 'this is against my rights' adequate
to her situation?

Justice in the higher sense – the kind that satisfies the heart's
outcry – requires more than equal cake. Weil does not deny that
injustice may take the form of a violation of a right. However,
as Peter Winch puts it, 'That is not the same as saying [. . .] that
this is what the injustice consists in, even in such cases.'* Once
we recognize that a state of affairs meeting someone's rights is
conceptually distinct from its being just in this way, Weil
believed, it follows that to be satisfied with the meeting of
rights is too often to settle for less than human beings need.
And to do so is to accept a simulacrum of the good.

Weil agreed with Philip that the renovation of France and
democratic values were necessary. But the means by which she
believed this could be achieved required the transformation of
the spiritual life of human beings and a reordering of political
community founded on the unconditional, eternal obligations
that human beings are owed merely because they are human.
What was needed was new civilization attentive to the reality of
human vulnerability and need, ordered by the higher values of
justice and truth – a civilization in which no one was deprived
of community or their own integrity, in which no one made
idols of their nation, their heroes or themselves. She did not
deny the *Rights of Man* (indeed, she deliberately discusses several
of its articles with approval), but rather aimed to provide them
with a philosophical and spiritual coherence that she believed
her predecessors in 1789 – and her contemporaries in 1943 –
had failed to deliver.

It is little wonder that this work divides its readers – after all,
such a country hardly seems deliverable. Soon after the appearance of its first edition in France in 1949, the prominent
personalist Emmanuel Mounier wrote that it was impossible
to imagine 'a text apparently less political'. This phrase is
sometimes cited as evidence that Mounier belongs to that category of interpreters who read Weil as a cloud-dwelling mystic

* See Peter Winch, *Simone Weil: 'The Just Balance'*, Cambridge: Cambridge
University Press, 1989, p. 181.

rather than as a practical philosopher firmly rooted in the worldly concerns of needs, work and political action. However, Mounier's review continues to say that it is impossible to imagine a text 'that also induces us in a more pressing way to reflect on what is political and what is not, to ask ourselves if we are not being permanently coerced by those who have an interest in maintaining a certain way of doing politics as being the only serious one.'* Philosopher Michel Alexandre claimed that it 'reopens everything', 'dominating Marx, and taking up the Gospel and Kant.'†

Despite its unwieldy, unworldly moments, it is wrong to dismiss *The Need for Roots*, as T. S. Eliot does, as a 'prolegomena to politics' whose author was a genius but whose message is fit for limited consumption by the young and idealistic.‡ In speaking to the problems of her time, Simone Weil spoke to the experience of hypocrisy in the face of hunger, indifference in the face of injustice and power that had forgotten its purpose. For Weil, it is not enough to say 'these we will always have with us' – we must resist the customs and culture that cultivate them.

To do so, and to accept many of the claims of this work, Weil believed a certain faith was necessary. Although it was not published in the first editions of *L'Enracinement*, Weil's manuscript for the work you are about to read includes a 'Profession of faith' as the preamble to her *Prelude*. It declares that:

> There is a reality situated outside the world, which is to say outside space and time, outside the mental universe of human beings, outside every domain that human faculties can attain.

* Emmanuel Mounier, 'Simone Weil: *L'Enracinement*', *Esprit* 18:1 (1950): pp. 172–4, p. 173.
† See Florence de Lussy, 'Présentation', ENR, p. 55.
‡ T. S. Eliot, 'Preface' to *The Need for Roots*, trans. Arthur Wills, London: Routledge, 2003, p. xiv.

It is to this reality that the need for an absolute good at the centre of the human heart responds, never finding any object to meet it in this world. [. . .]

The unique intermediary by which the good can descend into the milieu of men are those among men who have their attention and their love turned towards her.*

Faith, she would go on to write in *The Need for Roots*, is 'more realist than realist politics'.†

Weil's wide-ranging and idiosyncratic blend of philosophy, politics and mysticism has produced a diverse secondary literature – not to mention her use of classics, history and biblical sources. The book was divided into three sections by its first editors, each of which might seem, at first glance, easier to classify alone; but even so, trying to describe them individually is like dancing with a partner who keeps moving in directions you didn't expect. In the divisions imposed by Weil's editors, the first part contains the prelude for the new declaration, which, if not exactly what de Gaulle wanted, was what Weil thought France needed. The second is an essay on the concepts of uprootedness and re-rootedness. But how to describe the third? Florence de Lussy claims that it resolutely 'leaves the political domain' and classifies it as a 'metaphysico-religious meditation'.‡ But there are reasons to think that in Weil's picture true religion cannot leave the political domain. In her view, true religion is a call to love this world, not to retreat from it – and a politics that retreats from the truths of religion mistakes shadows for the fullness of reality.

Since the question of how to understand the whole of this text in relation to its parts is debated, and since discussion of the original editors' parts are prevalent in scholarly literature, I will briefly outline the division of the text that shaped Weil's twentieth-century reception in English. In Part I Weil lists fifteen needs of the human soul: order, freedom, obedience,

---

* Weil, 'Profession de foi', ELN, p. 96.
† See p. 163.
‡ 'Présentation', ENR, pp. 10–11.

responsibility, equality, hierarchy, honour, punishment, freedom of opinion, security, risk, private property, collective
property, truth, rootedness. Some of these correspond to articles of the *Declaration of the Rights of Man and the Citizen*,
and some to points raised by Philip's lecture, among other
interlocutors. In outlining each need Weil takes pains to distinguish between what truly nourishes the soul and 'poisons
which, for a time, may give the illusion of taking its place'.*

Her vision is radical. She conceives of order, for example, as
'a web of social relations such that no one is forced to violate
strict obligations in order to fulfil other obligations'. Imagine a
poor parent with an ill child. He is a labourer who is not paid
if he does not work. He needs to work, for his own sake, for
others', and to feed his child. He needs not to work, to care for
her. His obligations conflict in a way that societies should not
tolerate: human communities should not be ordered in such a
way that their members are 'wounded in their love of the good'.
What would human life have to be, not to be divided from oneself and others?

Of the fifteen needs Weil discusses, she claims that 'Rootedness' is 'perhaps the most important and least acknowledged
human spiritual need' but also among the hardest to define:

> A person is rooted through their real, active and natural partici-
> pation in the life of a community that keeps alive treasures of the
> past and has aspirations for the future. This participation is nat-
> ural in that it stems automatically from place, birth, occupation
> and the surrounding community. Every human being needs to
> have multiple roots and to derive almost all their moral, intel-
> lectual and spiritual life from the environment to which they
> naturally belong.†

In Part II she discusses uprootedness and the different forms
this social disease takes in contemporary contexts of labour,
including industrial labour, rural labour, prostitution and more.

* See p. 8.
† See p. 33.

Drawing on more than a decade's reflection on the value of work in capitalist societies, and first-hand experience of labour in factories and fields, Weil claims that the new civilization France should aspire to be would be 'a civilization built on the spirituality of work'.* But building such a civilization faces several challenges, including false conceptions of greatness and patriotism.

Invoking the lexicon of her predecessor Pascal, Weil describes human beings as capable of 'greatness' (*grandeur*) and 'baseness' (*bassesse*). For Pascal, 'greatness' refers to the heights humanity can reach. We glimpse it when we encounter those exemplars of excellence who make us wonder at human possibility and genius. 'Baseness', by contrast, refers to the depths – in seeing it we often wish to avert our gaze from what humanity is capable of. Pascal wrote that the greatest baseness of humanity was the search for glory, but that this was also the greatest mark of humanity's excellence.† We crave the admirable and to be admired: but in doing so we are not always discerning about the true object of our desires.

For Pascal, greatness occurs in different orders, and the occupants of one order are often incapable of seeing the greatness of others':

> The greatness of intellectual people is not visible to kings, rich men, captains, to all whose greatness is of the flesh.
>
> The greatness of wisdom, which is nothing if it does not come from God, is not visible to fleshly or intellectual people. They are three orders differing in kind.‡

* See p. 73.
† Blaise Pascal, *Pensées*, trans. A. J. Krailsheimer, London: Penguin, 1966, p. 179. Because the manuscript for Pascal's *Pensées* was left unfinished, different editions have proliferated with different numbering for the fragments. Louis Lafuma respects the provisional classification suggested by the order of MS copies, so in references to the *Pensées* I have provided the Lafuma fragment number preceded by the letter L. Here, L470.
‡ Pascal, *Pensées*, p. 124. L308. Translation adapted.

'Greatness' is an important feature of Weil's provocative challenge to her compatriots: what is our conception of glory? Is it any different from Hitler's?

Ranging widely over times, thinkers and texts, Weil offers a genealogy of French conceptions of patriotism from her distinctive axiological perspective. Appealing again to the 'regions' or 'domains' of justice, she distinguishes false patriotism from true patriotism. After the Revolution, the roots of French patriotism became unstable – they could no longer love the past or the greatness of France in the same way, having so violently broken with it. Weil blames 'uprooted intellectuals', the eighteenth-century *Encyclopédistes*, for the lack of rootedness in the liberation movement.* 'The feeling that went by the name of patriotism' in the post-revolutionary period, she says, 'was love of the sovereign nation, based to a large extent on pride in belonging.'†

But this is an ersatz love: 'The state is a cold thing that cannot be loved, but it kills and abolishes everything that could be loved, so we are forced to love it because that is all there is. Such is the moral torment of our contemporaries'.‡ True patriotism consists in 'compassion for one's country', because 'compassion' is the form of love that is fitting for things that are earthly, temporal, fallible and destructible. Some of Weil's contemporaries (before 1940) spoke of the 'eternal France'. But to do so, she thought, was to fail to love their country truly – to elevate something temporal to the eternal was idolatry.

In analysing the conditions that led to the Fall of France in June of 1940, Weil claims that one component was that the French had only France to be faithful to. In doing so she interrogates a core value of Republicanism – the distinctive form of French secularism, or *laïcité*. Prior to the Revolution of 1789, Roman Catholicism had been the state religion of France, tracing its history to the conversion of Clovis I in 508 CE. Article 10 of the *Declaration of*

---

* The *Encyclopédistes* contributed to the development of the *Encyclopédie*, edited by Denis Diderot and Jean le Rond d'Alembert, from 1751–1765. See p. 84.
† See p. 85.
‡ See pp. 87–8.

the Rights of Man and the Citizen states that 'No one may be disturbed on account of his opinions, even religious ones, as long as
the manifestation of such opinions does not interfere with the
established Law and Order.' In the nineteenth century, France
began a programme of national secularization – including forbidding religious instruction in schools – and in 1905 a law was
passed establishing state secularism.*

Weil agreed with the secularists that narrow and dogmatic religious education was harmful and to be avoided. But even so, she
did not think they had chosen the lesser evil. She thought it was a
greater harm not to teach children the 'spiritual treasures' that
were to be found in the religious texts and traditions of both
Christian and non-Christian civilizations. Moreover, she believed
it was a mistake to conceive of religion as a private matter; people
feel they were born for sacrifice, and in a context where the state
sets itself up as an absolute, 'there was no other form of sacrifice
left in the public imagination than [. . .] sacrifice offered to the
state'. To resist this void of values and the 'idolatrous tendency' of
totalitarianism, what is needed is 'an authentic spiritual life'.†

This is not to say, however, that idolatrous tendencies only
tempt secularists. Some Christians were also guilty of false patriotism of a different kind, for 'A Christian has only one country,
which is outside this world.' For the Christian, a certain love of
country is forbidden: 'for the proper object of love is good, and
"No one is good except God alone"'.‡

At its crux, Weil's objection to French patriotism was that
'universal French values' were morally incoherent and spiritually intolerable. They avoided facing their inherent contradiction,
namely that 'justice has no nationality'. The demands of our
obligations are not limited; countries have boundaries that –
when considered from a certain level – draw false limits. What
people need is 'a concept of patriotism subordinate to justice'.*

---

* The Jules Ferry educational reforms forbidding religious instructions in
schools were instituted in 1881–1882; the 1905 law is the *Loi du 9 décembre
1905 concernant la séparation des Églises et de l'État.*
† See pp. 98, 99.
‡ See p. 102.

We cannot look to any country's past and say that justice has always been served, that its history is only good. Writing against the danger of 'my country right or wrong' thinking, Weil claims that true love of country – compassion – is 'alert to good and evil and finds reasons to love in both'.*

That we have limitlessness obligations to others, she says, is 'a fundamental contradiction in the human condition'. It is not easy to bear, so we try to escape it by lying to ourselves – fleeing the weight for the easier burden of self-deception. Some try to escape through false mysticism: they flee the world, failing to see that 'It is only through the things and beings here on Earth that human love can break through to what lies beyond.' Some try to escape through idolatry, by making aspects of the finite world absolute. And some try to escape by denying obligations. But this, Weil says, is 'spiritual suicide'. For our souls hunger for truth like bodies for food, and the truth is that 'We must accept our situation, which subjects us to absolute obligations towards things that are relative, limited and imperfect.'†

In Part III – Rootedness – Weil turns to the problem of finding a method to inspire a people to turn towards this truth and outlines several obstacles to building this new civilization. She names four of particular concern: 'our false conception of glory; the deterioration of our sense of justice; our idolatry of money and the absence within us of any religious inspiration.' She returns to the importance of education and to the concept of greatness. Like patriotism, *grandeur* comes in true and false forms; human admiration does not always arise from worthy objects. What the new civilization needs is a manner of educating that enables the good to descend from its domain into the world of human matters.

Education – whether aimed at children or adults, individuals or a people, or even oneself – consists in creating motives. It is the job of teaching to impart what is beneficial, what is obligatory and what is good.‡

* See p. 134.
† See p. 122.
‡ See p. 144.

In her 'Profession of Faith', Weil claimed that the unique intermediary of the good was those exemplary human beings 'who
have their attention and their love turned towards [the good]'.*
Instead of cultivating admiration for the just and compassion-
ate, false greatness glorified conquest and injustice. It is an idol
that has been transmitted throughout the centuries, so much so
that:

> It is a general law. It also governs literature and the arts, for
> example. There is a certain dominance of literary talent over the
> centuries that echoes the dominance of political talent in space;
> they are dominances of the same kind, also temporal, also
> belonging to the sphere of matter and force, equally base. They
> can also be the subject of trade and commerce.†

To love the past in this false sense of greatness is to forget all
those whose greatness was not recognized, who left no words
or wars in their wake.‡

Are these thoughts of divine inspiration, human genius or
utopian delusion? The reader can only answer this question for
themselves. In any case, Weil's curious cocktail of Plato and
Pascal, Scripture and Karl Marx, is the best kind of challenging
companion – reading it offers many invitations to re-read your
society and yourself.

Simone Weil was an extraordinary woman, but there is no
doubt that she was very ordinary in one sense: she lacked perfection. During her lifetime she felt this lack keenly, but readers
today may find her imperfect in new ways. Given Weil's preoccupation with words and the evil they can inflict, some may
recoil from her seeming acceptance and repetition of the pre-
judices of her time. How can the thinker who scathingly criticized

---

* Weil, 'Profession de foi', ELN, p. 96.
† See pp. 178–9.
‡ Part of Weil's objection to personalism was that it capitulated to grandeur in
this aggrandizing sense: it made the value of human beings relative. This is not
merely a matter of class analysis – Weil's objection is not merely that the personalists were bourgeois – but that they failed to locate the true locus of
human value. See 'What Is Sacred?', p. 111.

French colonialism, the France 'bent on carving out its portion of yellow and black flesh across the world',* use words like *indigène* or savage? Or metaphors of slavery? Her use of biblical, classical and historical sources has alienated many on grounds of methodology, accuracy and ethics. She does not conform to contemporary academic expectations or neatly fit into any categories: she was Jewish and Christian with caveats; she drew selectively from texts and traditions in ways that may seem strange (or worse) to those who hold them dear. But, however she came to write them, these are the words she wrote – I hope they can still be read with the healthy scepticism that is midwife to curiosity. This work has been compared to Augustine's *City of God*, Plato's *Timaeus*, and Spinoza's *Tractatus Theologico-Politicus* – and should be read with no less openness and generosity.†

In a letter to her parents written during its writing Simone Weil described *L'Enracinement* her second 'great work' ('*grand oeuvre*'),‡ after *Reflexions sur la causes de la liberté et de l'oppression sociale* (1934).§ But she would not live to see the outcome of its impetus. The *Declaration of the Rights of Man and the Citizen* was included, after the war's end, in the constitution of the Fourth French Republic (1946). Many of its principles also informed the Universal Declaration of Human Rights, proclaimed by the United Nations General Assembly in Paris on 10 December 1948 as 'a common standard of achievements for all peoples and all nations'.¶

After her death in England in 1943, Weil's family was unable to retrieve her manuscripts until they returned to Europe from

---

* See p. 150.

† For Augustine, see Patrice Rolland, 'Avant-propos I', in NRF, p. 45; for Plato, see Chenavier, 'Avant-propos II', in NRF, p. 46; for Spinoza, Emmanuel Gabellieri, *Simone Weil*, Paris : Éditions Ellipses, 2001, p. 26.

‡ Simone Weil, Lettre à ses parents, 22 mai 1943. *Œuvres complètes VII 1, Correspondance I. Correspondance familiale*, Paris: Gallimard, 2012, p. 280.

§ 'Reflections on the Causes of Liberty and Social Oppression' (1934), in Simone Weil, *Oppression and Liberty*, trans. Arthur Wills and John Petrie, London: Routledge 2001.

¶ For the UN Declaration see https://www.un.org/en/about-us/universal-declaration-of-human-rights.

the United States after the war. Her parents entrusted the publication of the *Prelude to a Declaration of Obligations towards the Human Being* to Boris Souvarine (a founding member of the French Communist Party, and a close friend of Simone) who arranged for it to be published by Gallimard. In 1949 it appeared in their *Espoir* collection, edited by Albert Camus. There it was given the title by which it has since been known, *L'enracinement.**

Kate Kirkpatrick

---

* For more on Weil's manuscript and variants, see the two introductory essays by Florence de Lussy in ENR. Here, '*Histoire du manuscrit*', ENR, pp. 63–6. See also Springsted and Collins, 'Introduction'.

THE NEED FOR ROOTS

The concept of obligations takes precedence over that of rights, which are subordinate and relative to it. A right is not effective on its own, but solely in relation to the obligation to which it corresponds. The successful fulfilment of a right comes not from the person who possesses it, but from others who recognize that they have an obligation towards that person. The obligation takes effect once it is recognized. If an obligation is not recognized by anyone, it loses nothing of the plenitude of its being. But a right that is not recognized by anyone amounts to very little.[1]

It makes no sense to say that people have rights on the one hand and duties on the other. These terms express only differences of opinion. Their relationship is that of object and subject. A man, considered on his own, has only duties, including certain duties towards himself. Others, considered from his point of view, have only rights. He in turn has rights when he is considered from the point of view of others who recognize obligations towards him. A man alone in the world would have no rights, but he would have obligations.

The notion of rights, being of an objective order, cannot be separated from that of existence and reality. It appears when obligation descends into the realm of fact, and therefore always takes into account to some extent states of affairs and particular situations. Rights always appear to be associated with certain conditions. Obligation alone can be unconditional. The domain of obligations is situated above all conditions because it is above this world.

The people of 1789 did not recognize the existence of such a domain. They only recognized that of human matters. That is why they started from the notion of rights. But, at the same time, they wanted to lay down absolute principles. This contradiction resulted in a confusion of language and ideas which is largely responsible for the current political and social confusion. The domain of what is eternal, universal and unconditional is different from that conditioned by fact and contains different concepts, ones that link to the innermost recesses of the human soul.

Obligations are only binding on human beings. There are no obligations for collectivities as such. But there are obligations for all human beings who make up, serve, command or represent a collectivity, both in the part of their lives that is tied to the collectivity and in that which is independent of it.

Identical obligations bind all human beings, even though they correspond to different actions in different situations. No human being, whoever they are, can escape them under any circumstances without committing a crime, except in cases where, if two real obligations are incompatible, they are forced to relinquish one of them.

The imperfection of a social order is measured by the number of such conflicting situations it contains.

But, even in such a case, there is a crime if the relinquished obligation is not only relinquished but is also denied.

In the domain of human matters, the object of an obligation is always the human being as such. There is an obligation towards every human being through the mere fact that they are a human being, without the need for any other condition to be satisfied, and even if they do not recognize the obligation towards them.

[. . .]gard to all hum[an] beings

All human beings, in all individual or collective relations, are bound by a certain obligation towards every human being, and that solely from the fact that they are a human being, without any other condition being needed.

This obligation is not based on any de facto situation, or on legal precedent, or on customs, social structure or relations of force, or on the legacy of the past, or the supposed direction of history. Because no de facto situation can give rise to an obligation.

This obligation is not based on any convention because all conventions are modifiable according to the wishes of the contracting parties, whereas no change desired by humans can modify anything [*of this obligation*] at all.

This obligation is eternal. It echoes the eternal destiny of human beings. Only human beings have an eternal destiny. Human collectivities do not. Therefore, there are no direct eternal obligations to human collectivities. The only eternal obligation is that towards the human being as such.

This obligation is unconditional. If it is founded on something, that something does not belong to our world. In our world, it is founded on nothing. It is the only obligation related to human matters that is unconditional.

This obligation has not a foundation, but only a verification in the common consent accorded by the universal consciousness. It is expressed in some of the most ancient texts that have come down to us. It is recognized by all in every individual case where it is not opposed by interests or passions. It is the yardstick by which we measure progress.

The recognition of this obligation is expressed in a confused and imperfect manner, to a greater or lesser degree depending on each case, by what we call positive rights.[2] Insofar as positive rights are in contradiction with this obligation, to that precise extent they bear the hallmark of illegitimacy.

Although this eternal obligation echoes the human being's eternal destiny, this destiny is not its direct object. A human being's eternal destiny cannot be the object of any obligation because it is not subordinate to external actions.

The fact that a human being has an eternal destiny imposes only one obligation, that of respect. The obligation is only fulfilled if respect is effectively expressed, in a real and not a fictitious manner. This can only be done through the intermediary of humans' earthly needs.

Human conscience has never varied on this matter. Thousands of years ago, the Egyptians thought that a soul could not justify itself after death unless it could say: 'I let no one suffer from

hunger'.[3] All Christians know that one day they are likely to hear
Christ himself say to them: 'I was hungry and you fed me not'.[4]
Everyone imagines progress as being first and foremost reaching
a state of human society in which people will not suffer from
hunger. If we ask the question in general terms to anyone, nobody
thinks a man is innocent if, having an abundance of food and
finding on his doorstep someone three-quarters dead from hunger, he walks past without giving them anything.

It is therefore an eternal obligation to a human being not to
let them suffer from hunger when one has the opportunity to
help them. This obligation being the most obvious, it should
serve as the model for drawing up the list of eternal duties
towards all human beings. In the interests of rigour, this list
should be developed from this first example through analogy.

The list of obligations to human beings must correspond
therefore to the list of vital human needs that are comparable
to hunger.

Among these needs, some are physical, such as hunger itself.
These are easy enough to enumerate and include protection
against violence and the provision of shelter, clothing, warmth,
hygiene and care for the sick.

Others, among these needs are related not to physical life,
but to moral life. These too, however, are earthly and have no
direct connection with man's eternal destiny, so far as our intelligence can grasp. But like the physical needs, they are necessities
of life here below. In other words, if they are not satisfied, man
gradually falls into a deathlike, almost purely vegetative state.

These moral needs are much harder to identify and list than
the needs of the body. But everyone recognizes that they
exist. All the cruelties a conqueror can impose on subjugated
peoples – massacres, mutilations, organized famine, enslave-
ment and mass deportations – are generally considered to be
measures of the same ilk, although freedom or a native country
are not physical necessities. Everyone is aware that there are
cruelties that affect man's life without harming his body. They
are the ones that deprive man of a certain food necessary for
the life of the soul.

Obligations to human matters – unconditional or relative,

eternal or changing, direct or indirect – all derive, without exception, from human beings' vital needs. Those that do not directly concern a particular human being all have as their object needs that are comparable to that for food.

Respect is owed to a field of wheat, not for itself, but because it provides food for human beings.

In an analogous way, respect should be given to a collectivity of any kind – country, family, or other – not for itself, but because it provides food for a certain number of human souls.

This obligation in fact demands different attitudes and different actions according to different situations. But considered in itself, it is absolutely identical for all.

In particular, it is absolutely identical for those who are inside a given collectivity and for those who are outside it.

A very high degree of respect is owed to human collectivities, for a number of reasons.

First of all, each one is unique and, if destroyed, cannot be replaced. A sack of wheat can always be substituted for another sack of wheat. The food a collectivity gives its members' souls has no equivalent anywhere in the entire universe.

Secondly, by virtue of its duration, the collectivity is already part of the future. It contains food, not only for the souls of the living, but also for the souls of unborn beings who will enter the world in centuries to come.

Lastly, by virtue of the same duration, the collectivity has its roots in the past. It is the sole repository for the spiritual treasures amassed by the dead; it is the vehicle through which the dead can speak to the living. And the only earthly thing that has a direct connection to man's eternal destiny is the influence of those who have become fully aware of this destiny, passed on from generation to generation.

For all these reasons, the obligation towards an endangered collectivity can sometimes go as far as total sacrifice. But it does not follow that the collectivity is above the human being. It can also happen that the obligation to save a human being in distress must go so far as total sacrifice, without this implying any superiority on the part of the one being saved.

In certain circumstances, a farmer may have to risk exhaustion, sickness or even death in order to cultivate his field. But he is always aware that it is solely a question of bread.

Analogously, even when total sacrifice is demanded, a collectivity is never owed anything other than a respect on a par with that owed to food.

Very often the role is reversed. Some collectivities, instead of serving food, consume souls. In such cases there is a social disease, and the first obligation is to attempt treatment. In some circumstances, surgical methods may be required.

Here too, the obligation is identical for those inside the collectivity and for those outside it.

A collectivity may provide insufficient food for its members' souls. In such cases it must be improved.

And lastly, there are dead collectivities that do not devour souls but neither do they nourish them. If it is quite certain that they are dead and not a matter of a temporary fatigue, only then should they be annihilated.

The first question to be examined is what needs related to the life of the soul correspond to the body's needs for food, sleep and warmth. It is important to try to define and list them.

These needs must never be confused with desires, whims, fantasies or vices. It is also important to distinguish between the essential and the accidental. Man does not need rice or potatoes, but he does need food; he does not need wood or coal, but he does need heating. Likewise, for the needs of the soul,[5] we must recognize the different but equivalent satisfactions that fulfil the same needs. Similarly, it is important to distinguish between foods of the soul and the poisons which, for a time, may give the illusion of taking their place.

The lack of such a study makes well-intentioned governments act randomly.

Below are a few examples.

I

The main need of the soul, the one closest to its eternal destiny, is order – that is to say, a web of social relations such that no one is forced to violate strict obligations in order to fulfil other obligations. Only then does the soul suffer spiritual violence from external circumstances. Because someone who is prevented from fulfilling an obligation solely by the threat of death or suffering can rise above it, and will be wounded only physically. But if circumstances make actions required by several strict obligations incompatible, and they are unable to defend themselves, they are wounded in their love of the good.

Nowadays, there is a very high degree of disorder and incompatibility between obligations.

Anyone acting in such a way as to exacerbate this incompatibility is a maker of disorder. Anyone who acts in such a way as to reduce this incompatibility is a creator of order. Anyone who, to simplify matters, refuses certain obligations, has, in their heart, entered into a pact with crime.

Unfortunately, there is no method for reducing this incompatibility. It is not even certain that the idea of an order in which all obligations are compatible is not a fantasy. When duty descends to the level of facts, so many independent relationships come into play that incompatibility seems far more likely than compatibility.

But we have before us every day the example of the universe, where an infinite number of independent mechanical actions concur to create an order that remains fixed, despite variations. And so, we love the beauty of the world because we feel behind it the presence of something analogous to the wisdom we wished we possessed to satisfy our desire for the good.

To a lesser degree, truly beautiful works of art are examples of entities in which independent factors combine to form a single thing of beauty in a way that is impossible to understand.

Lastly, our awareness of our various obligations always stems from a desire for good that is unique, fixed and identical to itself for each man, from the cradle to the grave. This desire perpetually stirring inside us prevents us from ever resigning ourselves to situations where the obligations are incompatible. Either we resort to lying in order to forget they exist, or we struggle blindly to extricate ourselves from them.

The contemplation of authentic works of art, even more the contemplation of the beauty of the world and more still the contemplation of the unknown good to which we aspire, can sustain us in our effort to think continually about the human order which should be our first object.

The major makers of violence have taken encouragement from seeing how blind mechanical force is sovereign throughout the universe.

But if we look at the world more closely than they do, we will find greater encouragement if we consider how limited these innumerable blind forces are, working together in a balance, forced to compete against a unity by something we do not understand but which we love and call beauty.

If we constantly bear in mind the idea of a true human order, if we think of it as a purpose to which we owe total sacrifice when the opportunity arises, we will be in the situation of someone walking in the dark without a guide, but constantly focused on the direction they want to follow. For such a traveller there is great hope.

This order is the primary need, above even needs themselves. To be able to conceive this requires a knowledge of the other needs.

The first characteristic that distinguishes needs from desires, whims or vices, and food from delicacies or poisons, is that needs are limited, as are the foods that match them. A miser can never have enough gold, but if everyone is given unlimited bread, there will come a time when they will have enough. Food brings satiety. The same is true of the food of the soul.

The second characteristic, connected to the first, is that needs come in contrasting pairs, and must combine in a balance. Man needs food, but also an interval between meals; he needs warmth and coolness, rest and exercise. The same applies to the needs of the soul.

The so-called happy medium does not satisfy either of the contrary needs. It is a caricature of the true balance through which opposing needs are fully satisfied.

II

Freedom is a vital food for the human soul. In the concrete sense of the word, freedom means the possibility of choice. A real possibility, naturally. Wherever there is communal life, it is inevitable that choices will be restricted by rules that are necessary in the interests of the common good.

But freedom is not greater or lesser according to whether the restrictions are narrower or broader. The conditions for it to be fully achieved are less easily measurable.

Rules must be simple and reasonable enough for anyone who wishes to do so, and who has an average faculty of attention, can both understand the utility to which they correspond and the necessities of fact that impose them. Rules must emanate from an authority regarded not as a stranger or an enemy, but which is loved and seen to belong to those it governs. They must be stable, few and general enough to be assimilated into thought once and for all, and not create a conflict each time a decision has to be taken.

Under these conditions, although limited in reality, the freedom of people of good will is total to their way of thinking. Since the rules have been absorbed into their very beings, forbidden possibilities do not enter their minds and need not be rejected. Likewise, when it comes to food, for normal people, the habit of not eating repellent or dangerous things, dinned into us from childhood, is not felt as a restriction on their freedom. Only a child feels the limitation.

Those who lack good will or remain infantile are never free in any state of society.

When the possibilities of choice are so wide as to jeopardize the common good, people do not enjoy freedom. Because they need either to take refuge in irresponsibility, childishness and indifference – a refuge where they will find only boredom – or they feel overwhelmed by the responsibility in all circumstances by the fear of harming others. In such cases, people mistakenly believe that they have freedom, but because they are not enjoying it, they conclude that freedom is not a good.

III

Obedience is a vital need of the human soul. There are two kinds: obedience to established rules, and obedience to human beings regarded as leaders. It presupposes consent, not to each of the orders received, but consent granted for all time, subject only to the demands of conscience when the case arises. It must be generally recognized, and above all by leaders, that consent and not fear of punishment or the enticement of a reward is in fact the motivating force for obedience, ensuring that submission never entails servility. Furthermore, those who command must also be seen to obey, and the entire hierarchical structure must be working towards a goal whose value and even greatness is recognized by all, from the top down.

Since obedience is a necessary food for the soul, anyone who is permanently deprived of it is sick. Any collectivity governed by a sovereign leader who is accountable to no one therefore is in the hands of a sick person.

That is why, when a man is placed at the head of the social organization for life, they must be a symbol and not a leader, as exemplified by the British monarch; decency also requires that their freedom be more restricted than that of any man of the people. That way, effective leaders have someone above them even though they are leaders; on the other hand, they can replace one another, without interrupting continuity, and subsequently each receives the obedience due to them.

Those who subjugate human masses through coercion and cruelty deprive them of two vital foods – freedom and obedience – because these masses no longer have the power to give their inner consent to the authority subjecting them. Those who favour a state of affairs chiefly motivated by the enticement of gain, deprive people of obedience, for the consent that is the principle of obedience is not something that can be sold.

There are numerous indications that the people of our time had long been hungering for obedience. But this has been taken advantage of to give them slavery.

IV

Initiative and responsibility, the feeling of being useful and even indispensable, are vital needs of the human soul.

The unemployed experience total deprivation in this respect, even if they receive support so they can feed, clothe and house themselves. The unemployed count for nothing in economic life, and, for them, the ballot paper that represents their participation in political life is meaningless.

The situation of the manual labourer is barely any better.

Satisfying the need for responsibility requires a man to make frequent problem-solving decisions, big and small, concerning interests other than his own, but to which he feels committed. It also requires him to make an ongoing effort and to adapt his thinking to embrace the entire endeavour of the collectivity to which he belongs,[6] including areas in which he never has to make decisions or give advice. To do this, he must be acquainted with this endeavour, asked to take an interest in it, made aware of its value, usefulness, and, when appropriate, its greatness, and be given a clear idea of the part he plays in it.

A collectivity of any kind that does not give its members these satisfactions is flawed and must be transformed.

With strong personalities, the need to take the initiative can go as far as the need to be in charge. An intense local and regional life and a multitude of educational causes and youth movements must give everyone capable of it the opportunity to be in command at certain times in their life.

V

Equality is a vital need of the human soul. It consists of public, general, and effective recognition, concretely expressed through institutions and practices, that every human being is owed the same amount of respect and consideration because respect is due to every human being as such and has no degrees.

That means that the inevitable differences between people

must never suggest a disparity in the degree of respect. For these differences not to be felt as having this implication, there must be a certain balance between equality and inequality.

One combination of equality and inequality is equality of possibility. If anyone can attain the social rank corresponding to the function they are capable of fulfilling, and if education is so widely accessible that no one is deprived of skills by the mere fact of their birth, then all children have the same hope. Then everyone is equal in hope to everyone else, both for themselves when they are young, and later for their children.

However, this combination alone, without other factors, does not constitute a balance; on the contrary it contains great dangers.

First of all, for a man who is suffering from being in an inferior situation to know that his situation is due to his inadequacy, and that everyone else knows it, is not a consolation but a twofold cause of resentment. Depending on character, some may be ground down by this, others may turn to crime.

Then, in social life a sort of upwards suction movement is inevitably created. The result is a social disease if there is no downwards movement to counterbalance it. This means that if it really is possible for the child of a farmhand one day to be a minister, then it really should be possible for the child of a minister one day to be a farmhand. This second possibility is not realistic unless there is a very risky degree of social coercion.

If this kind of equality operates alone and without limits, it gives social life a degree of fluidity that breaks it down.

There are less crude ways of combining equality and difference. The first is proportion. Proportion is defined as the combination of equality and inequality, and everywhere in the universe it is the only balancing factor.

Applied to maintaining social balance, creating proportion would impose on each man burdens corresponding to the power and wellbeing he possesses, and corresponding risks in the case of incapacity or wrongdoing. For example, a boss who is incapable or guilty of wrongdoing towards his workers would have to suffer much more, in body and soul, than a manual worker who is incapable or guilty of wrongdoing towards his boss. Furthermore, all manual workers should know that it is so. This implies both a certain organization of risks and a conception of punishment in criminal law whereby social rank is considered an aggravating circumstance and plays a large part in determining the sentence. All the more reason why the exercise of high public office must involve serious personal risks.

Another way of making equality compatible with difference is to eliminate any quantitative element from differences as far as this is possible. Where there is only difference in nature, not in degree, there is no inequality.

Because money is seen as the sole, or almost sole, motive for nearly all actions and the sole, or almost sole, measure of all things, the poison of inequality has spread everywhere. Admittedly this inequality is mobile; it is not attached to people, because money is earned and lost; but it is still real.

There are two kinds of inequalities, corresponding to two different stimuli. Relatively stable inequality, like that of ancient France, leads to people idolizing their superiors – not without a mixture of repressed hatred – and submitting to their orders. Mobile, fluid inequality leads to a desire to rebel against it. It is no closer to equality than stable inequality, and it is just as unhealthy. In placing the emphasis on equality, the Revolution of 1789, in fact only sanctioned the substitution of one form of inequality for the other.

The more equality there is in a society, the less action there is of the two stimuli linked to the two forms of inequality, and consequently other stimuli are needed.

Equality is even greater when the different human conditions are regarded not as being either more or less than one another, but simply diverse. Let the profession of miner and that of minister simply be two different vocations, like those of poet and mathematician. Let the material hardships associated with being a miner contribute to the nobility of those who suffer them.

In wartime, if an army has the right spirit, a soldier is happy and proud to be under fire and not at headquarters; a general is happy and proud that the fate of the battle depends on his strategy, and, at the same time, the soldier admires the general and the general admires the soldier. Such a balance is an equality. There would be equality in social conditions if there were that same balance.

This implies that each condition should be given the esteem due to it, and that this esteem should not be feigned.

VI

Hierarchy is a vital need of the human soul. It comprises a certain veneration, a certain devotion, to superiors considered not in their persons or for the powers they exercise, but as symbols. What they symbolize is the domain that is above all humans, the expression of which in this world is made up of the obligations of each human being towards their fellows. True hierarchy presupposes that the superiors are conscious of this symbolic function and know that it is the only legitimate object of their subordinates' devotion. True hierarchy has the effect of ensuring that everyone morally accepts their place.

VII

Honour is a vital need of the human soul. The respect due to each human being as such, even when it is accorded, is not sufficient to satisfy this need because it is identical for everyone and is immutable. Honour, however, relates to a human being, considered not merely as such, but in their social sphere. This need is fully satisfied if each of the collectivities to which a human being belongs offers them a part in a tradition of greatness, and if that greatness is publicly recognized outside that collectivity.

For example, for the need for honour in professional life to be satisfied, each profession must be part of a collectivity that is truly capable of keeping alive the memory of the heritage of greatness, heroism, probity, generosity and genius created in the exercise of that profession.

All oppression creates a famine with regard to the need for

honour because the traditions of greatness belonging to the oppressed are not recognized, due to their lack of social prestige.

That is always the effect of conquest. Vercingetorix was no hero to the Romans. If the English had conquered France in the fifteenth century, Joan of Arc would have been generally forgotten, even to a large extent by us. Nowadays, we speak of her to the Annamites and the Arabs, but they know that we neglect to mention their heroes and saints, thus the state in which we maintain them denies them their honour.[7,8]

Social oppression has the same effects. [Georges]* Guynemer and [Jean] Mermoz are etched in the public consciousness thanks to the social prestige of aviation.[9,10] The sometimes incredible heroism of miners or fishermen hardly resonates within miner or fishing milieus.

The ultimate privation of honour is the total privation of consideration inflicted on some categories of human beings. In France, these include, in different ways, prostitutes, convicted criminals, police officers, and the sub-proletariat comprising immigrants and indigenous peoples from the colonies. Such categories should not exist.

Only crime should place the being who committed it outside social consideration, and punishment should rehabilitate them.

VIII

Punishment is a vital need of the human soul. There are two kinds, disciplinary and penal. The former offers assurance against infringement, which would be too exhausting a battle without external support. But it is the punishment of crime that is most essential to the soul. Through crime a man puts himself outside the web of eternal obligations that binds every human being to all others. He can only be reintegrated through punishment – fully if there is consent on his part, otherwise imperfectly. Just as the only way to show respect to the hungry is to give them food, so the only way to show respect to those

---

* Square brackets indicate translator's additions.

who have placed themselves outside the law is to reintegrate them by subjecting them to the punishment imposed by the law.

The need for punishment is not satisfied when the penal code is merely a process of coercion through terror, as is usually the case.

Satisfying this need requires most importantly that all matters relating to criminal law should be of a solemn and sacred character. The majesty of the law needs to be conveyed to the court, the police, the accused and the convict, even in minor cases, provided it results in the deprivation of freedom. Punishment must be an honour; it must not only eradicate the shame of the crime but should be regarded as an additional lesson that requires a greater degree of devotion to the public good. The harshness of the sentence should also reflect the nature of the obligations violated and not the interests of public security.

The discrediting of the police, the casualness of the magistrates, the prison system, ex-convicts' permanent loss of social status, the scale of penalties which provides for a much harsher punishment for ten petty thefts than for rape or some murders and even punishes simple affliction – all conspire to prevent there being anything in our society that deserves the name of punishment.

There should be a higher degree of impunity both for misdemeanours and crimes as we move down, not up, the social ladder. Otherwise, the suffering inflicted is experienced as coercion or even abuse of power and does not constitute punishment. Punishment only occurs if at some point, even afterwards, in the memory the suffering goes hand in hand with a sense of justice. Just as a musician awakens a sense of beauty through sound, so the penal system must be able to awaken a sense of justice in the criminal through pain, or even, if need be, through death. As is said of the apprentice who has injured himself that 'the vocation has entered his body', so punishment is a method of bringing justice into the soul of the criminal through the suffering of the flesh.

The question of how best to prevent a conspiracy at the top to obtain impunity is one of the thorniest political problems. It can only be resolved if one or more people are appointed to prevent such a conspiracy and are in a situation where they are not tempted to enter into one themselves.

IX

Freedom of opinion and freedom of association are often spoken of in the same breath. That is a mistake. Except in the case of natural groupings, association is not a need, but an expedient of practical life.

Conversely, total, unlimited freedom of expression for any opinion whatsoever, without any restriction or reservation, is an absolute need for the intellect. Therefore, it is a need of the soul because when the intellect is uneasy, the entire soul is sick. The nature and limits of the satisfaction of this need are part of the very structure of the different faculties of the soul. Because one same thing can be limited and unlimited, just as the length of a rectangle can be extended indefinitely while its width remains the same.

Human intelligence can be exercised in three ways. It can work on technical problems, in other words, seek the means to achieve a set goal. It can provide enlightenment when the will is torn between choices of direction and deliberation takes place. Finally, it can come into play alone, separated from the other faculties, in purely theoretical speculation from which any concern for action has been temporarily removed.

In a healthy soul, intelligence operates in these three ways in turn, with different degrees of freedom. In the first function, it is a servant. In the second, it is destructive and must be silenced the moment it starts to provide arguments to the part of the soul which, in anyone who is not in the state of perfection, always places itself on the side of evil. But when it operates alone and independently, it must have sovereign freedom. Otherwise, the human being is lacking in something essential.

The same applies to a healthy society. That is why it would be desirable to establish a reservoir of absolute freedom in the field of publishing, but in such a way that it is understood that the printed works do not bind the authors to any extent and do not contain any advice for readers. All the arguments in favour of evil causes could be set out with full force. It is good and salutary that they should be. Anyone would be able to applaud what they disapprove of most strongly. It would be common knowledge that the purpose of such books would not be to define the authors' stances on life's problems, but to contribute to preliminary research, to enumerate completely and accurately the facts relative to each problem. The law would prevent their publication from putting the author at risk in any way.

On the other hand, publications intended to influence so-called '*opinion*',[11] in other words that show how life should be conducted, constitute acts and must be subject to the same restrictions as all acts. In other words, they must not cause any illegitimate prejudice to any human being, and above all they must never contain any negation, express or implicit, of the eternal obligations to the human being, once these obligations have been solemnly recognized in law.

The distinction between the two domains – that which is external to action and that which is part of it – is impossible to formulate on paper in legal language. But that does not mean it is not perfectly clear. The dividing line between these domains is in fact easy to establish, provided there is a strong enough will to do so.

It is clear, for example, that the daily newspapers and the entire weekly press belong to the second domain. Magazines and journals too, because they all exert an influence on people's thinking; only those prepared to surrender this function would be able to boast total freedom.

The same goes for literature. It would be a solution for the recent controversy on the issue of morality and literature, and which has been clouded by the fact that all talented people, out of professional solidarity, were on the same side, and only fools and cowards on the other.[12]

But the position of the fools and cowards was nonetheless largely consistent with reason. Writers have an unacceptable tendency of trying to have it both ways. Never so much as in our time have they claimed and exercised the role of spiritual advisers. In the years leading up to the war, no one disputed that role except the scientists. The place in the country's moral life, formerly occupied by priests, was held by physicists and novelists, which is a measure of the value of our progress. But if writers were asked to be accountable with regard to the stances they took, they indignantly took refuge in the sacred privilege of art for art's sake.

Without a doubt, for example, Gide always knew that books like *The Fruits of the Earth* or *The Vatican Cellars* have had an influence on the way hundreds of young people live their lives in practice, and he was proud of it. There is therefore no reason to put such books behind the inviolable barrier of art for art's sake, or to imprison a boy who throws someone off a moving train.[13] We might as well invoke the privileged claim of art for art's sake in support of crime. At one point, the Surrealists were not so far from this. All the things that countless idiots have repeated ad nauseam, blaming our defeat on writers, is most certainly true, unfortunately.[14]

If, thanks to total freedom being granted to pure intellect, an author publishes writings contrary to the principles of morality recognized in the law, and if later that writer becomes a source of influence, it is easy to ask them if they are prepared to make it publicly known that these writings do not reflect their own views. If not, it is easy to punish them. If they are lying, it is easy to dishonour them. Besides, it should be acknowledged that once a writer takes their place among the influencers of public opinion, they cannot demand unlimited freedom of opinion. Again, a legal definition is impossible, but the facts are not that difficult to identify. There is no reason to restrict the sovereignty of the law to the domain of things that can be expressed in legal terms, since this sovereignty is also exercised through judgements of fairness.

Furthermore, the very need for freedom, so essential to the intellect, requires protection against suggestion, propaganda or influence through obsession. These are modes of coercion; a particular form of coercion does not involve fear or physical pain but is still a form of violence. Modern technology provides extremely effective tools. This coercion, by its nature, is collective, and human souls are its victims.

The state, of course, behaves criminally if it uses these means, except in cases of when it is urgent to protect the public interest. But it must also prevent the use of such techniques. Advertising, for example, should be strictly limited by law; the volume should be considerably reduced; advertising must be strictly prohibited from ever touching on topics belonging to the realm of thought.

In the same way, the press, radio broadcasts, and other media can be stifled, not only for damaging publicly recognized principles of morality, but also for baseness of tone and thought, bad taste, vulgarity and an insidiously corrupting moral tone. This can be done without affecting freedom of opinion in the least. For example, a newspaper can be closed down without the editorial staff losing the right to publish wherever they choose, or even, in less serious cases, to stay together and carry on publishing the same journal under another name. Only it will have been publicly shamed and risks being so again. Freedom of opinion is the right only, and with reservations, of the journalist and not the newspaper, because the journalist alone has the ability to form an opinion.

Generally speaking, all the problems relating to freedom of expression become clearer if we posit that this freedom is a need of the intellect, and that intellect resides solely in the individual human being. There is no collective exercise of the intellect. Consequently, no collective body can legitimately demand freedom of expression because no group has the slightest need for it.

Quite the contrary, protecting freedom of thought requires that the law prohibits a group from expressing an opinion. Because when a group begins to have opinions, it inevitably tends to impose them on its members. Sooner or later, individuals are prevented to a greater or lesser extent from expressing an opinion contrary to those of the group on a range of issues of varying degrees of magnitude, unless they leave. But breaking away from a group of which one is a member is always painful, or at least emotionally so. And while risk and the possibility of pain are healthy and necessary elements of action, they are unhealthy in the exercise of the intellect. A fear, even slight, always causes either a bowing or a hardening, depending on the degree of courage, and that is all it takes to distort the extremely delicate and fragile precision instrument that comprises intelligence. In this regard, even friendship is a great danger. Intelligence is eroded as soon as the expression of thought is preceded, explicitly or implicitly, by the little word 'we'. And when the light of intelligence is dimmed, it is not long before the love of good gets lost.

The immediate practical solution is the abolition of political parties. The struggle between parties, as it existed in the Third Republic, is intolerable; the single party, which is in fact the inevitable outcome, is the extreme degree of evil; there is no other possibility but a public life without parties. These days, such an idea sounds like something new and bold. Good, because we need something new. But in actual fact, it is simply the tradition of 1789. In the eyes of the people of 1789, there was no other possibility even; a public life such as ours over the past half-century would have seemed to them like a hideous nightmare; they would never have believed it possible that a representative of the people could abandon their dignity to the point of becoming a disciplined member of a party.

Rousseau, incidentally, had clearly shown that the struggle between parties automatically killed the Republic. He predicted the effects. It would be useful at this point for people to be encouraged to read *The Social Contract*. In fact, nowadays, wherever there have been political parties, democracy has died. It is well known that the English parties have traditions, a spirit, a function that makes them incomparable to anything else. It is also well known that the United States' rival teams are not political parties. A democracy where public life comprises the struggle between political parties is unable to prevent the formation of a party that has the stated aim of destroying it.[15] If it introduces exemption laws, it suffocates itself. If it does not, it is as safe as a bird faced with a snake.

It is important to distinguish between two types of groups: interest groups, for which organization and discipline would be permitted to a certain extent, and associations for promoting ideas (*groupements des idées*), from which they would be strictly banned. In the current situation, it is good to allow people to form groups to defend their interests, in other words, pay and the like, and to let these groups act within very narrow confines and under the constant eye of the government. But they must not be allowed to touch thinking. The groups where ideas are debated should not so much be groups as relatively fluid environments. When an action is formulated, there is no reason for it to be executed by anyone except those who agree with it.

In the labour movement, for example, such a distinction would put an end to a tangled confusion. In the period leading up to the war, workers were constantly being torn in three different directions. First, the battle for pay and then the remnants – increasingly weak but still breathing – of the old syndicalist spirit of the past, idealistic and libertarian to some degree, and lastly, the political parties. Often, during a strike, the workers who were suffering and fighting would have been quite incapable of saying whether it was about pay, or a resurgence of the old trade-union spirit, or about a political operation led by a party – and no one from the outside knew either.

Such a situation is impossible. When the war broke out, the trade unions in France were dead or dying, despite – or because of – their millions of members. They resumed an embryonic life, after a long stagnation, prompted to put up a resistance against the invader. That does not prove that they are viable. It is quite clear that they had been killed off, or nearly killed off, by two poisons, each one of which was deadly.

Unions cannot thrive if the workers are obsessed with money to the same degree as in the factory, doing piecework. Firstly, because it results in the kind of moral death always caused by the obsession with money. Then because in the current social conditions, the union, being then a permanent actor in the country's economic life, inevitably ends up being transformed into a single, mandatory trade organization toeing the official line. It has then become a corpse.

On the other hand, it is also clear that the union cannot exist alongside political parties. That is an impossibility of the order of mechanical laws. For an analogous reason, incidentally, the Socialist Party cannot coexist with the Communist Party because the latter has the quality of being a party, so to speak, to a much higher degree.

Moreover, the obsession with wages strengthens Communist influence because so acutely do questions of money affect almost everyone, while at the same time producing a boredom so lethal that the apocalyptic prospect of the Communist version of the revolution is essential by way of compensation. If the bourgeoisie does not have the same need for an apocalypse, it is because there is a poetry, a prestige, associated with large sums that somewhat tempers the boredom associated with money. Instead, when money is counted in small amounts, boredom is pure boredom. Besides, the bourgeoisie and petty bourgeoisie's taste for fascism shows that, in spite of everything, they too are bored.

France's Vichy government established unique and obligatory workers' organizations. It is unfortunate that these were called, in modern fashion, corporations, which actually means something that is so different and so beautiful. But it is fortunate that these dead organizations are there to pick up the dead part of union activity. It would be dangerous to abolish them. It is much better to entrust them with day-to-day campaigning for pay and so-called immediate demands. As for the political parties, if they were all rigorously banned in a general climate of freedom, it is to be hoped that it would at least be difficult for them to carry on a clandestine existence.

In this case, the workers' unions, if there is still a spark of real life in them, could gradually return to being a vehicle for workers' thinking, the organ of worker honour. According to the tradition of the French labour movement, which has always seen itself as responsible for the entire world, they would be interested in anything to do with justice – including, where appropriate, pay issues, but only from time to time and to save human beings from hardship. They should of course be able to exercise influence over trade organizations in accordance with the terms and conditions laid down by the law.

It is possible there would be only advantages in prohibiting trade organizations from going on strike, and allowing the unions to do so, with provisos, by weighing up the risks versus this responsibility, prohibiting any constraints, and protecting the continuity of economic life.

As for lockouts, there are no grounds for not banning them altogether.

Associations for promoting ideas could be authorized subject to two conditions. One, that there is no question of excommunication. Recruitment would take place freely through affinity, however without anyone being invited to sign up to a series of statements enshrined in written formulae. However, once accepted, a member could not be excluded other than for bringing the organization into disrepute or infiltration, an offence that would involve setting up an illegal organization and as a result incur a harsher punishment.

That would be a real measure of public good, experience having shown that totalitarian states are established by totalitarian parties, and that totalitarian parties are forged by excluding those with dissenting opinions.

The other condition could be that there must be a real circulation of ideas, and concrete evidence of this in the form of brochures, journals or typed newsletters discussing general problems. Too great a uniformity of opinion would make a group suspect.

Furthermore, all groups would be authorized to act as they saw fit, on condition they did not infringe the law or coerce their members through discipline.

As for interest groups, their oversight first requires a distinction to be made; the word interest sometimes expresses a need but sometimes it means something completely different. For a poor worker, interest means food, shelter and heating. For a boss, it means something else. When the word is understood in its primary sense, government action should chiefly focus on stimulating, supporting and protecting the defence of interests. In the opposite case, the interest groups' activities should be continuously monitored, restricted, and, when necessary, curtailed by the authorities. It goes without saying that the most stringent limitations and most painful punishments are appropriate for those who are inherently the most powerful.

So-called freedom of association has, until now, been the

freedom of associations. But associations are not meant to be free; they are instruments, they must be controlled. Freedom is only appropriate for human beings.

As for freedom of thought, it is true to say that without freedom of thought, there is no thought. But it is even truer to say that when there is no thought, it is not free either. There has been a lot of freedom of thought in recent years, but no thought. That is comparable to the situation of the child who, having no meat, asks for salt to put on it.

X

Security is an essential need of the soul. Security means that the soul is not hampered by fear or terror, except as a result of a combination of accidental circumstances and for rare and short periods. Fear or terror, as enduring states of mind, are almost deadly poisons, whether the cause is the likelihood of unemployment, or police repression, or the presence of a foreign conqueror, or the expectation of an impending invasion, or any other affliction that feels beyond human strength.

Roman masters would display a whip in the entrance hall in view of their slaves, knowing that the sight of it would reduce them to the half-dead state necessary for slavery. Conversely, according to the Egyptians, the righteous should be able to say after death: 'I have not caused fear to any person.'[16]

Even though permanent fear is only a latent state, and so is rarely experienced as suffering, it is still a disease. It is a semi-paralysis of the soul.

XI

Risk is an essential need of the soul. The absence of risk creates a kind of boredom that numbs in a different way from fear, but almost as much. Moreover, there are situations that create a vague anxiety without specific risks, transmitting both diseases at the same time.

Risk is a danger that causes a considered reaction, in other words, it does not overstretch the soul's resources to the point of crushing it through fear. In some cases, it contains an element of playfulness; in others, when a specific obligation pushes man to confront it, it is the greatest possible stimulus.

Protecting people against fear and terror does not imply the elimination of risk. On the contrary, it implies the permanent presence of a certain level of risk in all aspects of social life because the absence of risk diminishes courage to the point of leaving the spirit without any internal protection against fear when needed. All that is required is for risk to occur in conditions such that it does not turn into a sense of fatality.

XII

Private property is a vital need of the soul. The soul is isolated, lost, when not surrounded by objects that feel like an extension of the body's limbs. Any man is irresistibly inclined to mentally appropriate all the items he has long and continually used for work, pleasure, or life's necessities. And so, after a while, a gardener feels that the garden is his. But when a sense of ownership does not coincide with legal ownership, that man is continually under threat of experiencing a deeply painful wrench.

If private property is recognized as a need, it implies for everyone the possibility of possessing objects other than common consumer items. The forms of this need vary greatly depending on circumstances, but it is desirable for most people to own their home and some land around it, and, if possible, to own their work implements. The land and livestock are implements for the farmer's work.

The principle of private property is violated in the case of land that is worked by farm labourers and farmhands under the orders of a manager but is owned by city-dwellers who derive the revenues from it. Of all the people who have a relationship with this land, there is no one who, in some way or another, is a stranger to it. It is wasted, not from the point of view of the wheat, but from that of the fulfilment of the need for ownership that it could provide.

Between the above extreme and the other, in other words, the farmer and his family who cultivate the land he owns, there are many in-between cases where the need for human ownership is more or less unacknowledged.

XIII

Participation in collective goods does not consist of material enjoyment but in a sense of ownership, is just as important a need. It is a state of mind rather than a legal provision. Where there is a truly civic life, everyone has a sense of personal ownership of the public monuments and gardens and the lavishness displayed in ceremonies. Thus the luxury desired by almost every human being is granted even to the poorest of the poor. It is not solely the state that has to provide this satisfaction, but every kind of collectivity.

A large, modern factory is a waste when it comes to the need for ownership. Neither the workers nor the manager, who is under the thumb of a board of directors, nor the members of the board who never see it, nor the shareholders who are unaware of its existence, derive from it the slightest satisfaction of this need.

When forms of exchange and acquisition result in food wastage, both material and spiritual, they need to be transformed.

There is no natural connection between ownership and money. The link made today is solely the result of a system that has focused on money as the most powerful of every possible motive. Since this system is unhealthy, the two should be uncoupled.

The true criterion for ownership is that it is legitimate provided it is real. Or more specifically, the laws regarding property are all the better if they make good use of the possibilities contained in the goods of this world to satisfy the human need for common property.

Consequently, the current means of acquisition and possession must be transformed in the name of the ownership

principle. All types of possession that do not satisfy anybody's need for private or collective property can reasonably
be considered as worthless.

That does not mean that this asset should be transferred
to the state, but rather an effort is needed to make it a true
ownership.

XIV

Rootedness is perhaps the most essential and the most

XIV[17]

The need for truth is more sacred than any other, but it is never
mentioned. After realizing the quantity and enormity of the
material falsehoods spread unashamedly, we are afraid to read
even the books of the most reputable authors. We then read as
we would drink water from a dubious well.

There are people who work eight hours a day and make
great efforts to read in the evenings to educate themselves. They
do not have the leisure to check facts in great libraries. They
take the book at its word. Feeding them falsehoods should be
forbidden. What sense is there in professing that authors are in
good faith? They do not do physical work eight hours a day.
Society feeds them so that they can take the time and trouble to
avoid errors. It would not go down well for a pointsman causing a derailment to excuse himself saying he was acting in good
faith.

All the more reason why it is shameful to tolerate the existence of newspapers when it is common knowledge that no
member of staff would be able to keep their job unless they
were prepared occasionally to alter the truth.

The public distrusts the press, but this distrust affords them
no protection. Aware that newspapers contain truths and falsehoods, readers mentally divide the news they read between

these two categories, but randomly, according to their preferences. Thus they are vulnerable to misconceptions.

Everyone knows that when journalism merges with organized untruths, it is a crime. But we believe it is a non-punishable
crime. What in the world could possibly deem it unpunishable
once it has been acknowledged as criminal? Where on earth did
this strange notion of non-punishable crimes come from? This
is one of the most heinous distortions of the legal spirit.

Is it not time to proclaim that every detectable crime is pun-
ishable, and that we are determined, if we have the opportunity,
to punish all crimes?

Some simple public-health measures would protect the population from violation of the truth.

The first would be the institution of highly respected special
tribunals made up of trained, handpicked judges. They would
be required to punish all avoidable mistakes with public condemnation and would have the power to inflict prison or
prison-camp sentences for repeat offences, aggravated by
proven bad faith.

For example, an admirer of ancient Greece, reading in
Jacques Maritain's assertion that 'the greatest thinkers of
antiquity had not thought to criticize slavery,' would take Maritain to court over this statement.[18] They would invoke the only
major text on slavery that has come down to us, that by Aristotle. They would make the judges read the sentence 'some say
that slavery is absolutely contrary to nature and reason'.[19] They
would point out that nothing suggests that those few had not
been among the greatest thinkers of antiquity. The court would
blame Maritain for having published, when it was so easy for
him to avoid making such a mistake, a false assertion constituting, albeit unintentionally, a terrible slander against an entire
civilization. All daily, weekly and other newspapers, all magazines and radio would have an obligation to make the public
aware of the court's opprobrium, and Maritain's response, if
relevant. In his case, that might be difficult.

When *Gringoire* published verbatim a speech by a Spanish
anarchist billed as a speaker at a meeting in Paris but who, at

the last minute, was unable to leave Spain, such a court would not have been superfluous.[20] Bad faith being in such a case more blatant than two plus two makes four, jail or prison camp would not have been too harsh.

This system would allow anyone having identified an avoidable error in a printed text or radio broadcast to bring a case before these courts.

The second measure would be an absolute prohibition of propaganda of any kind via the radio or the daily press. These two instruments would be authorized solely for disseminating unbiased information.

These courts would be vigilant in ensuring that information is not biased.

For vehicles of information, they might have to judge not only erroneous statements, but also deliberate and biased omissions.

The circles in which ideas circulate would only be entitled to disseminate them in weekly, fortnightly or monthly publications. There is no need for a greater frequency if the intention is to make people think and not to overwhelm them.

The reliability of means of persuasion would be overseen by the same courts, which would be empowered to close down a publication if it distorted the truth too often. But its editors would be able to revive it under a new name.

In all of this there would not be the slightest infringement of civil liberties. There would be satisfaction of the most sacred need of the human soul, the need for protection against suggestion and untruths.

But, people will object, who will guarantee the judges' impartiality? The only guarantee, apart from their total independence is that they are from very different social backgrounds, that they are naturally endowed with a profound, clear and sharp intellect, and that they are trained in a school where they receive not a legal education but one that is firstly spiritual and secondly intellectual. They have to become accustomed to loving the truth.

The human need for truth cannot be satisfied if it is not possible to find people who love the truth for this purpose.

XV[21]

Rootedness is perhaps the most important and least known human spiritual need. It is one of the hardest to define. A human being is rooted through their real, active and natural participation in the life of a collectivity that keeps alive treasures of the past and has aspirations for the future. This participation is natural in that it stems automatically from place, birth, occupation and those around them. Every human being needs to have multiple roots and to derive almost all their moral, intellectual and spiritual life from the environment to which they naturally belong.

The exchange of influences between very different milieus is just as vital as rootedness in the natural environment. But a given milieu should receive external influences not as an addition, but as a stimulus that makes its own life more intense. It should only be nourished by external influences after digesting them, and the individuals making up that environment should only receive these influences through it. When a genuinely talented painter goes into a museum, their own originality is confirmed. The same should apply to the world's diverse populations and the different social milieus.

Every military conquest results in uprootedness, and in this sense conquest is almost always an evil. Uprootedness is minimal when the conquerors are invaders who settle in the conquered country, mingle with the population and put down roots themselves. This was the case of the Hellenes in Greece, the Celts in Gaul and the Moors in Spain. But when the conqueror remains a foreigner in the territory they now possess, uprootedness is an almost fatal disease for the subjugated population. The most extreme examples are when there are mass deportations, as in German-occupied Europe or in the Niger Bend, or when there is a violent repression of all local traditions, as in the French colonies in Oceania (if we are to believe Gauguin and Alain Gerbault).[22]

Even when there is no military conquest, money and economic domination can be such a powerful foreign influence that it results in the disease of uprootedness.

And finally, social relations within the same country can be highly dangerous contributory factors to uprootedness. Nowadays, across our country, conquest aside, there are two poisons spreading this disease. One is money. Money destroys roots wherever it goes because the drive to make money supplants all other incentives. This drive easily overshadows all other incentives because it requires so much less attention. Nothing is as clear or simple as a number.

INDUSTRIAL UPROOTEDNESS

Wage-earning is a social condition that is entirely and permanently dependent on money, especially since piecework forces every worker to be continuously counting pennies. This is the social condition where the disease of uprootedness is most acute. [Georges] Bernanos wrote that our workers are not immigrants like those of Mr Ford.[23] Today's main social difficulty comes from the fact that in a sense they are immigrants. Although they have stayed put geographically, they have been morally uprooted, exiled and re-admitted, as if out of forbearance, as muscle-power. Unemployment is, of course, uprootedness squared. The unemployed have no place in the factories, in their homes, in the parties or trade unions supposedly for them, in places of leisure, or in intellectual culture if they try to acquire it.

Because the second uprootedness factor is education such as it is conceived at present. The Renaissance created a division everywhere between the cultured class and the masses. But in separating culture from national tradition, it at least immersed it in the Greek tradition. Since then, the links with national traditions have not been renewed, but Greece has been forgotten. The result is a culture that has developed in a very restricted milieu, divorced from the world, in a confined atmosphere, a culture that is very much oriented towards and influenced by technology, heavily coloured by pragmatism, extremely fragmented by specialization, completely devoid both of contact with this world and openness to the outside world.

Nowadays, someone can belong to so-called cultured milieus, on the one hand without having any conception of human destiny, and on the other without knowing, for example, that not all the constellations are visible in all seasons. It is commonly believed that a humble farmer's son at elementary school today knows more than Pythagoras did because he obediently repeats that the Earth moves around the sun. But he does not actually gaze at the stars. This sun that he learns about in class has nothing to do with the one he sees. He is torn from the universe around him, just as Polynesian schoolchildren are torn from their past by being made to parrot: 'Our ancestors the Gauls were fair-haired.'

These days, what we call educating the masses is to take this modern culture – developed in a milieu that is so closed, flawed and indifferent to the truth – and to remove from it all that might still be left that is pure gold, through an operation called popularization, and to cram what is left over into the minds of the hapless souls eager to learn, as if feeding birds.

Furthermore, the desire to learn for the sake of learning, the desire for truth, has become very rare. The prestige attached to culture has become almost exclusively social, as much in the farmer who dreams of his son being a teacher, or the teacher who dreams of his son going to an elite university, as in society circles that toady to famous scholars and writers. Examinations exert the same obsessive power over students as wages over pieceworkers. A social system is profoundly sick when a farmer works the land believing that if he is a farmer it is because he was not clever enough to be a teacher.

For workers, the jumble of confused and more or less false ideas known as Marxism, a jumble which, since Marx's day, has only appealed to mediocre bourgeois intellectuals, is also completely alien, indigestible, and in itself devoid of sustenance for the workers because it has been gutted of almost all the truth contained in Marx's writings.[24] It is sometimes supplemented by popular science of even worse quality. All this can only exacerbate the workers' uprootedness.

Uprootedness is by far the most dangerous disease of human societies because it propagates itself. People who are truly

uprooted have only two possible ways to respond: either they
sink into an almost deathlike inertia of the soul, as did most
slaves in the days of the Roman Empire, or they throw themselves into an activity that always tends to uproot, often by the
most violent methods, those who are not yet, or are only partially, uprooted.

The Romans were a handful of fugitives who banded themselves together artificially into a city and deprived the
Mediterranean populations of their own lives, their homeland,
their traditions and their past, to such a degree that posterity has
accepted their own word that they were the founders of civilization in these lands. The Hebrews were escaped slaves, and they
exterminated or reduced to servitude all the populations of Pal-
estine.[25] At the time Hitler seized power over the Germans, they
were really, as he kept repeating, a nation of proletarians, that is
to say, uprooted peoples. Several factors contributed to a moral
sickness that descended into irresponsibility: the humiliation of
1918, inflation, over-industrialization and, above all, the extreme
gravity of the unemployment crisis. The Spanish and the English
who, from the sixteenth century onwards massacred or enslaved
populations of colour, were adventurers with almost no contact
with the profound life of their own country. The same can be
said of part of the French Empire, which was formed at a time
when French tradition was weakened. Those who are uprooted,
uproot. Those who are rooted do not uproot.

There are two diametrically opposed ideas contained within
the concept of revolution, often using the same slogans and
propaganda themes. One is the notion of transforming society so
that workers can be rooted in it; the other is to extend to society
as a whole the disease of uprootedness that has been inflicted on
workers. It should not be stated or thought that the latter operation can ever be a prelude to the former; that is false. They are
two paths going in entirely opposite directions.

Nowadays, the latter conception is much more frequent than
the former, both among activists and among the mass of workers. It follows that it tends to become increasingly prevalent as
uprootedness persists and its ravages spread. It is easy to understand that overnight, the damage can become irreparable.

On the conservative side, there is an analogous equivocation. A small number of people really want the workers to become rooted again, but their wish is accompanied by images, most of which, instead of relating to the future, are borrowed from a past that is partially fictitious. The others simply want to maintain the proletariat in the condition of human material to which it has been reduced, or to aggravate it.

And so those who truly desire good, already few in number, weaken themselves still further by splitting themselves between two hostile camps with which they have nothing in common.

The sudden collapse of France [in June 1940], which surprised everyone everywhere, simply showed how deracinated the country was. A tree whose roots are almost completely eaten away is felled at the first blow. If France has presented a more distressing spectacle than any other country in Europe, it is because modern civilization with its poisons was established there earlier than anywhere else except Germany. But in Germany the uprootedness took an aggressive form, whereas in France it took the guise of lethargy and stupor. This difference stems from causes that are chiefly hidden but can be found if we look for them. Conversely, the country that was most successful in resisting the first wave of German terror is the one where tradition is most alive and best preserved – that is to say England.

In France, the uprootedness of the proletarian condition had reduced a large proportion of the workers to a state of inert stupor and caused others to adopt a bellicose attitude towards society. The same money that had violently slashed the workers' roots had also gnawed at those of the bourgeois milieus, because wealth is cosmopolitan; the tenuous attachment to the country that might have remained intact was far superseded, especially after 1936, by fear and hatred towards the industrial workers. The agricultural workers too had been almost uprooted since World War I, demoralized by having served as cannon fodder, by money, which was becoming an increasing concern in their lives, and by far-too-frequent contact with the corruption of the cities. As for intelligence, it was almost extinguished.

The country's general sickness took the form of a kind of

stupor, which was the only thing preventing a civil war. France hated the war that threatened to stop the nation from sleeping. Stunned by the terrible blow of May and June 1940, France leaped into Pétain's arms so the country could carry on slumbering in a semblance of security. Since then, enemy oppression has turned this sleep into such a painful nightmare that France has stirred and is anxiously awaiting the outside help that will rouse the country.

As a result of the war, the disease of uprootedness has become so acute throughout Europe that we can rightly be appalled by it. The only glimmer of hope is that suffering has revived to some degree memories that were once almost dead, such as, in France, those of 1789.

As for the countries of the East, where for some centuries, but especially for the past fifty years, whites have carried the disease of uprootedness from which they suffer, Japan is an example of how severely the active form of the disease is taking hold. Indochina is an example of the passive form. India, where there is still a living tradition, is contaminated enough that those same people who speak publicly in the name of this tradition dream of establishing a modern Western nation in their country. China is very mysterious. Russia, which is still half-European, half-oriental, is just as mysterious, for it is not clear whether the energy that covers it with glory is the result, like in the case of Germany, of an active uprootedness – as the history of the last twenty-five years would suggest – or whether it is predominantly a question of the profound life of the people, that sprang from the depths of time and had remained underground almost intact.

As for the American continent, since settlement has primarily relied on immigration for several centuries, the dominant influence that it will probably exert greatly aggravates the danger.

In this almost desperate situation, the only help to be found here below is in the islands of the past that have remained alive on the surface of the Earth. It is not that we should approve of Mussolini's boasts about the Roman Empire or try to use Louis XIV in the same way.[26] Conquests are not life; they are death at the very moment they occur. Droplets of the living past should be jealously preserved, everywhere, in Paris or Tahiti or wherever, because there are not very many of them on the entire planet.

It would be vain to turn away from the past to think only of the future. It is a dangerous illusion to believe that such a possibility even exists. Opposing the future and the past is absurd. The future brings us nothing, gives us nothing; we are the ones who, in order to build it, must give it everything, give it our very lives. But in order to give, we must possess, and we possess no other life, no other sap, but only the treasures inherited from the past and digested, absorbed and re-created by us. Of all the needs of the human soul, there is none more vital than the past.

Love of the past has nothing to do with a reactionary political stance. Like all human activities, the sap of revolution is tradition. Marx was so conscious of this that he insisted on taking this tradition back to the remotest past by making class struggle the sole explanation for the whole of history.[27] Still at the beginning of the twentieth century, few things in Europe were closer to the Middle Ages than French syndicalism, the only reflection of the spirit of the guilds in France. The feeble remnants of this syndicalism are among the embers on which it is most urgent to blow.

For several centuries, white people have been destroying the past everywhere, stupidly, blindly, in their own countries and abroad. Although there has been real progress in some respects during this period, it is not because of this mania but in spite of it, spurred on by the little of the past that has remained alive.

Once destroyed, the past can never be retrieved. The destruction of the past is perhaps the greatest crime. Today, the preservation of the little that remains should become almost an obsession. We must stop the terrible uprootedness that is still being produced by the Europeans' colonial methods, even in their less cruel forms. In the wake of a victory, we must refrain from punishing our defeated enemies by even further uprooting them. When it is neither possible nor desirable to exterminate them, aggravating their madness would be crazier than the enemy. Above all, with any political, legal or technical innovation likely to have social repercussions, an arrangement must be sought that will enable human beings to put down roots again.

This does not mean confining them. On the contrary, giving them space has never been more essential. Rootedness and the proliferation of contacts are complementary. For example, if, wherever technology permits – and with a slight effort, this could be easily be possible – workers were to be widely dispersed, each one owning a house, a plot of land and a machine; and if, on the other hand, the Tour de France of the past could be revived for young people, at international level if necessary;[28] if workers were given frequent opportunities to do work placements in the assembly shop where the parts they make are put together with all the others, or to help train apprentices and had effective wage protection, the affliction of the proletarian condition would be eradicated.

The proletarian condition will not be destroyed with legal measures, be it the nationalization of key industries, the suppression of private property, or by giving the trade unions or factory representatives collective bargaining powers and control over hiring. All the proposed measures, whether they are labelled revolutionary or reformist, are purely legal, and it is not at the legal level that workers' affliction and the remedy for it are to be found. Marx would have understood this perfectly well if he had been true to his own thinking, for it is a self-evident fact that leaps off the best pages of *Capital*.[29]

It is not in the workers' demands that a remedy to their affliction can be found.[30] Deep in affliction body and soul, including the imagination, how could they imagine something that does not bear its stamp? If they make a violent effort to extricate themselves from it, they sink into apocalyptic fantasies or seek compensation in a worker imperialism that is no more to be encouraged than national imperialism.

What can be seen in their demands is the indication of their suffering. Their demands all, or nearly all, express the misery of being uprooted. If they want to control employment and nationalization, it is because they are haunted by the fear of being totally uprooted, of unemployment. If they want to abolish private property, it is because they are tired of being admitted to the workplace like immigrants allowed in as a favour. This is also the psychological motivation behind the factory occupations of June 1936.[31] For a few days, they experienced a pure, unalloyed joy on feeling at home in their workplaces; the joy of a child who does not want to think about the morrow. No one could reasonably believe that the future would be good.

The French workers' movement spawned by the Revolution was essentially a cry, more of protest than revolt, in the face of the merciless cruelty of fate towards all the oppressed. Relative to what can be expected of a collective movement, in this one, there was a great deal of purity. It ended in 1914; since then, there have been only echoes of it. The poisons of the surrounding society have corrupted even the sense of affliction. We must try to revive the tradition of it, but we cannot wish to resuscitate it. No matter how beautiful the sound of a cry of pain may be, we cannot wish to hear it again; it is more humane to want to heal the pain.

The concrete list of workers' sufferings provides the list of things to be changed. First of all, we must eradicate the shock experienced by the youngster who, at twelve or thirteen years of age, leaves school and goes to work in the factory. Some workers would be quite happy had that shock not left a permanently painful wound; but they themselves do not know that their suffering comes from the past. The child at school, whether a good or bad pupil, was a being whose existence was recognized and schooling sought to develop, appealing to their noblest instincts. Overnight, they become an adjunct to the machine, a little less than a thing, and no one cares that their impulse to obey is due to the basest motives, provided they obey. Most workers have had, at least at this point in their lives, this impression that they no longer exist, together with a kind of inner vertigo which intellectuals or the bourgeoisie very rarely experience, even when suffering a great deal. This first shock, received so early, often leaves an indelible scar, making the love of work definitively impossible.

It is necessary to vary the ways a worker needs to direct their attention during the course of a workday, and also the type of stimuli needed to combat laziness or exhaustion – stimuli which nowadays are only fear and money – the nature of obedience, the limited scope for initiative, skill and thought required of workers, the impossibility for them to be involved in the company's overall work through thinking and feeling, their sometimes total ignorance of the value, social usefulness and destination of the things they produce, the complete separation between work and family life. The list could go on.

Apart from the desire for reform, three kinds of factors are at play in the production system: technical, economic and military. These days, the importance of military factors in production reflects that of production in the conduct of war; in other words, it is sizeable.

From the military point of view, it is doubly absurd that thousands of workers should be crammed into huge industrial prisons where genuinely skilled workers are in very small numbers. Present military conditions require, on the one hand, that industrial production be scattered, and, on the other, that the greatest number of workers in peacetime consists of educated professionals, under whose orders, in the event of an international crisis or war, large numbers of women, young boys and older men can be placed in order to step up production immediately. The greatest contributory factor to the paralysis of British war production for so long was the lack of skilled workers.

But since the function of machine labourers cannot be performed by highly skilled professionals, this function should be abolished, except in the case of war.

It is so rare that military necessities are in alignment and not in contradiction with the highest human aspirations that when they are, advantage should be taken.

From a technical point of view, the relative ease of transporting energy in the form of electricity certainly permits a large degree of decentralization.

As for the machines, they have not yet been developed to the point where the production system can be transformed, but the adjustable automatic machines currently in use suggest that it should certainly be possible to achieve this with some effort, were that effort to be made.

Generally speaking, a reform of infinitely greater social importance than all the measures grouped under the label of socialism would be a transformation in the very conception of technical research. Until now, no one has ever thought that an engineer engaged in technical research on new types of machines could have anything other than the twin goal of increasing the profits of the company commissioning the research, and of serving the interests of the consumer. Because in such cases, when we speak of production interests, it is about producing more and cheaper. In other words, these interests are in fact those of consumption. The two words are constantly used interchangeably.

As for the workers who will give their muscle-power to this machine, no one thinks about them. No one even thinks that it is possible to think about them. At most, vague safety devices are occasionally provided, although in fact, severed fingers and factory stairs tacky with fresh blood every day are very frequent.

But this feeble trace of attention is the only one. Not only does nobody think of the workers' moral wellbeing, which would require too much imagination, but nor is there any concern to protect them from injury. Otherwise, another solution might have been found for the mines instead of that terrible pneumatic jackhammer, which makes the operator judder nonstop for eight hours.

Nor is there any thought as to whether the new machine, by tying up capital and imposing rigid production quotas, might increase the general risk of unemployment.

What use is it to the workers to obtain a wage increase and a relaxation of discipline as a result of struggle, if in the meantime engineers from a handful of firms inadvertently invent machines that wear them out body and soul, or aggravate their financial difficulties? What would be the use of partial or total nationalization of the economy if the mentality of these engineering firms has not changed? And so far, to our knowledge, where there has been nationalization, the mentality has not changed. Even Soviet propaganda has never claimed that Russia has found a radically new type of machine, worthy of being used by a 'dictatorial proletariat'.[32]

However, if there is one certainty that appears emphatically in Marx's writings, it is that a change in class relations will remain a pure illusion if it does not go hand in hand with a technology transformation, a transformation made concrete with new machines.

From the worker's point of view, a machine needs to have three features. First, it must be capable of being handled without exhausting muscles, nerves or organs, and also it must not cut or tear the flesh, other than in exceptional circumstances.

Secondly, in relation to the general risk of unemployment, the production system as a whole must be as flexible as possible, in order to be able to keep pace with fluctuations in demand. Consequently, the same machine must be multi-purpose, very varied if possible and even to some extent indeterminate. This is also a military necessity to enable the smoothest possible transition from a state of peace to one of war. Finally, such a machine would make work enjoyable because it would avoid the monotony so dreaded by workers because of the associated boredom and repugnance.

Thirdly, it should correspond to the work of a skilled professional. This too is a military necessity, and moreover it is essential to the workers' dignity and mental wellbeing. A working class made up almost entirely of good professionals is not a proletariat.

Extensive development of the automatic, adjustable, multipurpose machine would satisfy these needs to a large extent. The first models exist, and they certainly open up vast possibilities. Such machines eliminate the role of machine operator. In a huge company like Renault, few workers look happy; among the privileged few are operators of cam-driven variable-speed automatic lathes.

But the main thing is the very idea of posing, in technical terms, the problems concerning the repercussions of machines on the moral wellbeing of workers. Once the problems have been identified, the engineers have simply to solve them. They have solved many others. They just need the will to do so. For this, the places where new machines are being developed must no longer be immersed entirely in the web of capitalist interests. It is natural that the state should have a hold over them through subsidies. And why not the workers' organizations through bonuses? Not to mention other means of influence and pressure. If the workers' unions could become truly vibrant, there would have to be ongoing contact between them and the engineering firms where new technologies are being developed. The way could be paved for such contacts by creating an atmosphere favourable to workers in engineering schools.

Until now, engineers have never had any other goal than the needs of manufacturing. If they were to start taking account of the needs of those who manufacture, gradually the entire production system would be transformed.

This should be on the curriculum of engineering schools and all technical colleges – and taught as a subject that has real substance.

It is possible that there might be only benefits in setting in motion right now studies of this kind of question.

The subject of such studies would be easy to define. A pope once said: 'Dead matter emerges from the factory ennobled, while men are there corrupted and degraded.'[33] Marx expressed exactly the same idea in even more vigorous terms. The point is that all those who seek to achieve technical progress are convinced that of all the deficiencies apparent in the present state of manufacturing, the one in most urgent need of being remedied, is this: nothing must ever be done that makes it worse, and everything must be done to reduce it. From now on, for anyone with responsibilities in industry, this idea should be part of their sense of professional obligation, of professional honour. Instilling this idea into the universal consciousness would be one of the labour unions' essential tasks, if they were capable of fulfilling it.

If most of the workers were highly skilled professionals, quite often having to demonstrate ingenuity and initiative, responsible for their own output and machinery, the present labour discipline would no longer be necessary. Some could work at home, others in small workshops organized on a co-operative basis. Nowadays, authority in small factories is exercised in a manner that is even more unacceptable than in large ones because they follow the example of the bigger works. These workshops would not be small factories but industrial organizations of a new kind, with a new ethos; although small, the organic bonds between would be strong enough to form one large enterprise. In a large enterprise, for all its faults, there is a poetry of a particular kind which appeals to today's workers.

Piecework payment would no longer be a problem once the barracking of workers was abolished. This would be the normal mode of remuneration for work freely done, eliminating the obsession with speed at all costs. Obedience would no longer mean a submission of every second. A worker or group of workers would be given a certain number of orders to be fulfilled by a given date and have free choice in the way they organized the work. This would be very different from having to repeat the same movement ad infinitum, imposed by an order, up until the exact second when a new commission imposes a new movement for an unknown duration. There is a certain relationship with time that is suited to inert things, and another that is suited to thinking beings. It is wrong to confuse them.

Cooperatives or not, these little workshops would not be barracks. Workers would sometimes be able to show their wives their workplace and their machines, as they were so happy to do in June 1936, during the occupation. The children would come after school to meet their fathers and learn how to work, at an age when work is by far the most exciting game. Later, when they became apprenticed, they would already almost have a trade, and could choose to improve their skill or acquire a second one. Work would be brightened by poetry – that childlike wonderment – for their entire lifetimes, instead of being an enduring nightmare because of the shock of the first experiences.

Although, even in the current demoralized climate, farm

workers need far less stimulation than industrial workers, it may be because of the following difference. A child may already be unhappy in the fields when they are nine or ten years old, but almost always there has been a time when the work was a wonderful game for them, reserved for grown-ups.

If the majority of workers were to become almost happy, many seemingly essential and agonizing problems would not only be solved but eliminated. Even if they had not been solved, people would forget they had ever arisen. Affliction is a breeding ground for false problems. It creates obsessions. The way to appease them is not to satisfy them, but to make the affliction disappear. If a man is thirsty because of a stomach wound, it is not a drink he needs, but for the wound to be healed.

Sadly, only the fate of the young can be changed. A great effort will have to be made in the training of young workers, first of all through apprenticeship. The state will have to take charge of this because no other sector of society is capable of doing so.

Nothing better shows the essential failing of the capitalist class than employers' disregard for apprenticeship. In Russia this is called criminal negligence. This simple, easily grasped, indisputable truth cannot be overstated or over-publicized. For the past twenty or thirty years, employers have ignored the need to train competent professionals. The lack of skilled workers has contributed to the country's decline as much as any other factor. Even in 1934 and 1935, at the peak of the unemployment crisis, when production was at a standstill, mechanical and aviation plants needed highly skilled professionals but were unable to find any.[34] Workers complained that the tests were too difficult; the fact was they had not been trained to take those tests. How, under these conditions, would we be able to produce sufficient armaments? But even without the war, the skills shortage, which had worsened over the years, would eventually make economic life itself impossible.

It must be made known once and for all, to the entire country and to all concerned, that employers have shown themselves to be incapable of meeting the responsibilities that the capitalist system demands of them. They have a function to fulfil, but not this one, because experience has shown that it is too onerous and too vast for them. Once this is understood, they will no longer be feared, while they, on the other hand, will stop opposing the necessary reforms; they will remain within the modest confines of their natural function. This is their only chance of salvation, and it is because people fear them that there is so often talk of getting rid of them.

Bosses accused a worker caught having a drink of lack of foresight, but they themselves in their wisdom did not foresee that if you do not train apprentices, after twenty years you will have no more workers, at least none worthy of the name. They seem incapable of thinking more than two or three years ahead. Doubtless too, they secretly prefer to have in their factories a herd of unhappy, uprooted beings not entitled to any consideration. They did not know that while slaves are more completely subjugated than free men, their rebellion is also much more terrible. They have experienced this, but they have not understood it.

The failure of the trade unions to address the problem of apprenticeship is just as scandalous from another point of view. It was not their job to worry about the future of production, but since fighting for justice is their sole purpose, they should have been sensitive to the youngsters' moral suffering. The fact is, the unions abandoned the truly wretched factory-worker groups – the adolescents, the women, immigrants and foreign and colonial workers. Their combined suffering counted for much less in union life than the issue of a wage increase for categories of workers who were already well paid.

There is no better illustration of how difficult it is for a collective movement to be truly committed to justice, and for the afflicted to be truly defended. They cannot fight for themselves because affliction prevents them from doing so, and no one fights for them because human nature tends not to pay attention to the afflicted.

Only the JOC (*Jeunesse Ouvrière Chrétienne* – Young Christian Workers) was concerned with the affliction of adolescent workers.[35] The existence of such an organization is perhaps the only sure sign that Christianity has not died.

In the same way as the capitalists have betrayed their vocation by criminally neglecting not only the interests of the
people, not only those of the nation, but even their own, the
workers' unions have betrayed theirs by defending vested interests instead of protecting the most deprived workers. This, too,
should be made known, in case the day comes when they might
have the responsibility and the temptation to commit abuses of
power. Bringing the trade unions into line and transforming
them into single, compulsory organizations was the natural,
inevitable outcome of this changed attitude. In essence, the
Vichy government's action in this respect has been almost non-
existent. The CGT (*Confédération Générale du Travail* – General
Confederation of Labour) was not a victim of rape by the Vichy
regime; it had long been in no condition to be so.[36]

The state is not particularly qualified to defend the afflicted.
It is almost incapable of doing so, unless compelled by an obvious, urgent public-welfare requirement and by a ground swell
of public opinion.

As regards the training of young workers, the public welfare
need is as urgent and blatant as it could be. As for the ground
swell of public opinion, it has to be stimulated, and that must
begin now, by making use of the embryonic authentic trade-union
organizations, the JOC, study groups and youth movements,
even official ones.

The Bolsheviks fired up their people with the idea of developing a great industry. Could we not fire up our own people by
proposing the development of a new kind of working population? Such an aim would be commensurate with France's genius.

Young-workers' training must go beyond the purely vocational. It must, of course, include an education, like the training
of all young people, and that is why it is desirable that apprenticeship should not take place in schools, where it is always
done badly, but should be an immediate immersion in production itself. But it cannot be entrusted to the factories either.
Inventiveness is needed here. What is required is a combination
of the advantages of vocational establishments and those of a
factory apprenticeship, as well as those of the current type of
chantiers de compagnons,[37] and many others besides.

But the training of young workers, especially in a country like France, also means education, participation in an intellectual culture. They should feel at home in the world of thought.

What kind of participation and what kind of culture? This is a long-running debate. In the past, in some milieus, there was a lot of talk about a worker culture. Others maintained that there is no such thing as worker or non-worker culture, but just culture. The effect of this observation has been that the most intelligent and eager-to-learn workers have been treated like half-witted high-school students. Things may have been a little better at times, but on the whole, this is the principle of popularization as we understand it nowadays. The word is as awful as the thing. When we have something that is almost satisfactory to describe, we will have to find another word.

True, truth is one, but error is manifold; and in every culture, except in the case of perfection, which for humanity is only a limited case, there is a mixture of truth and error. If our culture were close to perfection, it would be situated above social classes. But since it is mediocre, it is to a large extent a culture for bourgeois intellectuals, and more particularly, for some time now, a culture for intellectual civil servants.

Pushing the analysis further, we would find that there is a great deal more truth in some of Marx's ideas than would first appear; but it is not the Marxists who will ever make such an analysis, for they would first have to look at themselves in a mirror, and that is too painful an operation for which only specifically Christian virtues provide sufficient courage.

What makes our culture so difficult to communicate to the people is not that it is too highbrow, but that it is too low. A singular remedy is offered, by lowering it even further before giving it to them in small doses.

There are two obstacles that make it difficult for the people to access culture. One is the lack of time and energy. The people have little leisure to devote to intellectual pursuits, and fatigue restricts the amount of effort they can make.

This obstacle is of no importance. At least it would not have any importance if the error of attributing it to them were not made. Truth illuminates the soul in proportion to its purity and not in any kind of quantity. It is not the quantity of the metal that matters, but the alloy content. And so, a little pure gold is worth a lot of pure gold. A little pure truth is worth as much as a lot of pure truth. Likewise, a perfect Greek statue contains as much beauty as two perfect Greek statues.

Niobe's sin was to ignore the fact that quantity has nothing to do with good, and she was punished for this by the death of her children.[38] We commit the same sin every day, and we are punished in the same way.

If a worker, in a year of dedicated effort and perseverance, learns some geometry theorems, as much truth will have entered his soul as into that of a student who, in the same amount of time, has devoted equal energy to higher mathematics.

Admittedly this is hard to believe, and perhaps would not be easy to demonstrate. At least it should be an article of faith for Christians, if they were to remember that truth is one of the pure blessings that the Gospel compares to bread, and that he who asks for bread is not given stones.

Material obstacles – lack of leisure, fatigue, lack of natural talent, sickness, physical pain – hinder the acquisition of the lower or average elements of culture, not that of the very precious wealth it contains.

The second obstacle to worker culture is that the condition of the worker, as with any other, corresponds to a particular sensibility. Consequently, there is something alien in what has been developed by and for others.

The remedy for this is an effort of translation. Not of popularization, but of translation, which is quite different.

This does not mean taking the truths – already far too poor – contained in the culture of intellectuals, and then degrading and mutilating them and voiding them of their flavour, but simply expressing them, in their fullness, in a language which, in the words of Pascal, makes them perceptible to the heart for those whose sensibility is shaped by their worker's condition.[39]

The art of transposing truths is one of the most essential and least known. What makes it difficult is that, in order to practise it, it is necessary to place oneself at the centre of a truth, and to have possessed it in its nakedness, behind the particular form in which it happens to be expressed.

Furthermore, transposition is a criterion for a truth. What cannot be transposed is not a truth; similarly, that which does not change its appearance according to the point of view is not a solid object, but an illusion. In thought too there is a three-dimensional space.

The search for suitable modes of transposition for transmitting culture to the people would be far more beneficial to culture than to the people. It would be an infinitely valuable stimulus for culture, which would emerge from the suffocatingly confined atmosphere in which it has been enclosed. It would no longer belong solely to the specialists. Because at present it does belong to specialists, top-down, only degraded as we go downwards. Just as we treat the workers as if they were high-school pupils who are a bit obtuse, we treat the pupils as if they were extremely tired students, and the students as if they were teachers who have suffered from amnesia and need to be re-educated. Culture is an instrument wielded by teachers to create teachers who will in turn create teachers.

Of all the current forms of the disease of uprootedness, the uprootedness of culture is not the least alarming. The first consequence of this disease is generally, in all domains, that because relationships are severed, each thing is seen as a goal in itself. Uprootedness breeds idolatry.

To take just one example of the deformation of our culture, the wholly justifiable concern to keep geometrical reasoning as a necessity means that geometry is presented to high-school students as something with absolutely no relation to the world. They will be interested in it only as a game, or to achieve good grades. How can they see any truth in it? Most of them will always be unaware that almost all our actions, whether simple or skilfully combined, are applications of geometric principles, that the universe we live in is a web of geometric relationships, and that geometrical necessity is the very one to which we are in fact subject, as creatures enclosed in space and time. Geometrical necessity is presented in such a way that it seems arbitrary. What could be more absurd than an arbitrary necessity? Necessity, by definition, is something that imposes itself.

On the other hand, when we want to popularize geometry and bring it closer to experience, we exclude demonstrations. All that remains are a few completely useless formulae. Geometry has lost its flavour, its essence. Its essence is to be a discipline that has necessity as its purpose – the same necessity which, in fact, is sovereign here below.

Both of these deformations could easily be avoided. There is no need to choose between demonstration and experience. It is as easy to demonstrate with wood or iron as with a stick of chalk.

There would be a simple way to introduce geometrical necessity in a vocational school, by combining study and practical experience. The students would be told: 'Here are a number of tasks to be carried out (making objects that meet certain conditions). Some are possible, some are impossible. Do the ones that are possible and convince me that the ones you don't do are impossible.' Through this window, all geometry can be incorporated into work. Execution is sufficient empirical proof of possibility, but for impossibility there is no empirical proof, there must be demonstration. The impossible is the concrete form of necessity.

As for the rest of science, everything that belongs to classical science – and it is not possible to incorporate Einstein and quantum theory into worker culture – proceeds mainly from a similar method, which consists of transporting the relations governing human labour into nature. Consequently, it belongs much more naturally to workers, if presented to them appropriately, than to high-school students.

This applies even more to the area of culture classified as 'the humanities' (*lettres*). Because the subject is always the human condition, and it is the people who have the most real, the most direct experience of the human condition.

On the whole, with some exceptions, second-class and lesser works are more suitable for the elite, and first-class works are more suitable for the people.

Think, for example, what a profound understanding could

result from an encounter between the people and Greek poetry, whose subject is almost always affliction! The question is how to translate and present it. For example, a worker who feels the dread of unemployment in the very marrow of his bones, would understand how Philoctetes feels when his bow is taken away, and his despair as he gazes at his useless hands. A worker would also understand that Electra is hungry, which a bourgeois, except in the present period, is absolutely incapable of understanding – including the editors of the Budé edition [of the classics].[40]

There is a third obstacle to worker culture and that is slavery. When it is truly exercised, thought is essentially free and sovereign. For a thinking being to be free and sovereign for an hour or two and a slave for the rest of the day is such a cruel wrench that in order to avoid being torn in two, it is almost impossible for that being not to relinquish the highest forms of thought.

If effective reforms were carried out, this obstacle would gradually be eliminated. Moreover, the memory of recent slavery and the vestiges of dying-out slavery would be a powerful mental stimulus during the liberation process.

A condition for a worker culture is a mix of so-called intellectuals – a dreadful name, but at present they do not deserve anything better – and workers. It is difficult for such a mix to be realized, but the present situation is conducive to it. Many young intellectuals have been thrown into slavery in the factories and fields of Germany. Others mixed with young workers in the *camps des compagnons*.[41] But there they gained valuable experience. Many were destroyed by it, or at least weakened in body and soul. But some were perhaps truly educated.

Such a precious experience is in danger of being wasted because of the almost irresistible temptation to forget humiliation and affliction as soon as it is over. Those prisoners who have returned should be approached immediately and urged to maintain the contacts they had made with workers under duress, to rethink their recent experience for them, with a view to bringing culture and the people closer together, and to take culture in a new direction.

Right now, the trade-union Resistance organizations could facilitate such a rapprochement. But in general, if there is to be an intellectual life in the workers' unions, they will need contacts with thinkers other than simply incorporating them into the CGT in professional organizations for protecting their own financial interests. That was the ultimate absurdity.

The natural relationship would be for a trade union to admit as honorary members, but with no voice in discussions on action, intellectuals who would place themselves at its service free of charge to run classes and libraries.

Among the generation which, because of its young age has been spared having to mix with workers under the constraint of captivity, it would be highly desirable for a movement to develop analogous to that of the Russian students fifty years ago, but with clearer ideas, and for students to volunteer for extended stints as labourers, mixing anonymously with the masses in the factories and fields.

In short, the abolition of the proletarian condition, which is defined above all by being uprooted, boils down to the task of constituting an industrial production and a culture of the mind where the workers are, and feel, at home.

Of course, the workers themselves would have a large part in creating this condition. But, by the nature of things, this part would grow as their true liberation is achieved. It would inevitably be minimal as long as the workers are ground down by affliction.

This problem of creating a truly new workers' condition is urgent and must be addressed without delay. A direction must be decided now. Because, as soon as the war is over, construction will take place, in the literal sense of the word. Houses and edifices will be built. What is erected will not be demolished again unless there is another war, and life will adapt to it. It would be paradoxical if the building blocks that are to determine the whole of society, perhaps for many generations to come, were left to assemble themselves at random. Consequently, it will be necessary to think clearly in advance about the organization of industrial enterprises in the near future.

If we were to avoid this necessity for fear of possible divisions, it would simply mean that we are not qualified to shape France's destiny.

And so, it is pressing to examine a plan for giving workers new roots, as suggested in the outline below.

Big factories would be abolished. A large company would consist of an assembly shop linked to numerous small workshops, each with one or several workers, scattered throughout the countryside. These workers, not specialists, would take turns working in the central assembly shop at certain periods, and these periods should be regarded as holidays. They would do half a day's work, and the rest of the time would be spent forging comradeships, developing company loyalty, attending technical talks to ensure that each worker understood the exact purpose of the parts they produce and the difficulties resolved thanks to others' work, as well as talks on geography so they could see where the products they help to make end up, which human beings use them, in what kind of milieu, what kind of daily life they lead, in what kind of human environment these products have a place, and what that place is. To this would be added general culture. A workers' college would be next to each central assembly shop. It would have close links with the company's management but would not be owned by it.

The machines would not belong to the company. They would belong to the tiny, scattered workshops, and these in turn would be owned by the workers, either individually or collectively. Each worker would also have a house and some land.

This threefold ownership of machine, house and land would be conferred [on male workers] by the state, at the time of their marriage, and on condition that they had successfully completed a demanding technical test, as well as an intelligence and general culture test.

On the one hand, the choice of machine should match the worker's preferences and know-how, and on the other, it should meet the very general production requirements. It should obviously be, as far as possible, an adjustable and multi-purpose automatic machine.

This threefold ownership could neither be inherited, nor sold, nor alienated in any way. (The machine alone could, in some cases, be exchanged.) Anyone benefiting from it would only be able to relinquish it altogether. In this case, it should be made not impossible but difficult for him to receive the equivalent later elsewhere.

When a worker dies, this property returns to the state, which of course must ensure the equivalent welfare of his wife and children. If the widow is capable of performing the work, she retains ownership.

All these gifts are financed through taxes, either direct taxes on company profits or indirect taxes on the sale of products. They are administered by a body made up of civil servants, company bosses, trade unionists and members of parliament.

This right of ownership can be withdrawn on the grounds of professional misconduct as determined by a court. This, of course, presupposes that similar penal measures are in place to punish professional misconduct by an employer.

A worker who wishes to become the owner of a small workshop would have to obtain the authorization of a professional body responsible for granting it at its discretion and would then be granted resources to purchase two or three additional machines, but no more.

A worker unable to pass the test would remain an employee. But he would be able to try again throughout his life, with no age limit. He could at any age and on several occasions apply to do a free placement of several months in a vocational training college.

These incapacitated workers would work either in small, non-cooperative workshops, as assistants to an employee working from home, or as labourers in assembly shops. But industry should only tolerate small numbers of them. Most should be encouraged into the manual or pen-pushing jobs that are essential to public services and commerce.

Until he is old enough to marry and settle down for life – in other words, twenty-two, twenty-five or thirty, depending on his character – a young worker would be considered as still in apprenticeship.

In childhood, schools should give children enough leisure so that they can spend hours and hours tinkering around their father's work. The half-day format – a few hours of study, a few hours of work – should continue for a long time. Then there should be a very varied way of life: travelling around in a sort of Tour de France, staying and working sometimes with individual workers, sometimes in small workshops, sometimes in different companies' assembly workshops, sometimes in youth groups such as 'Chantiers' or 'Compagnons' stays which, depending on preferences and abilities, could be repeated several times and last for periods ranging from a few weeks to two years, in workers' training schools. Moreover, these stays should, under certain conditions, be possible at any age. They should be entirely free of charge and should not lead to any kind of social advantage.

When the young worker, filled with variety and satiated, is thinking of settling down, he will be ready to put down roots. A wife, children, a house, a garden providing him with much of his food, a job binding him to a company he would love and be proud of, and which would be an open window on the world: that is enough for a human being's earthly happiness.

Of course, such a concept for young workers implies a total overhaul of barracks life.

As for pay, naturally and above all it would be necessary to avoid wages being so low as to leave the worker destitute – but this is hardly likely in such conditions – and then to avoid pay becoming a preoccupation that stops him from becoming attached to the company.

Corporate and arbitration bodies etc., should be conceived solely for that purpose – and should function in such a way that workers rarely need to think about money matters.

The profession of company manager should, like that of doctor, be among those which the state, in the public interest, allows to be exercised only subject to certain guarantees. These guarantees should relate not only to capability, but to moral elevation.

The capital invested would be much less than at present. A credit system could easily enable a young man who is poor but has the ability and vocation to be an entrepreneur to become one.

The company could thus become individual again. As for public limited companies, once a transitional system is in place, it might be better to abolish them altogether and declare them banned.

Of course, the variety of businesses would require very different approaches. The plan outlined here can only be put into operation following an extensive effort, including in the field of technical innovation, which would be crucial.

In any case, a mode of social life of this kind would be neither capitalist nor socialist.

It would eliminate the proletarian condition, whereas so-called socialism tends to throw everybody into it.

Its focus would not be, to cite the formula now in fashion, the interests of the consumer – these interests can only be crudely material – but human dignity in work, which is a spiritual value.

The disadvantage of such a social conception is that it has no chance of moving beyond empty words unless a number of free individuals are passionately and deeply committed to bringing it about. There is no certainty that such people can be found or galvanized.

Yet, failing this, it seems that the only choice is between different and almost equally appalling forms of affliction.

Although such a conception is a long way off, post-war reconstruction should have as its immediate objective the dispersal of industrial labour.

RURAL UPROOTEDNESS

The problem of rural uprootedness is no less severe than that of industrial uprootedness. Although the disease is less advanced, it is all the more scandalous because it goes against nature for the land to be farmed by people who have been uprooted. The same attention should be accorded to both problems.

Moreover, public attention should never be paid to industrial workers without the same attention being given to rural workers. For they are very touchy, very susceptible, and always haunted by the idea that they are being forgotten. It is certain that amid their present sufferings they find comfort in the assurance that their plight is being considered. But it has to be said that people think about them a great deal more when they are hungry than when there is plenty to eat, even those who had believed that their minds were on far higher things than physical needs.

When we speak of the people, industrial workers have a tendency – which should not be encouraged – to think that it must be only about them. There is absolutely no justification for this, other than the fact that they make more noise than rural workers. They have managed to convince the intellectuals who are sympathetic towards the people of this. The result has been a kind of hatred among the rural classes for 'the left', as it is called in politics, except when they have fallen under the influence of Communism, and where anticlericalism is the main driving force, and no doubt in a few other cases as well.

The animosity between rural and industrial workers in France goes back a long way. There is a late-fourteenth-century lament in which the peasants give a heart-rending enumeration of the cruelties to which they are subjected by all classes of society, including craftsmen. In the history of popular movements in France, unless I am mistaken, rural and industrial workers have hardly ever found themselves side by side. Even in 1789, it was perhaps more of a coincidence than anything else.

In the fourteenth century, peasants were by far the most afflicted. But even when they are materially better off – and when they are, they are barely aware of it because the factory workers who came to spend a few days' holiday in the country gave in to the temptation of boasting – they are always plagued by the feeling that everything happens in the cities, and that they are 'out of it'.[42]

Of course, this thinking is aggravated by the advent of the wireless and cinemas in the countryside, and by the circulation of newspapers such as *Confidences* and *Marie Claire*,[43] compared with which cocaine is harmless.

Given that this is the situation, first of all we need to invent and put into practice something that will make the rural workers feel that they are 'in it'.[44]

It is perhaps regrettable that in the official broadcasts from London, a lot more has always been said about the industrial workers than about them. Admittedly, they have a much, much smaller role to play in the Resistance. But perhaps that is all the more reason to demonstrate again and again that everyone is aware of their existence.

It must be borne in mind that the French people cannot be said to be in favour of a movement when this is not true of the majority of rural workers.

We should make it a rule never to promise something new and better to the industrial workers without promising the same to the rural workers. Prior to 1933, the Nazi Party's great skill was to present itself to the factory workers as specifically a workers' party, to the rural workers as specifically a rural workers' party, to the petty bourgeois as specifically a petty bourgeois party, and so on. This was easy for them because they lied to everyone. We should do the same, but without lying. That is difficult, but not impossible.

In recent years, rural uprootedness has been as lethal a danger to the country as industrial-worker uprootedness. One of the severest symptoms was seven or eight years ago, when the depopulation of the countryside continued in the midst of an unemployment crisis.[45]

It is obvious that rural depopulation ultimately leads to social death. It can be said that things will not go that far. But we have no idea. So far, we have not found any way to stop it.

Two things should be noted in relation to this phenomenon. One is that white people carry this disease with them wherever they go. It has even spread to Black Africa, even though for thousands of years this was undoubtedly a continent of villages. At least when they were not being massacred, tortured or enslaved, these people knew how to live happily on their land. Contact with us is causing them to lose that capacity. This might make us wonder whether even the Africans, albeit the most primitive of the colonized peoples, might not in fact have more to teach us than we to teach them. The benefits we have given them are comparable to those of given by the financier to the cobbler [in Lafontaine's fable].[46] Nothing in the world makes up for the loss of joy in work.

The other point is that the seemingly unlimited resources of the totalitarian state are powerless against this disease. In Germany, there have been official, formal, and oft-repeated admissions of this fact. In a sense, that is good, since it gives us the opportunity to do better than them.

The destruction of wheat stocks during the economic crisis made a big impact on public opinion, and rightly so, but on reflection, the desertion of the countryside in times of industrial crisis is even more scandalous, if that is possible. Clearly there is no other hope of solving the worker problem. There is no way to prevent the worker population from being a proletariat if it is constantly being swollen by the exodus of rural workers breaking away from their past lives.

The war has shown how serious the disease is among rural workers because the soldiers were young farm workers. In September 1939, rural workers were heard to say: 'It is better to live German than to die French.' What had been done to them to make them think they had nothing to lose?

We need to acknowledge one of the greatest difficulties in politics. Whereas the factory workers are suffering badly from feeling exiled in this society, the rural workers, on the other hand, believe that only the industrial workers are at home in it. The rural workers do not see the intellectuals who support the workers as supporters of the oppressed, but as supporters of the privileged. The intellectuals are completely unaware of this attitude.

The inferiority complex of those working in agriculture is so great that millionaire farmers find it natural for retired petty bourgeois neighbours to treat them with the colonial disdain reserved for natives. An inferiority complex has to be very strong for it not to be erased by money.

And so, the more pressure there is to provide moral satisfaction to the workers, the more important it is to provide the rural workers with that same moral satisfaction. Otherwise, the resulting imbalance would be dangerous for society and rebound on the workers themselves.

The rural workers' need for roots first of all takes the form of a thirst for property. It truly is a thirst in them, and a healthy and natural one. They are certain to be won over by being offered such hopes, and there is no reason not to do so if we consider the need for property as sacred, rather than the legal titles that lay down the terms of ownership. There are many possible legal provisions for gradually transferring land into the hands of those who farm it but do not own it. Nothing can justify a city-dweller's right to land ownership. Large-scale agricultural ownership is justifiable only in certain cases, for technical reasons, and in such cases, it is possible to conceive of agricultural workers intensively farming their own plot of land, growing vegetables and the like, and at the same time applying extensive farming methods with modern tools to vast areas owned by them in common, in the form of a cooperative.

A measure that would touch the heart of agricultural workers would be one that considered the land as a means of work, and not as an asset in the distribution of inheritances. Then we would no longer witness the scandalous plight of a farmer indebted for life to a government-official brother who works less and earns more.

Even small pensions for the elderly might have far-reaching benefits. Unfortunately, 'pension' is a magic word that draws young rural workers to the city. Humiliation of the old is often more pronounced in rural areas, and a little money, given in honourable conditions, would give them status.

By contrast, too much stability produces an effect of uprootedness among rural workers. A smallholder starts ploughing alone at the age of fourteen; at that age, work is poetry, exhilarating, even though he barely has the strength. A few years later, this youthful enthusiasm is exhausted, he knows his job, the physical strength required is overwhelming and far exceeds the work to be done; there is nothing else to do other than what he has been doing every day for several years. He then begins to spend the week dreaming about what he will do on Sunday. From that moment, he is lost.

The smallholder's first full contact with work at the age of fourteen, that initial headiness, should be celebrated with a

solemn feast that would make it enter deep into his heart forever. In the most Christian villages, such a feast should have a
religious character.

But also, three or four years later, the thirst returns and must
be satisfied. For a young agricultural worker, there is only one –
travel. All young farm workers should be given the opportunity
to travel without spending money, in France and even abroad,
not in the cities, but in the countryside. This would involve
organizing something similar to the Tour de France for them.[47]
It could include educational and cultural opportunities. Because
often the best young farm workers, having left school at thirteen and thrown themselves into work, often feel the desire to
study again when they are about eighteen or twenty. This also
happens to young industrial workers. Exchange systems could
make it possible for young people to travel, even those whose
families rely on them. It goes without saying that these trips
would be entirely voluntary. But parents would not be allowed
to stop them.

It is hard to imagine how powerful the idea of travel is among
rural workers, and the importance that such a reform would
have on their morale, even when still only a promise, and even
more so once it has become common practice. The youth, having travelled the world for several years without ever ceasing to
be an agricultural worker, would return home, his restlessness
assuaged, and would settle down.

Perhaps something similar would be needed for the young
women; they need something to replace *Marie Claire*, and we
cannot leave them *Marie Claire*.

Military life has been a terrible uprooting factor for young
rural workers, to the extent that ultimately military training
has had the opposite effect from its intended purpose; young
men had learned the military drill but were less eager to fight
than before because anyone finishing their military service
emerged as anti-militarist. This is living proof that it is not in
the interests of the military machine to allow the military the
sovereign right to take two years or even one year of every life.
Just as capitalism cannot be allowed to control the professional
training of young people, the army cannot be allowed to

control their military training. The civilian authorities must be involved, and they must do so in such a way that constitutes an education and not a corruption.

Contact between young rural workers and young factory workers during military service is not at all desirable. The latter seek to impress the former, which is damaging to both. Such contacts do not bring about real closeness. Only common action brings people closer together, and, by definition, there is no common action in the army since it is about preparing for war in peacetime.

There is no reason to set up barracks in cities; barracks for young rural workers could very well be built a long way from any town.

Admittedly the owners of licensed brothels would lose out. But there is no point considering any kind of reform unless there is the determination to put an end to the public authorities' collusion with these people and to abolish an institution that shames France.

Let it be said in passing that we have paid dearly for this disgrace. Prostitution established as an official institution, in accordance with a specifically French system, has largely contributed to corrupting the army and has completely corrupted the police.[48] This is likely to lead to the decline of democracy because it is impossible for a democracy to survive when the police, who represent the law in the eyes of the citizens, are openly held in contempt by the public. The English cannot understand how there can be a democracy in which the police are not held in affectionate respect. But their police do not have a flock of prostitutes for their amusement.

If it were possible to surmise exactly what factors contributed to our disaster, it might transpire that all our shameful behaviours – like this one, and colonial greed, and our ill-treatment of foreigners – have played their part in our downfall. A great deal can be said of our affliction, but not that it is undeserved.

Prostitution is a typical example of how the disease of uprootedness replicates itself: the professional prostitute's situation is uprootedness taken to its extreme, and a handful of prostitutes has a vast power to contaminate. It is obvious that we will not have a healthy rural population so long as the state persists in bringing young farm workers and prostitutes together. So long as the rural population is not healthy, the working class cannot be healthy either, and nor can the rest of the country.

Moreover, nothing would be more popular among rural workers than the plan to reform the military service system to take their moral wellbeing into consideration.

The problem of the culture of the mind arises for rural as well as factory workers. They too need a translation that is tailored to them, not to factory workers.

In all matters of the spirit, rural workers have been brutally uprooted by the modern world. They once had everything a human being needs when it comes to art and thought, in a form specific to them, and of the highest quality. From Restif de la Bretonne's writings about his childhood, it would seem that the most fortunate rural workers of that time had a fate that was infinitely preferable to that of their most fortunate counter-parts of today.[49] But this past, although so close, cannot be retrieved. We must find ways of preventing the rural workers from remaining alienated from the culture of the mind avail-able to them.

Science should be presented to rural and factory workers in very different ways. For the factory workers, it is natural that everything should be dominated by mechanics. For the rural workers, at the heart of everything should be the wondrous cycle by which solar energy, absorbed into the plants, captured by chlorophyll and concentrated in seeds and fruits, enters the one who eats or drinks, passes into their muscles and is expended in cultivating the land. Everything related to science can be understood in terms of this cycle because the notion of energy is at the centre of everything. If the awareness of this cycle were to become part of the rural worker's thinking, it would infuse their work with poetry.

Generally speaking, the essential purpose of all education in the villages should be to enhance awareness of the beauty of the world, to the beauty of nature. True, tourists have discovered that rural workers are not interested in landscapes. But when you share the rural workers' exhausting day's labour, which is the only way to talk with them openly, you hear them express regret that their work is too demanding for them to be able to enjoy the beauties of nature.

Of course, enhancing someone's sensitivity to beauty is not achieved by saying, 'Look how beautiful it is!' It is not so simple.

The educated classes' recent interest in folklore should help give agricultural workers the feeling that they have a place in human thinking. The present system suggests that anything to do with ideas is the exclusive preserve of the cities, apart from a small, very tiny share, because rural workers are thought not to have the capacity to conceive of a large one.

This is the colonial mentality, only to a lesser degree. Just as an indigene from the colonies influenced by a little European education despises their own people more than a cultured European would, so it often happens with a teacher who is the son of a farmer.

The first condition for agricultural workers to become morally re-rooted in the country is that the profession of rural teacher should be something special, something specific, and their training should be totally, not partially, different from that of an urban teacher. It is utterly absurd to produce teachers from the same mould for [a working-class district of Paris, like] Belleville and for a small village. It is one of the many absurdities of an era whose hallmark is stupidity.

The second condition is that rural teachers know agricultural workers and do not look down on them; this cannot be achieved simply by recruiting them from the agricultural milieu. A very large component of the training they receive should be devoted to the folklore of all countries, presented not as an object of curiosity, but as something important. They should learn about the part shepherds played in the first attempts at human thinking, speculations about the stars, and also, as evidenced by the comparisons that recur everywhere in ancient texts, notions of good and evil; they should be introduced to literature about rural life – Hesiod, Piers Plowman,[50] the laments of the Middle Ages, the few contemporary works that are authentically rural; all this, of course, without prejudice to general culture. After this initial preparation, trainee teachers could be sent to serve for a year as farmhands, anonymously, in a different region, and then brought back together again in ordinary schools to help them process their experience. The same applies to teachers in working-class districts and factories. However, such experiences require moral preparation, otherwise they can result in contempt or repulsion instead of compassion and love.

It would also be a very good thing if the Church could make the role of parish priest or village pastor something specific. When we think of how frequently Christ took inspiration from agricultural life for his parables, it is scandalous that religion should be absent from daily life in an entirely Catholic French village, relegated to a few hours on Sunday. But many of these parables do not appear in the liturgy, and those that do attract little attention. Just as the stars and the sun the teacher speaks of are found in school textbooks with no reference to heaven, so the vine, the wheat, and the sheep mentioned in church on Sundays have nothing in common with the vine, the wheat or the sheep in the fields to which the farmer dedicates a little of his life every day. Christian agricultural workers are also uprooted from their religious life. The idea of representing a village without a church in the 1937 Exposition was not as absurd as many have said.[51]

Just as the members of the JOC, the young Christian workers' association, rejoice in the idea of Christ the worker, so the agricultural workers should take pride in the sections of the parables of the Gospel devoted to the life of the fields and in the sacred function of bread and wine, and this should give them the sense that Christianity is something that belongs to them.

The controversies around *laïcité* (secularism) have been one of the main sources of poisoning of rural life in France. Sadly, these arguments look set to go on for a long time. It is impossible to avoid taking a position on this issue, and it seems at first almost impossible to find one that is not very bad.[52]

It is certain that neutrality is a lie. The secular system is not neutral; it conveys to children a philosophy that is on the one hand vastly superior to Saint-Sulpice-type religion, and on the other hand vastly inferior to authentic Christianity, which is very rare nowadays.[53] Many teachers embrace this philosophy with a religious fervour.

Freedom of teaching is not a solution. The word is meaningless. A child's spiritual formation belongs to no one, not to the child, who is in no position to do anything with it, nor to the parents, nor to the state. Family rights so often invoked are nothing more than a weapon. A priest who, when given a natural opportunity to do so, refrains from speaking of Christ to a child of a non-Christian family, would be a priest of little faith. To keep secular schools as they are, and at the same time to allow or even encourage competition from faith schools is absurd from both the theoretical and practical points of view. Private schools, whether faith-based or not, should be authorized, not on the basis of a principle of freedom, but on the basis of public usefulness in each particular case when the school is good, and subject to inspection.

Allowing the clergy to be involved in state education is not a solution. If it were possible, it would not be desirable, and it is not possible in France without a civil war.

Ordering teachers to talk to children about God, as the Vichy government did a few months ago on the initiative of Monsieur Chevalier, is a joke in very poor taste.[54]

Allowing secular philosophy to retain its official status would be an arbitrary measure, unjust in that it does not reflect any scale of values and would plunge us straight into totalitarianism. For, although secularism has aroused a certain degree of almost religious zeal, that degree is weak, by the nature of things, and we live in an age of ardent passions. The only obstacle to totalitarianism's idolatrous tendency can be found in an authentic spiritual life. If children are accustomed to not thinking of God, they will become fascists or Communists out of a need to give themselves to something.

We see more clearly what justice requires in this domain when the notion of rights is replaced by that of obligations linked to need. A young soul awakening to thought needs the wealth amassed by the human race over the centuries. It is wrong for a child to be brought up in a narrow Christianity that prevents them from ever becoming capable of realizing that there are treasures of pure gold in non-Christian civilizations. Secular education does children a greater wrong. It conceals these treasures, and those of Christianity as well.

The only justifiable and practically feasible attitude that French state education can have towards Christianity is to regard it as a treasure trove of human thought among many others. It is utterly absurd that a holder of a French baccalaureate should have read poems from the Middle Ages, Polyeuctus, *Athalie*, *Phaedra*, Pascal, Lamartine, philosophical doctrines imbued with Christianity such as those of Descartes and Kant, the *Divine Comedy* or *Paradise Lost*, but has never opened the Bible.

Future teachers and professors simply need to be told that religion has always played a central role in the development of human culture, philosophy and civilization in all countries, except recently in some parts of Europe. An education in which religion is never mentioned is absurd. On the other hand, just as in history we talk a lot about France to French children, it is natural that being in Europe, if we talk about religion, it should be, above all, about Christianity.

Consequently, for slightly older children, there should be classes at all levels of the curriculum that could be called religious history, for example. The children would be read passages from the Scriptures, especially the Gospel. Commentary would be in the very spirit of the text, as should always be the case. Dogma would be spoken of as something that has played a crucially important role in our countries, and in which people of the utmost integrity have believed with all their hearts; and the fact that dogma has been the pretext for inflicting many cruelties should not be concealed. But above all we would seek to make children aware of the beauty it contains. If they ask: 'Is it true?', the reply should be: 'It is so beautiful that it certainly contains a great deal of truth. As to whether it is wholly true or not, try to become capable of recognizing truth when you grow up.' It would be strictly forbidden to exclude from commentaries anything that implied a denial of dogma, and likewise anything that implied an affirmation. Any teacher who so wished and who had the requisite knowledge and pedagogical skills would be free to speak to the children not only about Christianity but also, although with much less emphasis, about any other authentic branch of religious thought. Religious thought is authentic when it is universal in its orientation. (This is not the case with Judaism, which is linked to a concept of race.)

Should such a solution be applied, it is to be hoped that religion would gradually cease to be something for or against, in which people take sides in the same way as in politics. We would then see the eradication of the two camps – those of the teacher and the parish priest – which have created a kind of underlying civil war in so many French villages. Contact with Christian beauty, presented simply as beauty to be savoured, would subtly instil spirituality into the mass population, if the country is capable of it, far more effectively than any dogmatic teaching of religious beliefs.

The word beauty in no way implies that religious matters should be considered in the manner of aesthetes. Their viewpoint is sacrilegious, not only in matters of religion, but even in matters of art. It consists in treating beauty as entertainment, manipulating it and gazing at it. Beauty is something that is consumed; it is sustenance. If Christian beauty were offered to the people simply as beauty, it should be as beauty that nourishes.

In rural schools, attentive, regular and frequently commentated reading of excerpts from the New Testament featuring rural life could do much to restore the lost poetry to agricultural labour. If both the entire spiritual life of the soul and all scientific knowledge related to the material universe were oriented towards the act of work, work would have its rightful place in people's thinking. Instead of being a kind of prison, it would be attuned to this world and the other.

Why, for example, should a farmer sowing a crop not be reminded, even without inner words, of some of Christ's utterances: 'unless a kernel of wheat falls to the ground and dies';

'the Word of God can be likened to a seed'; '[...] mustard seed
[...] indeed is smaller than all seeds'.[55] And also, be reminded
of the dual mechanism of growth, by which the seed consumes
itself and, with the help of bacteria, reaches the surface, and
that by which solar energy, transmitted through light and captured by the green of the stem, is compelled to rise. The analogy
that makes the mechanisms of life on Earth a mirror of supernatural mechanisms, if one can use this expression, then is
resoundingly alive, and so-called work fatigue causes it to enter
the body. The suffering that is always related to some extent to
the exertion of work becomes the pain that makes the beauty
of the world penetrate to the human being's very core.

A similar method can imbue the work of the manual labourer
with the same significance. It is just as easy to conceive.

Only in this way would the dignity of work have a solid
foundation. Because, ultimately, there is no true dignity that
does not have a spiritual root and is therefore of a supernatural
order.

The task of the community school is to confer more dignity
on work by infusing it with thinking, and not to make the
worker a compartmentalized thing that sometimes works and
sometimes thinks. Of course, a farmer who sows must take care
to scatter the grain correctly rather than remember lessons
learned in school. But the object of attention is not the entire
content of thought.[56] A happy young woman, pregnant for the
first time, who is sewing a layette, is thinking about sewing correctly. But she does not forget for one moment the child she is
carrying inside her. At the same time, somewhere in a prison
workshop, a woman inmate is sewing, also thinking about sewing correctly because she is afraid of being punished. Both
women are doing the same work at the same time, and they are
concentrating on the same technical difficulty. Nevertheless,
there is a gulf of difference between one task and the other. The
entire social problem consists of shifting workers from one of
these two conditions to the other.

What is needed, is for this world and the other, in their dual
beauty, to be present and associated with the act of work, like
the unborn child in the making of the layette. This association

can take place by presenting thoughts in a way that puts them in direct relation with the specific gestures and operations of each task, through a profound assimilation that allows them to penetrate the very substance of the being, and through a habit imprinted on the memory and linking those thoughts to the movements of work.

Today, we are not capable of such a transformation, either intellectually or spiritually. It would be an important step were we capable of starting to prepare for it. Of course, school would not be enough. It would require the participation of all the sectors where there is something akin to thought: the Church, trade unions, literary and scientific milieus. And, dare we suggest, political milieus.

The particular mission, the vocation of our era, is the constitution of a civilization based on the spirituality of work. The ideas that pave the way for this vocation and can be found scattered in the works of Rousseau, George Sand, Tolstoy, Proudhon, Marx, in papal encyclicals and elsewhere, are the only original thoughts of our time, the only ones we have not borrowed from the Greeks. It is because we did not live up to this great thing that was being born in us that we threw ourselves into the abyss of totalitarian systems. But if Germany is defeated, perhaps our bankruptcy will not be irrevocable. Perhaps we still have an opportunity. We cannot think about it without anguish; if we have it, mediocre as we are, how will we ensure we do not miss it?

This vocation is the only thing big enough to offer to the people instead of totalitarian idols. If it is not offered in such a way as to make them feel its greatness, they will remain in thrall to the idol, which will be coloured red instead of brown. If people are given the choice between butter and guns, although they prefer butter by far, a mysterious fatality compels them to choose guns, despite themselves. Butter is too lacking in poetry, at least when people have it, but it takes on a kind of poetry when they do not have it. They cannot admit to their preference for it.

Right now, the United Nations, especially America, is busy telling the starving people of Europe: our guns will provide you with butter. This arouses only one reaction, the thought that they are in no hurry. When this butter arrives, people will throw themselves on it; and immediately afterwards they will turn to anyone who will show them pretty guns, decently wrapped in any old ideology. Do not think that, being exhausted, they will only want wellbeing. Nervous exhaustion caused by recent affliction prevents people from attaining wellbeing. It compels them to seek oblivion, either through unbridled hedonism – as was the case after 1918 – or in some evil fanaticism. Affliction that has bitten too deeply creates a disposition to affliction that compels people to throw themselves and others into it. Germany is a case in point.

The afflicted people of continental Europe need greatness even more than bread, and there are only two kinds of greatness: genuine greatness, which is of the spiritual order, and the old lie of conquering the world. Conquest is the ersatz for greatness.

The contemporary form of authentic greatness is a civilization built on the spirituality of work. It is a thought that can be put forward without risking any disunity. The word spirituality does not imply any particular affiliation. In the present climate, the Communists themselves would probably not reject it. Moreover, it would be easy to find in Marx quotes which all boil down to a criticism of the lack of spirituality addressed to capitalist society; this implies that there must be some spirituality in the new society. Conservatives would not dare to reject this formula. Neither would the radical, secular or Freemason milieus. Christians would seize upon it with joy. It could lead to unanimity.

But such a formula can only be reached for with trepidation. How can we go near it without defiling it, without making a lie of it? Our age is so poisoned with lies that it turns everything it touches into a lie. And we are of our time, we have no reason to believe that we are better than it.

To discredit such words by throwing them into the public domain without infinite precautions would do irreparable harm and kill any hope that the corresponding thing might appear. These words must not be linked to a cause, a movement, or even a regime, or with a nation. Harm must not be done to them as it was by Pétain with the words *'Travail, Famille, Patrie'* (Work, Family, Fatherland), or by the Republic with the words *'Liberté, Égalité, Fraternité'* (Freedom, Equality, Fraternity). They must not become a motto.

If they are proposed publicly, it must be only as the expression of an idea that goes far beyond the people and collectivities of today, and which we commit in all humility to keeping in mind as a guide in all things. If this modesty has less appeal to the masses than more vulgar attitudes, it does not matter. It is better to fail than to succeed in doing harm.

But this thought need not be launched with a fanfare in order gradually to seep into people's minds because it responds to the concerns of everyone at the present moment. People all repeat, in slightly different ways, that we are suffering from an imbalance due to a purely material development of technology. The imbalance can only be repaired by a spiritual development in the same domain, that is, in the domain of work.

The only difficulty is the painful and unfortunately all too justifiable mistrust of the masses, who regard any formula that is slightly lofty as a trap to deceive them.

A civilization built on a spirituality of work would be the highest degree of rootedness of humanity in the universe, consequently the opposite of our current situation, which consists in an almost total uprootedness. It is therefore, by definition, the aspiration that is commensurate with our suffering.

UPROOTEDNESS AND NATION[57]

There is another form of uprootedness still that needs to be analysed to gain a basic understanding of our main disease. And that is uprootedness that could be called geographical, in other words, relating to collectivities that correspond to specific territories. The very significance of these collectivities has practically disappeared, except in one instance – the nation. But there are and have been many others. Some are smaller, sometimes tiny: towns or a cluster of villages, provinces, regions;

others encompass several nations or several parts of nations. The nation alone has taken the place of all of these. The nation, in other words, the state, since the only definition of the word nation is all the territories recognizing the authority of the same state. It is fair to say that in the present times, money and the state have replaced all other bonds.

For a long time now, the nation alone has played the part considered to epitomize the mission of the collectivity with regard to the human being, and that is to provide links between the past and the future via the present. In this sense, it can be claimed that it is the only form of collectivity in today's world. The family does not exist. What we call family is a small group of human beings around each of us: father and mother, husband or wife, children, and siblings who are already slightly removed. In recent times, amid the general distress, this small group has become an almost irresistible force of attraction, to the point of sometimes making us forget any kind of duty. But it was the only place where a little living warmth could be found amid the icy chill that had suddenly descended; it was an almost animal reaction.

But these days, no one thinks of their forebears who died fifty, or even twenty or ten years before they were born, nor of their descendants who will be born fifty, or even twenty or ten years after their death. As a result, from the point of view of the collectivity and its proper function, the family does not count.

Occupation does not count either. The guild was a link between the dead, the living and the unborn, in the context of a particular craft. There is nothing today that even remotely fulfils such a function. French syndicalism around 1900 may have made a few vague attempts in this direction, but these were quickly stamped out.

Ultimately, the village, town, region, province – all the geographical units smaller than the nation – have almost ceased to count. As have those that encompass several nations or parts of nations. When, for example, a few centuries ago, people said 'Christianity', it had a very different emotional resonance from today in Europe.

In short, when it comes to matters of the temporal order,

humanity's most precious asset – in other words, continuity in time beyond the limits of human existence, both backwards and forwards – has been entirely handed over to the state.

And yet it is precisely at this time, when the nation is subsisting on its own, that we have witnessed the sudden and vertiginously rapid disintegration of the nation. It has stunned us to the point that we find it extremely difficult to reflect on this.

In June and July 1940, the French people were not suddenly taken unawares by bandits lurking in the shadows who stole their country. They were a people who opened their hands and let their country fall to the ground. Later, but after a long interval, they made desperate efforts to retrieve it, but someone had trampled on it.

Now the sense of nationhood has returned. The words 'to die for France' have taken on an emphasis they had not had since 1918. But the movement of rebellion that roused the French people to action was largely triggered, to say the least, by hunger, cold, the hateful omnipresence of foreign soldiers with all the power to command, the separation of families and, for some people, exile and captivity. The clearest proof of this is the difference between the Occupied Zone and the rest of France. By nature, there is no more patriotic feeling north of the Loire compared to the south. The difference in situations has produced different mindsets. The example set by the British Resistance and the hope of a German defeat were also important factors.

France has no reality today other than memories and hope. The Republic has never been as beautiful as under the Empire,[58] the country is never more beautiful than under the oppression of a conqueror, if we have the hope of seeing it intact again. For this reason, the present intensity of national feeling is no indicator of how effective it will really be in stabilizing public life after France is liberated.

The immediate dissolution of this feeling in June 1940 is a memory filled with so much shame that people would rather put it out of their minds and dream only of the recovery to come. In private life, too, people are always tempted to gloss over their own shortcomings and find a way of reckoning in which they do not count. To give in to this temptation is to destroy the soul; it is the ultimate temptation that must be overcome.

We have all succumbed to this temptation, for this public shame that has been so profound that it has wounded each one of us in our inner sense of our own honour. Were it not for this temptation, reflecting on such an extraordinary phenomenon would have already led to a new doctrine, a new conception of patriotism.

From the social point of view especially, the need to think about the concept of patriotism cannot be avoided. Not to rethink it, but to think about it for the first time because, unless I am mistaken, it has never been thought about. Is that not odd, for a concept that has played, and still plays, such a role? That shows what little importance we place on thinking.

Over the past twenty-five years, the notion of patriotism had lost all credibility among French workers. The Communists awakened it after 1934, with a great fanfare of tricolour flags and singing of the *Marseillaise*. But they did not have the slightest difficulty in putting it back to sleep shortly before the war. It was not in the name of patriotism that they started the Resistance. They did not adopt it again until about nine months after the defeat. Little by little, they adopted it in its entirety. But it would be naive to see this as a genuine reconciliation between the working class and the country. The workers are dying for the country – this is only too true. But we are living in an era so mired in lies that even the virtue of blood willingly sacrificed is not enough to restore the truth.

For years, the workers were taught that internationalism is the most sacred obligation, and patriotism the most shameful bourgeois prejudice. Then more years were spent teaching them that patriotism is a sacred duty, and anything else was a betrayal. How, ultimately, could they be guided other than by gut reactions and propaganda?

There will be no healthy workers' movement unless it finds a doctrine that assigns a place to the notion of patriotism – a clearly defined, limited, place. This need is even more evident among the worker milieus because workers have been discussing the problem of patriotism for a long time. But it is a need shared by the entire country. It is inadmissible that the word, which today is almost continually used in conjunction with the word 'duty', has hardly ever been the subject of any study. In general, there only appears to be one mediocre page of Renan's work on the question that can be cited.[59]

The nation is a recent construct. In the Middle Ages, loyalty was owed to the lord, the city, or both, and beyond to territorial communities that were not very distinct. The feeling we call patriotism did exist, sometimes to a very intense degree, but its focus was not a territory. Depending on the circumstances, that feeling covered varying areas of land.

The fact is, patriotism has always existed, as far back as human history goes. Vercingetorix really died for Gaul; the Spanish tribes who resisted the Roman conquest sometimes to the point of extermination, died for Spain, and knew it, and said so; the dead of Marathon and Salamis died for Greece; at the time when Greece had not yet been reduced in the provinces and had the same relation to Rome as Vichy France has to Germany; the children of the Greek cities threw stones at the collaborators and called them traitors, with the same indignation that we feel today.

What had never existed until recently was a permanent, concrete object of patriotic sentiment. Patriotism was nebulous, shifting, and it broadened or narrowed according to affinities and threats. It was confused with different loyalties, towards men, lords or kings, or to cities. The whole formed something very muddled, but also very human. The terms used to express the sense of obligation that each one feels towards their country were often 'the public' or 'the public good' – a term that can mean a village, a city, a province, France, Christendom or the entire human race.

People also spoke of the kingdom of France. This term was a mixture of obligation to the country and loyalty to the king. But two obstacles prevented this dual feeling from ever being pure, not even in Joan of Arc's time. It should not be forgotten that the people of Paris were against Joan of Arc.

The first obstacle was that after Charles V, France, to use Montesquieu's vocabulary, ceased to be a monarchy and plunged into a state of despotism from which it only emerged in the eighteenth century.[60] These days, we find it so natural to pay taxes to the state that we cannot imagine the moral turmoil amid which this custom was established. In the fourteenth century, the payment of taxes, bar exceptional contributions made for war, was regarded as a disgrace, a shame reserved for conquered countries, the hallmark of slavery. The same sentiment is expressed in the Spanish *Romancero*, and also in Shakespeare's 'That England ... hath made a shameful conquest of itself'.[61]

As a child, Charles VI, abetted by his uncles through corruption and atrocious cruelty, brutally forced the people of France to accept an absolutely arbitrary, freely renewable tax, which literally starved the poor and was squandered by the lords. This is why the English under Henry V were first greeted as liberators, at a time when the Armagnacs were the party of the rich and the Burgundians that of the poor.

The French people, brutally subjugated at one fell swoop, had only mere stirrings of independence until the eighteenth century. Throughout this period, they were regarded by other Europeans as the ultimate slave people who were like cattle, at the mercy of their sovereign.

But at the same time, a suppressed and even more bitter hatred for the king took root deep in the hearts of this people, a hatred whose tradition never died out. It can already be felt in the heart-rending complaint of the peasants at the time of Charles VI and must have partially explained the mysterious popularity of the League in Paris. After the assassination of Henry IV, a twelve-year-old child was put to death for publicly saying that he would do the same to little Louis XIII. Richelieu began his career with a speech in which he asked the clergy to proclaim the damnation of all regicides. He gave as his reason that those who planned to do such a thing were driven by a zeal far too fanatical to be deterred by any temporal punishment.

This hatred was at its most virulent at the end of Louis XIV's reign. Having been crushed by a terror of equal intensity, it exploded eighty years later, in keeping with history's disconcerting custom, and it was poor Louis XVI who received the blow. That same hatred prevented a true restoration of the monarchy in 1815. Even today, it absolutely prevents the Count of Paris from being freely accepted by the people of France, despite the support of a man like Bernanos.[62] In some respects, this is a pity: many problems could be solved if he were, but that is how it is.

Another source of poison in the love of the French for the kingdom of France is the fact that in every age, some of the territories placed under obedience to the King of France felt like conquered lands and were treated as such. It has to be acknowledged that the forty kings who, over a thousand years, made France what it is today, often employed a brutality worthy of our era. If there is a natural correspondence between the tree and the fruit, it is not surprising that the fruit is in fact far from perfect.

Bar a few rare exceptions, history is witness to acts of atrocity as horrendous, if not more so, as the conquest by the French of the territories south of the Loire at the beginning of the thirteenth century. These territories, where there was a high degree of culture, tolerance, freedom and spiritual life, displayed an intense patriotism for what they called their 'language', the word by which they designated their country. For them, the French were foreigners and barbarians, as the Germans are to us. To instil terror from the start, the French began by exterminating the entire city of Béziers, and they achieved the desired effect. Once the land was conquered, they installed the Inquisition. A muted discontent continued to simmer among these populations, which later drove them to embrace Protestantism with ardour. D'Aubigné wrote that despite considerable differences in doctrine,[63] this was directly inspired by the Albigensians.[64] The religious fervour shown in Toulouse to the remains of the Duke of Montmorency, beheaded for rebelling against Richelieu, illustrates the strength of the hatred towards the central power in these parts. The same latent protest saw them throw themselves enthusiastically into the French Revolution. Later, they became radical-socialist, secular and anticlerical. Under the Third Republic, they no longer hated the central power, they had largely seized and exploited it.

It is noticeable that each time, their protest took on a more intense character of uprootedness and a lower level of spirituality and thought. It is also noticeable that since being conquered, these lands made a rather feeble contribution to French culture, whereas before they had been so brilliant. French thought owes more to the Albigensians and the troubadours of the twelfth century, who were not French, than to anything produced by these territories in the following centuries.

Burgundy was the seat of an original and extremely brilliant culture that did not survive it. At the end of the fourteenth century, the cities of Flanders had fraternal and clandestine relations with Paris and Rouen, but wounded Flemings preferred to die than to be cared for by the soldiers of Charles VI. These soldiers went on a plundering expedition to Holland and brought back wealthy bourgeois captives whom they decided to kill. A mercy movement offered them their lives if they were prepared to become subjects of the King of France. They replied that once dead, their bones would refuse to be subjected to the authority of the King of France, were that possible. A Catalan historian of the same period, telling the story of the Sicilian Vespers, writes, 'The French, who, wherever they rule, are as cruel as it is possible to be.'[65]

The Bretons were desperate when their sovereign, Anne, was forced to marry the King of France. If these people were to come back today, or rather a few years ago, would they have good reason to think they had been mistaken? No matter how discredited the Breton independence movement may be thanks to its leaders and the shameful ends they are pursuing, it is certain that this propaganda responds to something real, both in actual fact and in the feelings of these populations. There are latent treasures in the Bretons that have not been able to emerge. French culture does not suit them, but their own culture is unable to germinate, and so they remain at the very bottom of the social ladder. The Bretons make up the majority of illiterate soldiers; Breton women reportedly make up the majority of prostitutes in Paris. Independence would not be a remedy, but that does not mean that the disease does not exist.

Franche-Comté, free and happy under the very long-ago suzerainty of the Spanish, fought in the seventeenth century not to become French. The people of Strasbourg wept when they saw Louis XIV's troops enter their city in full peacetime, without any prior declaration, in a violation of promises made worthy of Hitler.

Paoli, the last Corsican hero, displayed his heroism by preventing his country from falling into French hands.[66] There is a monument to him in a church in Florence, but in France, but there is little mention of him. Corsica is an example of the danger of contagion that goes with uprootedness. After having conquered, colonized, corrupted and damaged the people of that island, we suffered them in the form of police prefects, police officers, warrant officers, school supervisors and other such functions, as a result of which they in turn treated the French more or less as a conquered people. They also helped to give France a reputation for brutality and cruelty, among many indigenous peoples of the colonies.

When the kings of France are praised for having assimilated the conquered countries, the main truth is that they largely uprooted them. It is an easy assimilation process, within everyone's reach. People who have been uprooted from their culture either remain without a culture or are given crumbs of the culture the conquerors are willing to share with them. In both cases, they do not stand out, they appear to be assimilated. The real feat is to assimilate peoples who preserve their culture, albeit modified. This feat is rarely achieved.

Under the *Ancien Régime*, the French were intensely conscious of being French in all of France's glorious moments in the thirteenth century, when the whole of Europe converged on the University of Paris; in the sixteenth century, when the Renaissance, already extinguished or not yet kindled elsewhere, had its centre in France, in the early years of Louis XIV's reign, when the prestige of the arts was equal to that of arms. Even so, it was not the kings who melded these disparate territories together. It was solely the Revolution.

Already in the eighteenth century, in very different milieux in France, alongside appalling corruption, there was a burning, pure flame of patriotism. Witness the young rural worker, the brilliantly gifted brother of Restif de la Bretonne who became a soldier almost as a child out of pure love for the public good and was killed at the age of seventeen.[67] But it was already the Revolution that produced this. Throughout the century, revolution was in the air, keenly awaited, longed for.

The Revolution merged the populations subject to the crown of France into a single mass, and this through the exhilaration of national sovereignty. Those who had been forcibly made French became so by willing consent; many of those who were not French wanted to become so. From that moment on, being French meant being the sovereign nation. If all peoples everywhere had become sovereign, as was hoped, France could not lose the glory of having begun. Moreover, borders no longer mattered. Foreigners were only those who remained slaves to tyrants. Foreigners with a truly republican soul were gladly welcomed as honorary French citizens.

And so, in France there was this paradox of a patriotism based not on love of the past, but on the most violent rupture with the country's past. And yet the Revolution had a past in the murkier park of France's history; all that was related to the emancipation of the serfs, the freedom of the cities, social struggles, the uprisings of the fourteenth century, the beginning of the Burgundian movement, the Fronde, writers such as d'Aubigné, Théophile de Viau and Retz.[68] Under Francis I, a popular militia plan was rejected because the lords objected that if it were implemented, the grandsons of the militiamen would be lords and their own grandsons would be serfs. Such was the magnitude of the growing underground force that was driving this people.

But the influence of the Encyclopaedists – all uprooted intellectuals obsessed with the idea of progress – prevented any effort to evoke a revolutionary tradition. Moreover, the long terror of Louis XIV's reign created a void that was hard to bridge. It is because of it that, despite Montesquieu's efforts to the contrary, the liberation movement of the eighteenth century found itself without historical roots; 1789 was truly a rupture.

The feeling that at the time was called patriotism had as its object only the present and the future. It was love of the sovereign nation, based to a large extent on pride in belonging. Being French seemed to be not a matter of fact, but a free choice, like modern-day affiliation to a party or a Church.

As for those who clung to France's past, their attachment took the form of personal and dynastic loyalty to the king. They had no qualms about seeking assistance from foreign rulers. They were not traitors. They remained faithful to what they believed they owed fidelity to, just like those who put Louis XVI to death.

The only people at that time who were patriots in the later sense of the word were those who appeared in the eyes of their contemporaries and of posterity as arch traitors, people like Talleyrand, who served not all regimes, as he was reputed, but France under different regimes.[69] But for these people, France was neither the sovereign nation nor the king; it was the French state. Subsequent events proved them right.

Because, when it became evident that national sovereignty was an illusion, it could no longer serve as an object of patriotism. On the other hand, royalty was like those plants felled and not replanted. Patriotism had to change its meaning and shift its focus to the state. But, from that point, it ceased to be popular. Because the state was not created in 1789, it dated back to the beginning of the seventeenth century and played a role in the people's hatred of royalty. That was how, through a historical paradox which, at first glance, seems surprising, patriotism switched social classes and political sides; it had been on the left, now it was on the right.

The change was complete following the Commune and the beginnings of the Third Republic. The massacre of May 1871 was a blow from which French workers perhaps did not recover psychologically. That was not so long ago. A worker who is now aged fifty may have listened as a child to his father's terrified recollections of it. The army of the nineteenth century was a specific creation of the French Revolution. Even soldiers under the Bourbons, Louis-Philippe or Napoleon III experienced a violent inner struggle when it came to obeying orders to shoot at the people. In 1871, for the first time since the Revolution, apart from the short interlude of 1848, France had a republican army. This army, made up of decent young men from the French countryside, began massacring the workers with an unprecedented excess of sadistic pleasure. No wonder it was such a shock.

The main cause was undoubtedly the need to compensate for the shame of defeat, the same need that led us a little later to conquer the unfortunate Annamites.[70] Evidence shows that once the corresponding psychological mechanisms come into play, there is no cruelty or baseness that decent people are not capable of, unless there is a supernatural operation of grace.

The Third Republic was a second shock. People are capable of believing in national sovereignty while evil kings or emperors stifle it; they say to themselves: if only we were rid of them! But when they are rid of them and democracy is established – and even then – the people are clearly not sovereign, confusion is inevitable.

1871 was the last year of this brand of French patriotism, born in 1789. The German imperial prince, who later became Frederick II, a humane, reasonable and intelligent man, was greatly surprised by the intensity of this patriotism encountered everywhere during the campaign. He could not understand the Alsatians who barely knew any French but spoke a dialect very close to German and had been brutally conquered very recently, wanted nothing to do with Germany. He realized that the reason was their pride in belonging to the country of the French Revolution, to the sovereign nation. The annexation cut them off from France, perhaps partially helped maintain that state of mind until 1918.

Initially, the Paris Commune had been not a social movement, but an eruption of patriotism and even acute chauvinism. Throughout the nineteenth century in fact, Europe was worried by the aggressive direction French patriotism had taken. The [Franco-Prussian] war of 1870 was the direct result of this, since France had not prepared for this war, but had nevertheless declared it without any satisfactory motive. The people's dreams of imperial conquest had remained alive throughout the century. At the same time, they hailed the independence of the world. Conquering the world and liberating the world are two forms of glory that are incompatible, but which reconcile very well in dreams.

This fervent popular sentiment simmered down after 1871. Two causes, however, maintained a semblance of continuity in patriotism. Number one, resentment of defeat. At that time, there were no satisfactory grounds for blaming the Germans: they had not committed any aggression and they had more or less refrained from atrocities, but we had the bad grace to blame them for the violation of the rights of the peoples of Alsace-Lorraine, a largely Germanic population, from the time of our first expeditions to Annam. But we resented them for having defeated us, as if they had violated a divine, eternal, inalienable right of France to victory.

In our present hatreds, for which unfortunately there are so many all-too-justifiable causes, this singular feeling also plays a part. It was also one of the factors influencing some early collaborators: if France were going to be defeated, they thought, it could only be because there had been a misdeal, an error, a misunderstanding of its natural place as victor. And so, the easiest, least painful process, the least excruciating way of making this crucial rectification, was to change sides. This way of thinking prevailed in some Vichy milieus in July 1940.

But, above all, what prevented French patriotism from disappearing during the Third Republic, after it had lost nearly all its living substance, was that there was nothing else. The French had nothing other than France to be faithful to, and when they abandoned it for a while, in June 1940, we saw how a people bound to nothing by any loyalty was reduced to a terrible and pitiful spectacle. That is why, later, they once again clung exclusively to France. But if the French people regain what is now called sovereignty, the same difficulty as pre 1940 will resurface because the reality designated by the word 'France' will be a state above all.

The state is a cold thing that cannot be loved, but it kills and abolishes everything that could be loved, so we are forced to love it because that is all there is. Such is the moral torment of our contemporaries.

This is perhaps the real cause of this phenomenon of the leader, which has arisen everywhere and surprises so many. At present, in every country, in every cause, there is a man to whom personal loyalty is pledged. The need to embrace the steely coldness of the state has made people, by contrast, avid to love something made of flesh and blood. This phenomenon is not about to end, and, however disastrous the consequences have been so far, it may still have some very painful surprises in store for us because the famous Hollywood art of creating stars out of any human material means that anyone can offer themselves for the adoration of the masses.

Unless I am mistaken, the idea of the state as an object of loyalty appeared for the first time in France and Europe with Richelieu. Before him, people might have spoken in tones of religious devotion of the public good, the country, the king, the lord. Richelieu was the first to adopt the principle that anyone exercising a public office owes their full loyalty not to the public, not to the king, but to the state and nothing else. It would be difficult to define the state in a rigorous manner. Unfortunately, however, there can be no doubt that the word designates a reality.

Richelieu, who had the clarity of thinking so common at that time, clearly illuminated this difference between morality and politics, around which so much confusion has since arisen. He said that we must be careful not to apply the same rules to the salvation of the state as to that of the soul because the salvation of souls takes place in the other world, whereas the salvation of states takes place only in this one.[71]

That is a cruel truth. A Christian should draw only one conclusion from this: instead of the total, absolute, unconditional fidelity owed to the salvation of the soul, that is, to God, the cause of the salvation of the state is one to which limited and conditional fidelity is owed.

But although Richelieu believed himself to be a Christian, no doubt sincerely, his conclusion was quite different. It was that the man responsible for the salvation of the state, and his subordinates, must employ to this end all effective means, without exception, and, if need be, sacrifice to it their own persons, their sovereign, the people, foreign countries, and every kind of obligation.

This is, with much more greatness, the doctrine of Maurras whose slogan is 'Politics first'.[72] But Maurras, quite logically, is an atheist. This cardinal, by positing as an absolute one thing whose entire reality resides here on Earth, committed the crime of idolatry. Besides, metal, stone and wood are not actually dangerous. The object of the real crime of idolatry is always something analogous to the state. It is this crime with which the devil tempted Christ by offering him the kingdoms of this world. Christ refused.[73] Richelieu accepted. He had his reward. But he always believed he was acting out of devotion, and, in a sense, that was true.

His devotion to the state deracinated France. His policy was to systematically kill all spontaneous life in the country, so as to prevent anything from opposing the state. If his actions to do so seem to have had limitations, it is because he was just beginning, and he was skilful enough to proceed gradually. It is enough to read Corneille's dedications to realize the degree of vile servitude to which he had lowered people's spirits.[74] Since then, in order to preserve our national glories from shame, it has been said that this language was simply the polite convention of the day. But that is a lie. For further evidence, it is enough to read the writings of Théophile de Viau.[75] Only the latter died prematurely from the consequences of an arbitrary imprisonment, whereas Corneille lived to a ripe old age.

Literature is of interest only as a sign, but it is a sign that does not deceive. Corneille's servile language shows that Richelieu wanted to enslave people's very minds. Not to his person, because in his self-denial he was probably sincere, but to the state he represented. His conception of the state was already totalitarian. He applied it as far as possible by subjecting the country, as far as the means available at the time permitted, to a police regime. He thus largely destroyed the country's moral life. If France submitted to this repression, it was because the nobles had so ravaged the country through absurd and atrociously cruel civil wars, that it agreed to pay that price for civil peace.

After the eruption of the Fronde, which, in its early days, in many ways heralded [the Revolution of] 1789, Louis XIV came to power in the spirit of a dictator rather than a legitimate sovereign. That is evident in his words '*l'État, c'est moi*' ('I am the state'). This is not the thinking of a king. Montesquieu explained this very clearly, in veiled terms. But what he could not yet see in his time was that there were two stages in the decline of the French monarchy. The monarchy after Charles V degenerated into personal despotism. But, from Richelieu onwards, it was replaced by a state machine with totalitarian tendencies, which, as Marx says, not only survived through all the upheavals, but was honed and stepped up with each regime change.

During the Fronde and under Mazarin, despite public suffering, France breathed morally. Louis XIV found the country to be teeming with brilliant geniuses which he recognized and encouraged. But, at the same time, he continued Richelieu's policy much more intensely and, within a very short time, reduced France to a moral wilderness, not to mention appalling material hardship.

If we read Saint-Simon, not as a literary and historical curiosity, but as a testament to the life that human beings actually lived, we are filled with horror and disgust at the strong degree of mortal boredom, such a general abjection of heart, soul, and mind. La Bruyère, Liselotte's letters, all the documents of the time, read in the same spirit, give the same impression.[76] Going back even a little further, it seems clear, for example, that Molière did not write *The Misanthrope* for fun.

Louis XIV's regime was in fact already totalitarian. Terror and denunciations ravaged the country. The idolatry of the state, represented by the sovereign, was organized with a brazenness that was a challenge to all Christian consciences. The art of propaganda was already very well known, as can be seen in the naive confession of the chief of police to Liselotte concerning the order not to allow the publication of any book on any subject that did not contain effusive praise of the king.

Under this regime, the uprootedness of the French provinces and the destruction of local life was even greater. The seventeenth century was a lull. The operation by which the Revolution replaced the king with national sovereignty had only one drawback: national sovereignty did not exist. As with Roland's horse, the only thing wrong with it was that it was dead.[77] There was, in fact, no known process for bringing about something real corresponding to these words. This left only the state, which naturally benefited from the zeal for unity – 'unity or death' – that arose from the belief in national sovereignty. Hence further destruction of local life. Aided by war, which, from the outset, is the mainspring of this entire history – the state, under the Convention and the Empire, became increasingly totalitarian.

Louis XIV had damaged the French Church by associating it with the cult of his person and imposing obedience on it, even in matters of religion. The Church's servility to the sovereign was largely to blame for the anticlericalism of the following century. But when the Church committed the unforgiveable error of linking its fate to that of the monarchical institutions, it cut itself off from public life. Nothing could better serve the state's totalitarian aspirations. This would result in the secular system, a prelude to the avowed veneration of the state as such that is in favour today.

Christians are defenceless against the secular mindset (*esprit laïque*). They either give themselves over entirely to political action, to party action, in order to place temporal power in the hands of a clergy, or of a clergy's entourage, or they resign themselves to being themselves irreligious in the entire secular part of their own lives, which is generally the case today, to a far greater degree than those concerned realize. In both cases the proper function of religion, which is to imbue all secular life, public and private, with light without ever dominating it, is abandoned.

During the nineteenth century, the railways wreaked terrible havoc in uprooting people. In the Berry region, George Sand still saw customs that were perhaps thousands of years old, the memory of which would have vanished were it not for her notes.[78]

The loss of the past, both collective and individual, is the great human tragedy, and we have discarded ours the way a child tears off rose petals. It is above all to avoid this loss that peoples desperately resist being conquered.

But in the totalitarian state, the public authorities subdue the people they are responsible for and fail to spare them the afflictions that come with conquest, in order to have a better instrument for conquering external foes. That is how things were done in France in the past and more recently in Germany, not to mention Russia.

The expansion of the state exhausts the country. The state eats the country's moral substance, lives on it and grows fat on it, until the food runs out, which reduces it to listlessness due to famine. France had come to this point. In Germany, on the contrary, state centralization is very recent, so the state has all the aggressiveness that comes from an overabundance of high-energy food. As for Russia, popular life is so intense there that the question is whether, ultimately, it will be the people who eat the state, or rather bring it down.

The Third Republic, in France, was very singular: one of its most singular features was that its entire structure, outside the intricacies of parliamentary life, came from the Empire. The French taste for abstract logic makes people very susceptible to being fooled by labels. The English have a kingdom with a republican content; we have a Republic with an imperial content. Still now, the Empire itself is linked, over and above the Revolution, by unbroken ties to the monarchy; not to the ancient French monarchy, but to the totalitarian, police monarchy of the seventeenth century. The figure of Fouché is a symbol of this continuity.[79] Throughout all the changes, the French state's repressive apparatus continued uninterrupted, with an ever-increasing capacity for action.

As a result, the state remained the target of bitterness, hatred and revulsion once reserved for a monarchy that had become a tyranny. We have experienced the following paradox, so strange that we could not even be aware of it: a democracy where all public institutions and everything related to them were openly loathed and despised by the entire population.

No Frenchman had the slightest scruples about stealing or swindling the state when it came to customs duties, taxes, subsidies, or any other matter. This excludes some civil servants, but they were part of the state machinery. If the bourgeoisie went much further than the rest of the country in behaviour of this kind, it is only because they had many more opportunities. The police are so profoundly despised that for many French people this feeling is part of the eternal moral structure of the honest man. Guignol is authentic French folklore, which dates back to the *Ancien Régime*, and has not aged.[80] The adjective *policier* is one of the harshest insults in French, and it would be interesting to know if there are equivalents in other languages. Yet the police are nothing other than the strong arm of the public authorities. The feelings of the French people with regard to this body have remained the same since the times when, as Rousseau observes, the peasants had to hide the fact that they had a little ham.

Similarly, all political institutions aroused repulsion, derision and contempt. The very word 'politics' had become pejorative to a degree that was unbelievable in a democracy. 'He's a politician', 'all this is politics' – these expressions were merciless condemnations. In the eyes of some French people, the very profession of parliamentarian – because it was a profession – had something ignominious about it. Some prided themselves in refraining from any contact with what they called 'politics', except on election day, or even including that day; others regarded their parliamentary deputy as a kind of servant, a being created and brought into the world to serve their own particular interests. The only sentiment that tempered the contempt for public affairs was the party spirit, at least among those infected by this disease.

It would be futile to look for an aspect of public life that aroused in the French the slightest sense of loyalty, gratitude or affection. In the heyday of secular zeal, there was teaching; but for a long time now, teaching has been seen by parents and children alike as nothing more than a machine for providing qualifications, in other words, employment. As for social laws, the French people, insofar as they were satisfied with them, never looked upon them as anything other than concessions wrenched from the reluctance of the public authorities through violent pressure.

No other interest took the place of that which was lacking in public affairs. With each successive regime destroying local and regional life at a faster pace, it had finally disappeared. France was like those sick people whose limbs are already cold and whose heart alone is still beating. Almost nowhere was there a pulse of life, except in Paris; starting from the suburbs, moral death was beginning to weigh down on the population.

In those outwardly peaceful pre-war days, the tedium of small French provincial towns was perhaps as cruel as more visible atrocities. Human beings condemned to spend those unique, irreplaceable years between the cradle and the grave in dreary boredom: was that not as appalling as hunger or massacres? It was Richelieu who began to cast this pall of boredom over France, and, since then, the atmosphere has become ever more unbreathable. By the time of the war, it had reached the point of suffocation.

If the state morally killed everything that was smaller than itself, territorially speaking, it also turned territorial borders into prison walls to confine thoughts. If we look a little more closely at history, beyond the textbooks, it is amazing how certain eras almost devoid of material means of communication surpassed our own for the richness, variety, fertility and intensity of life in the exchange of ideas across vast territories. This is true of the Middle Ages, of pre-Roman antiquity, of the period immediately preceding historical times. Nowadays, with the wireless, aviation, the development of transport of all kinds, printing and the press, the modern phenomenon of the nation compartmentalizes even something as naturally universal as science. Borders, of course, are not impassable, but just as crossing them requires going through endless tedious and annoying formalities, so any contact with foreign ideas in any domain requires a mental effort to cross the border. It is a considerable effort, and many people are not willing to make it. Even among those who are, the fact that an effort is required prevents organic bonds from being formed across borders.

True, there are international Churches and political parties. But when it comes to the Churches, it is an unbearable outrage that the priests and the faithful are asking God at the same time, with the same rites, the same words, and, presumably, an equal degree of faith and purity of heart, for military victory for one or other of two enemy sides. This outrage dates back a long time, but, in our century, religious life is more subservient than ever to that of the nation. As for the political parties, either they are international only in the imagination, or internationalism takes the form of total subservience to one particular nation.

Lastly, the state has also eradicated all ties that could offer a focus for loyalty outside public life. Just as, by abolishing the trade corporations or guilds, the French Revolution stimulated technical progress, so it has done damage morally, or at least it has consecrated and completed an already partially accomplished damage. It cannot be over-emphasized that today, when these words are used in any milieu whatsoever, they have nothing in common with the former corporations or guilds.

Once guilds disappeared, in people's individual lives work became a means to an end: money. Somewhere in the constitutive texts of the League of Nations there is a sentence stating that labour would no longer be a commodity.[81] That was a joke in the ultimate bad taste. We live in a century in which many decent people, who think they are a long way from what Lévy-Bruhl called the 'pre-logical mentality', believed in the magical efficacy of the word far more than any savage in the Australian outback.[82] When you take an essential product out of commercial circulation, you provide another mode of distribution for it. No such provision was made for work, which, of course, has remained a commodity.

Conscientiousness then is simply a form of commercial probity. In a society based on trade, the greatest social condemnation is reserved for theft and swindling, and in particular swindling by the merchant who sells rotten goods while guaranteeing that they are good. Similarly, when a person sells their labour, probity requires them to provide merchandise of a quality commensurate with the price. But probity is not loyalty. There is a great gulf between these two virtues.

There is a strong element of loyalty in workers' comradeship, which has long been the dominant motivation of syndical life. But several obstacles have prevented this loyalty from providing a solid support for moral life. On the one hand, the commercialism of social life has extended to the labour movement too, putting issues of pay to the fore; but the more money concerns dominate, the more the spirit of loyalty disappears. On the other hand, insofar as the workers' movement is revolutionary, it escapes this disadvantage but contracts the weaknesses inherent in any rebellion.

Richelieu, some of whose observations are so remarkably lucid, says he has recognized from experience that, all things being equal, rebels are always half as strong as the defenders of official power. Even if people believe they are supporting a good cause, the feeling of being in revolt weakens. Without such a psychological mechanism, there could be no stability in human societies. This mechanism explains the Communist Party's hold. Revolutionary workers are only too happy to have a state behind them – a state that gives their action the official character, the legitimacy and the reality that the state alone confers, and which at the same time is geographically located too far away for them to feel disenchanted. In the same way, the Encyclopaedists, deeply uncomfortable with being in conflict with their own sovereign, hungered for the favour of the rulers of Prussia or Russia.[83] This analogy helps explain why worker militants with revolutionary leanings who had resisted the prestige of Russia could not help giving in to that of Germany.

Apart from those who have given themselves entirely to the Communist Party, the workers cannot find in class loyalty a precise enough or clearly defined focus to give them inner stability. Few concepts are as indeterminate as that of social class. Marx, whose entire system was based on it, never sought to define it, or even simply to study it. The only information on social classes that can be drawn from his work is that they are in conflict. That is not enough. Nor is it one of those concepts which cannot be defined in words but are clear in the mind. In the absence of a definition, it is even more difficult to conceive of it, or to feel it than it is to define it.

However singular it may be, the loyalty implicit in a religious affiliation also counts for little in modern life. Despite obvious and considerable differences, a similar effect is produced both by the English system of a national Church and by the French system of the separation of Church and state. It is just that the latter seems more destructive.

Religion has been declared a private matter. According to current ways of thinking, this does not mean that it lies hidden in the soul, in that profoundly secret place, out of reach even of the conscience. It means that it is a matter of choice, opinion, taste – whim almost – something like choosing a political party or even a tie, or that it is a matter of family, education, or social situation. Having become a private affair, it loses the obligatory character reserved for public affairs, and consequently no longer has an undisputed claim on loyalty.

Much is said revealing that this is so. How often do we hear this platitude: 'Catholics, Protestants, Jews or free thinkers, we are all French', repeated exactly as if they were small territorial divisions, as one would say to a person from Marseilles, Lyon or Paris, 'we are all French'. Texts emanating from the Pope read: 'Not only from the Christian point of view, but more generally from the human point of view . . .' as if the Christian point of view, which either makes no sense or claims to encompass all things in this world and in the next, were less generally applicable than the human point of view. It is hard to conceive of a more terrible admission of bankruptcy. This is how '*anathema sit*' is paid for.[84] Ultimately, religion, downgraded to the status of a private matter, is reduced to the choice of a place to go and spend an hour or two on Sunday morning.

The comical thing is that religion, that the relation of a human being with God, is not regarded today as too sacred for the intervention of any external authority but is included among the things that the state leaves to the whim of the individual, as being of little importance in public affairs. At least this has been the case in the recent past. This is the current meaning of 'tolerance'.

So, there is nothing other than the state to which loyalty can cling. That is why, up until 1940 it was not denied. Because people feel that a human life without loyalty is a terrible thing. Among the general debasement of all the words that have to do with moral concepts, the words 'traitor' and 'betrayal' have lost none of their force. People also feel that they were born for sacrifice, and there was no other form of sacrifice left in the public imagination than military sacrifice, that is sacrifice offered to the state.

It was indeed solely the state. The illusion of the Nation, in the sense that the people of 1789 and of 1792 understood the word, which at that time caused tears of joy, was a thing of the past that had been completely abolished. The very word nation has changed its meaning. In our century, it no longer refers to the sovereign people, but to all the populations recognizing the authority of the same state; it is the architecture formed by a state and the country dominated by it. When we speak today of the sovereignty of the nation, it means only the sovereignty of the state. A dialogue between one of our contemporaries and a person from 1792 would result in some very amusing misunderstandings. Not only is the state in question not the sovereign people, but it is the same inhuman, brutal, bureaucratic, police state bequeathed by Richelieu to Louis XIV, by Louis XIV to the Convention, by the Convention to the Empire, and by the Empire to the Third Republic. Furthermore, it is instinctively recognized and hated as such.

Thus we have seen this strange thing, a state, an object of hatred, repulsion, derision, contempt and fear, which, in the name of patriotism, demanded absolute loyalty, total devotion and supreme sacrifice, and obtained them, from 1914 to 1918, to an extent that surpassed all expectations. It set itself up as an absolute here on Earth, in other words, as an object of idolatry; and it was accepted and served as such, honoured with an appalling number of human sacrifices. Idolatry without love: what could be sadder or more monstrous?

When someone immerses themselves deeper in devotion than is in their heart, there is inevitably a violent reaction, a kind of emotional revulsion. This is often seen in families, when an invalid needs care that goes beyond the affection they inspire. They are the object of a resentment that is repressed because it is inadmissible, but always present like a hidden poison.

The same thing happened between the French and France after 1918. They had given the country too much. They had given France more than they had in their hearts.

The entire movement of unpatriotic, pacifist, internationalist ideas post 1918 claimed to be in the name of the war dead and the veterans. And it truly did largely emanate from veteran milieus, although, admittedly, there were also fervently patriotic veterans' associations. But their patriotism rang hollow and lacked persuasive force. It resembled the language of people who, having suffered a great deal, feel a continuous need to remind themselves that their suffering had not been in vain. Because suffering that is disproportionate in relation to the impulses of the heart can lead to one of two attitudes: people either reject the cause for which they have endured too much, or they cling to it with a kind of despair.

Nothing has done more harm to patriotism than references to the role played by the police behind the lines, repeated ad nauseam. Nothing could hurt the French more than forcing them to acknowledge the presence, supporting the country, of the police state, the traditional target of their hatred. At the same time, excerpts from the sensationalist pre-1918 press emphasizing this role played by the police, reread calmly afterwards with disgust, made them feel they had been duped. There is nothing that a Frenchman is less capable of forgiving. The very words that expressed patriotic sentiment having been discredited, it fell, in a way, into the category of inadmissible feelings. There was a time, not so long ago, when the expression of patriotic sentiment, in at least some worker milieus, would have had the effect of a breach of behavioural codes.

All the testimonies concur in suggesting that the bravest in 1940 were the veterans of World War I. We can only conclude that their reactions after 1918 had a more profound influence on the souls of the children close to them than on their own. This is a very common and understandable phenomenon. The characters of those who were eighteen years old in 1914 had been formed in the preceding years.

It has been said that schools at the beginning of the twentieth century forged a youth for victory, and that schools post 1918 forged a defeated generation. There is certainly a lot of truth in this. But the post-1918 schoolteachers were veterans. Many of the children who turned ten between 1920 and 1930 had teachers who had fought in the war.

If France suffered the effect of this reaction more than other countries, it is due to a much more acute uprooting, corresponding to a much older and more intense centralization of the state, to the demoralizing effect of the victory, and to the licence allowed to all forms of propaganda.

The balance was also ruptured with regard to the concept of patriotism; this was compensated by a rupture in the opposite sense, in the domain of pure thought. Because in the midst of a total vacuum the state had remained the only entity qualified to demand fidelity and sacrifice of people, the notion of patriotism was posited as an absolute value. The country was beyond good and evil. This is expressed in the English saying: 'my country right or wrong'.[85] But often, we go further. We will not admit that our country can be wrong.

No matter how reluctant people from all walks of life may be to make the effort of critical examination, a glaring absurdity, even if they do not acknowledge it, puts them in a state of disquiet that weakens the spirit. Ultimately, there is nothing more integral to common human daily life than philosophy, but an implicit philosophy.

To posit the country as an absolute that evil cannot defile is a glaring absurdity. The country is another name for the nation, and the nation is a collection of territories and populations brought together by historical events in which chance plays a large part, as far as human intelligence can judge, and where good and evil are always mingled. The nation is a fact, and a fact is not an absolute. It is a fact among other analogous facts. There is more than one nation on the face of the Earth. Ours is certainly unique. But each of the others, considered in itself and with love, is just as unique.

Before 1940, it was fashionable to talk of 'eternal France'. These words are a kind of blasphemy. The same applies to the very moving pages written by great French Catholic writers on the vocation of France, the eternal salvation of France, and other similar themes. Richelieu was much more insightful when he said that the salvation of states only takes place here on Earth. France is a temporal, earthly entity. Unless I am mistaken, it has never been said that Christ died to save nations. The idea of a nation called by God as a nation belongs only to ancient law.

Pagan antiquity as it is called would never have made such a crude confusion. The Romans believed they were chosen, but only for earthly dominion. They were not interested in the next world. Nowhere does it appear that any city, any people, believed themselves singled out for a supernatural destiny. The Mysteries, which in a way constituted the official route to salvation, like today's Churches, were local institutions, but it was recognized that they were all equal to one another. Plato describes how man, assisted by grace, breaks free from the cave of this world; but he does not say that a city can break free. On the contrary, he represents the collectivity as something animal that impedes the salvation of the soul.

Antiquity is often accused of recognizing only collective values. In reality, this error was committed solely by the Romans, who were atheists, and by the Hebrews, and by the latter only until the Babylonian exile. But if we are mistaken in attributing this error to pre-Christian antiquity, we are also mistaken in not recognizing that we are continually committing it, corrupted as we are by the dual Roman and Hebrew tradition, which too often prevails in us over pure Christian inspiration.

Today's Christians find it difficult to recognize that, if we give the word patriotism the strongest possible meaning, a complete meaning, a Christian has only one country, which is outside this world. Because the Christian has only one father, who is not of this world. 'Store up for yourselves treasures in heaven [. . .] For where your treasure is, there your heart will be also.'[86] It is therefore forbidden to have one's heart on Earth.

Christians today do not like to ask the question of the respective rights over their hearts of God versus their country. The German bishops ended one of their most courageous protests by saying that they refused ever to be made to choose between God and Germany.[87] And why do they refuse? Circumstances can always arise that involve a choice between God and some earthly object, and there must never be any doubt as to this choice. But the French bishops would have said the same thing. Joan of Arc's popularity over the last quarter century was not entirely healthy; it was a convenient way of forgetting that there is a difference between France and God. Yet this inner cowardice before the prestige of the idea of patriotism did not render patriotism more energetic. The statue of Joan of Arc was placed prominently in every church in the country during those terrible days when the French abandoned France.

'If any man come to me, and hate not his father, and mother, and wife, and children, and brethren, and sisters, yea, and his own life also, he cannot be my disciple.'[88] If it is prescribed to hate all these, in a certain sense of the word hate, it is certainly forbidden to love one's country, in a certain sense of the word love. For the proper object of love is good, and 'No one is good except God alone'.[89]

This is self-evident, but, by some curse, our century is completely oblivious to it. Otherwise, it would have been impossible for a man like Père de Foucauld, who had chosen out of charity to be the witness of Christ amid non-Christian populations, to have believed he was entitled to provide information to the Second Bureau about these same populations.[90]

It would be salutary for us to reflect on the terrible words of the devil to Christ, pointing to all the kingdoms of this world and saying, 'All power has been given to me.'[91] No kingdom is exempt.

What did not shock the Christians did however shock the workers. A tradition still recent enough to be not quite dead makes the love of justice the central inspiration of the French labour movement. In the first half of the nineteenth century, this ardent love took up the cause of the oppressed of the entire world.

As long as the country comprised the people forming a sovereign nation, there was no problem with its relationship to justice. Because it was accepted quite arbitrarily, and by a very superficial interpretation of *The Social Contract*, that a sovereign nation does not commit injustice against its members or its neighbours; it was assumed that the causes of injustice all derive from the non-sovereignty of the nation.

But when behind the country stands the old state, justice is far removed. In the modern form of patriotism, there is not much talk of justice. Above all, nothing is being said that makes any connection between patriotism and justice. No one dares to assert that there is an equivalence between the two notions, especially not to the workers, who, through social oppression, feel the chill steel hand of the state and realize confusedly that the same chill hand must exist in international relations. When there is a great deal of talk of patriotism, little is said about justice; the sense of justice is so strong among the workers, even if they are materialists, because they have always felt being deprived of it, so a form of moral education in which justice is virtually absent cannot exercise any hold over them. When they die for France, they need to believe that they are dying for something much greater, that they are part of the universal fight against injustice. For them, as the famous saying goes, patriotism is not enough.

It is the same wherever there is a flame or a spark of true spiritual life, however imperceptible. For this fire, patriotism is not enough. And for those for whom it is absent, patriotism, with its highly exacting demands, is far too elevated; it can only be a strong enough stimulus in the form of the blindest national fanaticism.

It is true that people are capable of compartmentalizing their minds, each section holding an idea that has its own life, unrelated to the others. They dislike making either a critical effort or an effort at synthesis and will not impose this on themselves without violence.

But in fear, in anguish, when the flesh recoils in the face of death, in the face of too much suffering, in the face of excessive danger, every human being, no matter how uneducated, has a reasoning mechanism that finds arguments to prove that it is legitimate and good to avoid this death, this suffering, this danger. This proof can be good or bad, depending on the case. At any rate, at the time, the consternation of flesh and blood gives them an intensity of persuasive force that no orator has ever achieved.

There are people for whom things do not happen this way, either because their nature shields them from fear, or because their flesh, blood and guts are oblivious to the threat of death or pain, or because there is such a degree of unity in their minds that the reasoning mechanism does not kick in. In still others, this mechanism operates, exerting its powers of persuasion, but these are despised. This itself presupposes either an already high degree of inner unity or powerful external stimuli.

Hitler's astute observation about propaganda, that is that brute force alone cannot prevail over ideas, but can easily do so by throwing in a few ideas, no matter how poor their quality.[92] This observation also provides the key to inner life. The tumults of the flesh alone, however violent, cannot prevail over an idea. But their victory is easy if they communicate their persuasive power to another idea, no matter how bad. That is the import- ant point. No thought is too weak to function as an ally of the flesh. But the flesh needs thought as an ally.

That is why, whereas in ordinary times people – even cul- tured people – live with the most enormous inner contradictions without any discomfort, in moments of great crisis, the slightest flaw in the inner system acquires the same importance as if the most lucid philosopher were standing somewhere, mischie- vously ready to take advantage of it. And this is true of every man, no matter how ignorant.

In moments of extreme crisis – which are not necessarily those of the greatest danger but the times when humans find themselves faced with turmoil in their guts, blood and flesh, alone and without external stimuli – those whose inner life pro- ceeds entirely from one single idea are the only ones able to resist. This is why totalitarian systems create people who are immune to all trials and tribulations.

Patriotism can be this single idea only in a Hitlerian-style regime. This could easily be proved, down to the finest detail, but that is pointless since there is so much evidence. If patriot- ism is not this idea, and if it nevertheless has a place, then either there is an inner inconsistency and a hidden weakness in the soul, or there must be some other idea, dominating everything else, and in relation to which patriotism holds a clearly recognized, limited and secondary place.

This was not the case under our Third Republic. That was not the case in any milieu. What was everywhere, was moral incoherence. The inner reasoning mechanism was active in people's minds between 1914 and 1918. Most of them resisted with tremendous toughness, by this reaction which often pushes men to plunge blindly, for fear of dishonour, from the opposing side to the one where fear is pushing. But when the soul is exposed to pain and danger by this impulse alone, it very quickly becomes exhausted. Those anxiety-fed arguments unable to influence the course of action bite even deeper into the soul, and their influence is exerted after the event. This is what happened after 1918. And those who had given nothing and were ashamed of it were quick for other reasons to be infected. This mood was transmitted to the children who would later be asked to die.

It is clear just how far the internal disintegration of the French people has gone when we think that still today the idea of collaboration with the enemy has not lost all prestige. On the other hand, if we seek comfort in the show of resistance, if we say to ourselves that the resistance fighters have no difficulty in finding their inspiration both in patriotism and in an array of other motives, we must at the same time tell ourselves again and again that France as a nation is at the moment aligned with justice, general happiness and things of the sort, in other words, in the category of beautiful things that do not exist. The Allied victory will rescue France from that category and re-establish the country in the realm of facts; many difficulties that seemed to have been overcome will reappear. In a sense, affliction simplifies everything. The fact that France went down the route of resistance more slowly and later than most of the occupied countries shows that we would be wrong to be unconcerned about the future.

The extent of our regime's moral incoherence is evident if we think of school. Morality is part of the curriculum, and even teachers who did not like to teach morality dogmatically, inevitably taught it in a vague way. The central notion of this morality is justice and the obligations that entails towards our neighbour.

But when it comes to history, morality is no longer an issue. It is never a question of France's external obligations. Sometimes France is described as just and generous, as if morality were an extra, a feather in the cap, a crowning glory. Slight doubt may hang over the conquests France has made and lost, such as Napoleon's; never the ones it has kept. The past is only the history of France's growth, and it is accepted that this growth is always a good thing in every respect. No one ever asks whether in growing, France has not destroyed. To question whether France may have destroyed things of value would seem like the most terrible blasphemy. [Georges] Bernanos says that the members of *Action Française* see France as an infant that is required only to grow and put on weight. But they are not the only ones.[93] It is the general way of thinking which is always implicit in the way we look at the country's past, even if it is not overtly expressed. And the comparison with a child is still too respectable. The creatures required only to get fat are rabbits, pigs and chickens. Plato sums up this thinking in comparing the collectivity to an animal. And those blinded by its prestige, that is everyone except those who are predestined, 'call just and beautiful the things that are necessary, being incapable of discerning and teaching what a distance separates the essence of what is necessary from the essence of what is good'.[94]

Everything is done so that children feel – and this is something they feel naturally – that things relating to the country, the nation and its growth have an importance that sets them apart from everything else. And it is precisely in regard to these things that justice, consideration for others, strict obligations that place limits on ambitions and appetites – all the morality to which the lives of children are subjected – is never mentioned.

What conclusion can we draw from this, except that morality ranks among matters of lesser importance, that its place is in the lower domain of private life, along with religion, profession, or choice of doctor or supplier?

But if morality itself is thus debased, no other system is offered as a substitute. Because the higher prestige of the nation is linked to the glorification of war. It provides no motivation in peacetime, except in a regime that is on a permanent war footing, like that of the Nazis. Other than in such a regime, it would be dangerous to remind too many people that this country, which demands its children's lives, has another face: the state, with its taxes, customs and police. This is carefully avoided and so it never occurs to anyone that it is unpatriotic to hate the police and to defraud the customs and income tax authorities. A country such as England is to some extent an exception because of a centuries-old tradition of freedom guaranteed by the authorities. And so, the double moral standards in peacetime undermine the power of eternal morality without putting anything in its place.

This duality is omnipresent, present all the time, and not only in schools. It is there almost daily in ordinary times for all the French – when they read the newspaper and in conversations with their families or in cafés: they are thinking for France, in the name of France. From then on, and until they return to their private persona, they lose even the memory of the virtues that they acknowledge in a vague and abstract way that it is their obligation to practise. When it is a question of the self, and even of one's family, it is recognized to some extent that one should not boast too much, that one should be wary of one's own judgments when one is both judge and judged, that one should ask oneself whether others are not at least partially right, that one should not put oneself forward too much, that one should not think only of oneself; in short, that limits should be put on egotism and pride. But when it comes to national egotism and national pride, not only is there an unlimited licence, but the highest possible degree is imposed by something resembling an obligation. Consideration for others, admission of one's own mistakes, modesty, voluntary curbing of desires, in this domain become crimes, sacrileges. Among several sublime words that the Egyptian *Book of the Dead* puts in the mouth of the just man after death, perhaps these are the most poignant: 'I have never been deaf to words of justice and truth.'[95] But on the international front, it is generally considered a sacred duty to turn a deaf ear to words of justice and truth if they are contrary to the interests of France. Or do we believe that words contrary to the interests of France can never be just and true? That would come down to exactly the same thing.

There are lacks of taste which, in the absence of morals, good upbringing prevents people from committing in their private lives, but which seem completely natural at national level. Even the most odious benefactress would be hesitant to gather together her protégés to tell them of the great advantages they are being given and the gratitude they owe in return. But a French governor of Indochina has no compunction in using such language in the name of France, even immediately after the most appalling acts of repression or the most shocking famines, and he expects – he imposes – answers that echo his words.

This is a custom inherited from the Romans. They never inflicted cruelty or granted favours without vaunting their generosity and clemency. No one was granted an audience to make a request, even for simple relief from the most terrible oppression, unless they began with words of praise. They thus defiled the act of supplication, which had previously been honourable, by imposing lies and flattery on it. Conversely, in The Iliad, never does the language of a Trojan kneeling before a Greek to beg for his life carry the slightest hint of flattery.

Our patriotism derives directly from the Romans. That is why French children are encouraged to look to Corneille for inspiration. It is a pagan virtue, if these two words are compatible. The word pagan, when applied to Rome, truly and justifiably has the horror-freighted meaning given to it by early Christian polemicists. They really were an atheist, idolatrous people, worshipping not stone or bronze statues, but also themselves. It is this self-idolatry that they bequeathed to us under the name of patriotism.

So dual morality is a far more glaring scandal if instead of secular morality, we think of Christian virtue, of which secular morality is merely a version for the general public, a diluted solution. Christian virtue has as its core, its specific essence, humility, the freely consented downward movement. It is through this that the saints are like Christ. 'Jesus, who, existing in the form of God, did not consider equality with God a thing to be grasped, but emptied himself. [. . .] Although he was a son, he learned obedience through what he suffered.'[96]

But when the French think of France, for them, pride is a duty, according to the current conception; humility would be a betrayal. This betrayal is perhaps the one for which the Vichy government is most bitterly blamed. We are right because its humility is unseemly: it is that of the slave who flatters and lies to avoid a beating. But in such matters, a seemly humility is alien to us. We do not even imagine it is possible. To even conceive of its possibility, we would already have to make a tremendous effort of the imagination.

In a Christian soul, the presence of the pagan virtue of patriotism is corrosive. It passed from Rome into our hands without having been washed clean. Strangely enough, the barbarians, or those so called, were baptized almost without difficulty during the invasions, but the legacy of ancient Rome was never baptized, probably because it couldn't be, even though the Roman Empire made Christianity a state religion. It would be hard to imagine a crueller insult. As for the barbarians, it is not surprising that the Goths easily adopted Christianity, if, as people believed at the time, they were of the blood of the Getae, the most righteous of the Thracians, whom Herodotus called the immortalists because of their profound faith in eternal life.[97] The legacy of the barbarians combined with the Christian spirit to produce this unique, inimitable, perfectly uniform thing called chivalry. But there was never a fusion between the spirit of Rome and the spirit of Christ. If fusion had been possible, the Apocalypse would have lied in representing Rome as the woman seated on the beast, the woman full of the blasphemous names.

The Renaissance was a resurrection firstly of the Greek, then of the Roman spirit. It was only in this second stage that it was corrosive to Christianity. It was in this second stage that the modern form of nationality was born, the modern form of patriotism. Corneille was right to dedicate his *Horace* to Richelieu, and to do so in terms in which baseness is twinned with the overweening pride that inspires tragedy.[98] This baseness and pride are inseparable, as we can see today in Germany. Corneille himself is an excellent example of the asphyxia that suffocates Christian virtue when it comes into contact with the Roman spirit. His *Polyeucte* would seem comical to us if were we not blinded by habit.[99] Polyeuctus, under his pen, is a man who has suddenly understood that there is a much more glorious territory to conquer than the earthly kingdoms, and that there is a particular means of achieving it immediately. He sets out to conquer it, heedless of anything else, and in the same state of mind as when he was previously at war in the service of the Emperor. Alexander wept, it is said, for having to conquer only the globe. Corneille appears to have believed that Christ had come down to Earth to remedy that shortcoming.

If patriotism invisibly corrodes both Christian and secular virtue in peacetime, the opposite happens in times of war, and this is quite natural. When there is moral duality, it is always the virtue demanded by the circumstances that suffers the harm. The inclination to choose the easy option naturally gives the advantage to the kind of virtue which, in fact there is no need to exercise: to the morality of war in peacetime and to that of peace in wartime.

In peacetime, because of the impermeable partition that divides them from patriotism, justice and truth are downgraded to the rank of purely private virtues, like politeness, but when the country demands the supreme sacrifice, this same separation deprives patriotism of the total legitimacy which alone can spur a total effort.

Since we have become accustomed to considering the growth during which France has devoured and digested so many lands as an absolute good and free from any shadow, how can propaganda inspired by exactly the same thinking, and putting only the name of Europe in the place of that of France, not seep into a corner of our soul? Current patriotism consists of an equation between absolute good and a collectivity corresponding to a territorial space, namely France. Anyone who mentally changes the territorial component of the equation and puts in its place a smaller area, such as Brittany, or a larger one, such as Europe, is regarded as a traitor. Why is that? It is completely arbitrary. Habit prevents us from realizing how arbitrary it is. But at the moment of supreme crisis, this arbitrariness allows our inner sophism mechanism to take hold.

As for the new Europe that a German victory would forge, the present collaborators have the same attitude that Provençal, Breton, Alsatian and Franc-Comtois people are asked to have towards the past with regard to the conquest of their country by the King of France. Why should the difference between these two epochs change the notions of good and evil? Between 1918 and 1919, it was common to hear from decent people who hoped for peace: 'In the past there was war between provinces, then they united to form nations. In the same way nations will unite on every continent, then across the entire world, and that will be the end of all war.' This was a very widespread popular belief; it was based on the extrapolative reasoning that was so influential in the nineteenth century and again in the twentieth century. The good people who spoke in this way had a general idea of France's history, but in expressing these sentiments, they did not take into account the fact that national unity had been achieved almost exclusively through the bloodiest conquests. But if they remembered this in 1939, they also remembered that they had always thought those conquests to be a good thing. No wonder that, at least somewhere in their soul, they began to think: 'Perhaps it is necessary to go through this for progress, for the accomplishment of history?' They were able to say to themselves: 'France won a victory in 1918 but did not succeed in uniting Europe; now Germany is trying to achieve this, so let us not stand in the way.' Admittedly, the cruelties of the German system should have made them stop. But it is possible that they were either unaware of them, or that they assumed they were created by false propaganda, or that they judged them to be of little importance since they were inflicted on inferior populations. Is it more difficult to ignore the cruelties of the Germans towards the Jews or the Czechs than those of the French towards the Annamites?

[Charles] Péguy used to say that those who died in a just war were blessed.[100] It must follow that those who kill them unjustly are afflicted. If the French soldiers of 1914 died in a just war, then this is certainly also the case, at least to the same degree, for Vercingetorix.[101] If people think that way, how do they feel about the man who held him in chains for six years in a pitch-black dungeon, then paraded him before the Romans and had his throat slit? But Péguy was an ardent admirer of the Roman Empire. If we admire the Roman Empire, why blame Germany for trying to reconstitute it, using almost identical methods over a wider territory? This contradiction did not prevent Péguy from dying in 1914. But it was this contradiction, although not formulated or acknowledged, that prevented many young people in 1940 from going into the firing line in the same spirit as Péguy.

Either conquest is always evil, or it is always good, or it is sometimes good and sometimes evil. In the latter case, we need a criterion for discrimination. Taking as a criterion that conquest is good when it expands the nation one happens to belong to by birth, and evil when it diminishes it, is so contrary to reason that it is only acceptable for people who have consciously decided, once and for all, to abandon reason, as is the case in Germany. But Germany can do this because it lives by a romantic tradition. France cannot, because regard for reason is part of the national heritage. Some French people may say they are hostile to Christianity, but both before and after 1789, all movements of thought that took place in France claimed to be based on reason. France cannot abandon reason in the name of patriotism.

That is why France is ill at ease in its patriotism, even though it was France that invented modern patriotism in the seventeenth century. We should not think that what is called France's universal vocation makes it any easier for the French than for others to reconcile patriotism and universal values. It is the contrary that is true. It is harder for the French because they cannot completely succeed either in eliminating the second term of the contradiction, or in separating the two terms with an impermeable barrier. They find the contradiction within their patriotism itself. But because of this, they have to invent a new patriotism. If they do, they will fulfil, what was up to a certain point in the past, the function of France, in other words, thinking about what the world needs. And at present, the world needs a new patriotism. It is at this time, when patriotism is causing bloodshed, that this effort to invent a new form must be made. We must not wait until it has once again become a topic that is discussed in the salons and universities and on café terraces.

It is easy to say, like Lamartine: 'My country is everywhere that France's influence shines [. . .]. 'Truth is my country.'[102] Unfortunately, this would only make sense if France and truth had equivalent meanings. It happened, it happens, it will happen that France lies and is unjust because France is not God, far from it. Christ alone was able to say: 'I am the truth.'[103] That is not permitted to anything else on Earth, neither individuals nor collectivities, even less collectivities. Because it is possible for a person to attain a degree of holiness such that it is Christ who lives in them. On the other hand, there is no holy nation.

There was once a nation that believed itself to be holy, and that did not turn out well. Furthermore, it is strange to think that in that nation, the Pharisees were the resistance fighters and the tax collectors the collaborators, and to recall what Christ's relationship was with each of them.

This should make us think that our resistance might be a spiritually dangerous, even spiritually bad, position, if among the motives we are unable to keep the patriotic impulse within just limits. It is this very danger that is expressed, in the very vulgar language of our time, by those who, sincerely or not, say they fear that this movement will turn to fascism, because fascism is always linked to a certain type of patriotic sentiment.

France's universal vocation cannot, without being dishonest, be evoked with unalloyed pride. If people lie, they betray it in the very words they use to evoke it; if they remember the truth, shame must always be mingled with pride because there is something uncomfortable in all the historical examples that can be offered. In the thirteenth century, France was a centre for the whole of Christendom. But at the very start of that century, it destroyed for ever a burgeoning civilization south of the Loire that was already a shining beacon; and it was during that military operation and associated with it that for the first time France established the Inquisition. That is a huge stain. The thirteenth century is when the Gothic replaced the Norman, polyphonic music supplanted Gregorian chant, and, in theology, Aristotle's constructs superseded Platonic thinking. From then on during that century, there is no doubt that French influence equated to progress. In the seventeenth century, the influence of France again spread throughout Europe. But the military prestige associated with that influence was achieved through unacceptable means, at least for those who love justice. Furthermore, whereas the French classical conception produced splendid works in the French language, it exerted an equally destructive influence abroad. In 1789, France became the hope of the peoples. But, three years later, the country went off to war, and, from the first victories, set out to conquer rather than to liberate. Had it not been for England, Russia and Spain, France would have imposed on Europe a unity perhaps barely less repressive that that promised today by Germany. In the second half of the last century, when people realized that Europe isn't the world, and that there are several continents on this planet, France once again aspired to a universal role, but succeeded only in creating a colonial empire emulating that of the British. And in the hearts of many people of colour, France is now associated with sentiments that are intolerable.

And so, the contradiction inherent in French patriotism recurs throughout French history. We should not conclude that since France has lived with this contradiction for so long, it should continue. First of all, if we acknowledge a contradiction, it is reprehensible to put up with it. And then, the fact is, France nearly died from a crisis of French patriotism. Everything suggests that France would be dead if English patriotism were not fortunately of a more robust nature. But we cannot transport it over here. It is our own patriotism that needs to be revived. It still needs reviving. It is showing new signs of

life because the German soldiers on our soil are the best possible propagandists for French patriotism, but they will not be
here for ever.

This entails a terrible responsibility. Because what we are
talking about is recreating the country's soul, and there is such
a strong temptation to do this by dint of lies and partial truths,
that it requires more than heroism to insist on the truth.

The crisis of patriotism has been twofold. To use the vocabulary of politics, we could say that there is a crisis on the left and
a crisis on the right.

On the right, among the bourgeois youth, the disconnect
between patriotism and morality, combined with other causes,
had completely discredited all morality, but patriotism was
barely any more prestigious. The spirit expressed by the words
'Politics first' had spread much further than Maurras' influence
itself. But those words contain an absurdity because politics is
merely a technique, a set of processes. It is like saying 'mechanics first'. The question that immediately springs to mind is:
Politics for what? Richelieu would reply: for the greatness of
the state. And why for this purpose and not for any other?
There is no answer to that question.

That is the question that must not be asked. So-called realist
politics, passed on from Richelieu to Maurras, not without
having been dented on the way, only makes sense if this question is not asked. There is a simple condition to ensure it isn't.
When the beggar [pleading for alms] said to Talleyrand: 'Sir, I
must live', Talleyrand replied: 'I do not see the necessity'.[104] But
the beggar saw very well the necessity. Similarly, Louis XIV
saw very well the necessity for the state to be served with a
total devotion because the state was him. Richelieu thought of
himself only as its number-one servant, however, in a way, he
possessed it, and for that reason identified with it. Richelieu's
conception of politics only makes sense to those who, either
individually or collectively, feel either masters of their country
or capable of becoming so.

From 1924, the bourgeois youth no longer felt that France
belonged to it. The workers were making way too much noise.
On the other hand, they were suffering from that mysterious

exhaustion that overwhelmed France after 1918, the causes of which are doubtless physical for the most part. Whether alcoholism is to blame, or the anxious state of the parents who bore and raised these young people, or some other cause, the young generation has been showing unmistakeable signs of fatigue for a long time. Young Germans, even in 1932, when the authorities were taking no notice of them, had an incomparably greater vitality, despite the very harsh and prolonged deprivations they had suffered.

This weariness made the bourgeois youth feel incapable of being in control of the country. And so, to the question 'Politics for what purpose?' the obvious answer was 'to be established in power by others'. By others meaning by foreigners. There was nothing in the moral system of these young people able to curb this desire. The shock of 1936 made it even more profound, and irrevocable. They had not suffered any harm, but they had been afraid; they had been humiliated, and – the unforgivable crime in their eyes – humiliated by those they considered their inferiors. In 1937, the Italian press quoted an article from a French student magazine in which a young Frenchwoman wrote that she hoped Mussolini would find time, among his many commitments, to come and restore order in France.

However unappealing this social milieu may be, no matter how criminal their subsequent attitude was, they are human beings, and afflicted human beings. The problem with them can be described in these terms: how to reconcile them with France without delivering the country into their hands.

On the left, in other words, especially among the workers and among left-leaning intellectual sympathisers, there are two quite distinct currents, although sometimes, but not always, both coexist within the same being. One is the current stemming from the French working-class tradition, which visibly dates back to the eighteenth century, when so many workers read Jean-Jacques [Rousseau], but which perhaps has underground roots in the first town-emancipation movements. Those inspired solely by this current are committed to the idea of justice. Unfortunately, today, they are quite rare among workers and extremely rare among intellectuals.

There are such people in all the so-called left-wing milieus – Christians, syndicalists anarchists and socialists, and in particular there are some among the Communist workers, because Communist propaganda talks a great deal about justice. In this it follows the teachings of Lenin and Marx, strange as that may seem to those who have not fully grasped the intricacies of the doctrine.

These people are all deeply internationalist in times of peace because they know that justice has no nationality. Often, they are internationalist during a war until there is a defeat. But the crushing of their country immediately arouses an absolutely solid, pure patriotism deep in their hearts. Those people will be permanently reconciled with their country if they are offered the concept of a patriotism subordinate to justice.

The other current is a riposte to the bourgeois attitude. In offering the workers the purportedly scientific certainty that they will soon be the sovereign masters of the terrestrial globe, Marxism has given rise to a workers' imperialism akin to national imperialism. Russia appears to have provided experimental proof of this. Moreover, we rely on Russia to take charge of the hardest part of the action that should result in the overthrow of power.

For those who are morally exiled and immigrants, who chiefly experience the state's repressive side and who, through a centuries-old tradition are on the margins of the social categories targeted by the police and are themselves treated as such each time the state leans towards reaction, there is an irresistible temptation. A great, powerful, sovereign state, commanding a territory that is much vaster than their own country, tells them: 'I belong to you, I am yours. I exist only to help you, and very soon I will make you the absolute masters in your own country.'

For their part, rejecting this friendship would be about as easy as it would be for someone who has had nothing to drink for two days to refuse water. A few people, who have made a great effort to do so, have been so exhausted by this effort that they gave in without a fight at the first pressure from Germany. Many others only appear to resist, but in reality they are simply standing aside out of fear of the risks involved in the action they are committed to once they have signed up. Those people, whether numerous or not, are never a force.

The USSR, outside of Russia, is really the workers' country. This was patently visible on the faces of the French workers when they gathered around the newspaper kiosks to read the headlines announcing the first major Russian defeats. It was not the thought of the repercussions of these defeats on Franco-German relations that caused the despair in their eyes because the English defeats never affected them in this way. They felt threatened with losing more than France. They felt something similar to what the early Christians might have felt had they been given material evidence that the resurrection of Christ was a fiction. In general, there is probably a great deal of similarity between the frame of mind of the early Christians and that of many Communist workers. They too are expecting an impending, earthly disaster, all of a sudden establishing absolute good here on Earth forever, and at the same time their own glory. Martyrdom was easier for the early Christians than it was for those of the following centuries, and infinitely easier than for Christ's disciples, for whom, at the moment of supreme crisis, it had been impossible. Likewise, today the sacrifice is easier for a Communist than for a Christian.

The USSR being a state, patriotism towards it entails the same contradictions as any other. But it does not result in the same weakening. On the contrary. When a contradiction is felt, even vaguely, it gnaws at the feelings; when it is not felt at all, feelings are all the more intense since they simultaneously benefit from incompatible motives. That way, the USSR has all the prestige of a state and the cold brutality that permeates the politics of a state, especially a totalitarian one. And at the same time, it has all the prestige of being just. If the contradiction is not felt, it is partly because of the distance, and partly because the USSR promises absolute power to those who love it. Such a hope does not diminish the need for justice, but rather makes it blind. Since each person thinks they are sufficiently capable of justice, they also believe that a system in which they were

powerful would be perfectly just. That is the temptation that
the devil made Christ endure. People continually succumb to it.

Although these industrial workers driven by worker imperialism are very different from the fascist young bourgeois and
are a more beautiful type of human being, there is a similar
problem concerning them. How can they be made to love their
country enough without placing it in their hands? Because it
cannot be placed in their hands; they cannot even be given a
privileged position in it because that would be a glaring injustice with regard to the rest of the population, especially the rural
workers.

The present attitude of these workers towards Germany
should not blind us to the gravity of the problem. Germany
happens to be the enemy of the USSR. Before this was the case,
there was already discontent among the workers, but it is a
vital necessity for the Communist Party continually to stoke
discontent. And this discontent was 'against German fascism
and British imperialism'. Against France, there was no question. Furthermore, from the summer of 1939 to the summer of
1940, a year that was decisive, Communist influence in France
was exercised entirely against the country. It was not going
to be easy to turn the hearts of these workers towards their
country.

Among the rest of the population, the crisis of patriotism has
not been so acute; it has not gone so far as denial in favour of
something else; there has just been a sort of extinction. Among
the rural workers, that is probably because they feel they do
not count, other than as cannon fodder for interests alien
to theirs; among the petty bourgeoisie, it must be due chiefly
to boredom.

In addition to all the specific causes of disaffection there is
another very general one which is like the reverse of idolatry.
Under the name of 'nation' or 'homeland', the state has ceased
to be an infinite good, in the sense of a good to be served with
devotion. On the contrary, everyone saw it as an unlimited
good to be consumed. Once idolatry had been eradicated, the
absolute associated with the state remained attached to it and
took on this new form. The state appeared to be an infinite

cornucopia that distributed riches in proportion to the pressures it was under. And so, people were always resentful that it was not allocating more. It seemed as if it was refusing to grant all the things that it did not supply. When the state asked for something, it was a demand that appeared paradoxical. When it imposed, it was an intolerable constraint. People's attitude towards the state was that of children, not towards their parents but towards adults whom they neither loved nor feared; they make constant demands but will not obey.

How can people suddenly switch from this attitude to the boundless devotion required by war? But even during the war, the French believed that the state had victory somewhere in its coffers, along with other treasures that it couldn't be bothered to bring out. Everything was done to encourage that opinion, as is evident in the slogan '*Nous vaincrons parce que nous sommes les plus forts*' ('We shall win because we are the strongest').

Victory was going to liberate a country where everyone would have been almost exclusively occupied in disobeying, for either noble or base reasons. People listened to radio broadcasts from London, read and distributed banned publications, travelled with false papers, hid wheat, worked in a slovenly manner, bought and sold on the black market, and boasted of it to friends and family. How would these people be made to understand that all this was over, that from now on, they would have to obey?

People will also have spent those years dreaming of satiation. Those are the dreams of beggars, in the sense that they think only of receiving good things without giving anything in return. The public authorities will take care of distribution; how then to prevent this insolent-beggar attitude – which was that of the citizens towards the state already before the war – from becoming markedly more pronounced? And if it is directed towards a foreign country, America for example, the danger is even greater.

A second very common dream is that of killing. Killing for the most laudable reasons, but basely and without risks. Whether the state will succumb to the contagion of this diffuse terrorism, as is to be feared, or whether it will try to contain it, in both cases the repressive, police arm of the state, traditionally so loathed and despised in France, will be to the fore.

The government that will emerge in France after the country's liberation will be faced with the triple danger caused by this bloodlust, this begging complex and this inability to obey.

There is only one remedy. Give the French something to love. And first of all, give them France to love. Create the reality that corresponds to the name of France so that, such as it is, in its truth, people can love it with all their souls.

The nub of the contradiction inherent in patriotism is that the country is limited, whereas the demand is unlimited. At the moment of extreme peril, the state demands everything. Why would a person grant everything to something that is limited? On the other hand, refusing to give everything if the need arises is to abandon the state completely since its preservation cannot be assured at a lesser price. And so, people always appear to fall short of, or to go beyond, what they owe the state, and if they go beyond, as a reaction, they come back later owing even more.

This contradiction is only superficial. Or to be more precise, it is real, but seen in its truth, it boils down to one of those fundamental contradictions of the human condition, which we need to recognize, accept and draw on to rise above what is human. Never in this universe is there equality in magnitude between an obligation and its object. The obligation is infinite, its object is not. This contradiction weighs on the day-to-day life of all human beings, without exception, including those who would be completely incapable of articulating it, even confusedly. All the processes that people believe they have found to rid themselves of it are lies.

One of these consists of recognizing only obligations towards what is not of this world. A variant of this process constitutes false mystics, false contemplation. Another is the practice of good works carried out in a certain spirit, 'for the love of God', as people say, the afflicted saved being only the material for the action, an anonymous opportunity to demonstrate one's goodness to God. In both cases there is mendacity because: 'For he that loveth not his brother whom he hath seen, how can he love God whom he hath not seen?'[105] It is only through the things and beings here on Earth that human love can break through to what lies beyond.

Another process consists of admitting that here on Earth there are one or several objects enclosing this absolute, this infinite, this perfection that are essentially linked to obligation as such. That is the lie of idolatry.

The third process consists of denying all obligations. It cannot be proved by a geometrical demonstration that this is an error because obligation is of an order of certainty much higher than the domain of proofs.[106] In actual fact, this denial is impossible. It constitutes a spiritual suicide. And humans are made in such a way that spiritual death is accompanied by psychological illnesses which are themselves fatal. In actual fact, the self-preservation instinct prevents the soul from doing more than approaching such a state and, even then, it is overcome with a deadly boredom that transforms it into a wilderness. Nearly always, or rather almost certainly always, someone who denies all obligations is lying to others and to themselves; and they know it. There is no one who does not sometimes make judgements on good and evil, if only to blame another.

We must accept our situation, which subjects us to absolute obligations towards things that are relative, limited and imperfect. To identify these things and what their demands of us might consist of, we simply need to see clearly what their relationship is to good.

For the country, the notions of rootedness and vital milieu are sufficient. They do not need to be established through proof because, for some years, they have been verified experimentally. In the same way as there are culture mediums for some microscopic creatures, indispensable habitats for some plants, there is a certain part of everyone's soul and ways of thinking and behaving circulating from one human being to another that can only exist in the national milieu, and which vanish when a country is destroyed.

These days, the French all know what they were missing when France foundered. They know it in the same way they know what is missing when there is nothing to eat. They know that part of their soul adheres so closely to France that when France is taken away from them, it remains glued to it, like skin to a burning object, and is thus ripped off. And so there is a thing to which every French soul is glued, the same for all: unique, real although intangible, and as real as things that can be touched. And so, anything that threatens France with destruction – and in some circumstances an invasion is a threat of destruction – is equivalent to the threat of a physical mutilation of all French people, their children and their descendants ad infinitum. Because there are populations that have never recovered from having once been conquered.

That is sufficient for the obligation towards the country to be self-evident. It exists alongside others; it does not make people give everything, always, but makes them give everything sometimes. Just as a miner must sometimes give everything when there is an accident in the mine and comrades' lives are at stake. That is accepted, recognized. The obligation towards one's country is just as obvious when the country is concretely under threat as a reality. It is today. The reality of France has become palpable to all French people through absence.

Never have people dared deny their obligation towards the country other than by denying the reality of the country. Extreme pacifism, according to Gandhi's doctrine, is not a denial of this obligation, but a particular means of accomplishing it. As far as we know, this means has never been applied; notably not by Gandhi, who is much too realistic. If it had been applied in France, the French would not have put up armed resistance to the invader; but they would never have accepted doing nothing, in any domain, that might help the occupying army. They would have done their utmost to hinder it, and they would have maintained this attitude indefinitely, without compromise. It is clear that they would have perished in much greater numbers and much more painfully. It is the imitation of the Passion of the Christ on a national scale.

If an entire nation were close enough to perfection for it to be suggested that it imitate the Passion of the Christ, it would certainly be worth doing so. It would disappear, but this disappearance would be infinitely better than the most glorious survival. But this is not the case. Very likely, almost certainly, it cannot be the case. It is only the soul, in its innermost solitude that is capable of being given an orientation towards such perfection.

However, if there are people whose vocation is to seek this impossible perfection, the public authorities are obliged to allow them to do so, and moreover, to give them the means. Britain recognizes conscientious objection. But that is not enough. For these people, we must make the effort to invent something which, without involving either direct or indirect participation in strategic operations, is a presence in the war itself, and a presence that is much more arduous and dangerous than that of the soldiers.

That would be the sole remedy against the disadvantages of pacifist propaganda. Because it would permit, without injustice, the shaming of those who refused such a gesture on the grounds of total or almost total pacifism. Pacifism is only likely to cause harm through the confusion between two forms of repugnance: revulsion for killing and revulsion for dying. The first is honourable, but very weak; the second, almost inadmissible, but very powerful; the combination of the two creates a very strong motive, which is not inhibited by shame, and in which the second revulsion alone is active. The French pacifists of recent years were loath to die but not at all to kill, otherwise in July 1940 they would not have rushed so hastily into collaborating with Germany. The small number who found themselves in this milieu because of their genuine revulsion at murder were sadly deceived.

Distinguishing between these two revulsions eliminates any danger. The influence of the revulsion against killing is not dangerous; first of all, it is good because it stems from good; but it is weak, and regrettably there is no likelihood it will stop being so. As for those who are weak faced with the fear of death, they should be shown compassion because every human being, unless they are fanatical, is at least susceptible to this weakness; but if they turn their weakness into an opinion to be spread, they become criminal, and then it is necessary and easy to dishonour them.

Defining the country as a vital milieu avoids the contradictions and lies that erode patriotism. There is a certain vital milieu, but there are also others. It is the product of a tangle of causes in which good and evil, just and unjust are mingled, and as a result it is not the best possible. It has perhaps been constituted at the expense of another combination that is richer in vital emanations, and if that is the case, regrets would be justified. But past events are over; this milieu exists and should be preserved as it is as a treasure because of the good it contains.

In many cases, the populations conquered by the soldiers of the King of France suffered a wrong. But so many organic connections have grown over the centuries that a surgical remedy would only add further damage. The past is only partially repairable, and this can only be done by a local and regional life that is authorized and encouraged unreservedly by the public authorities within the framework of the French nation. On the other hand, the disappearance of the French nation, far from going some way to repairing the damage of the past conquest, renews it with considerably increased gravity; if a few centuries ago populations suffered a loss of vitality as a result of being subdued by the French military, they will be morally killed by a new wound inflicted by the Germans. In this sense only is there truth in the saying according to which there is no incompatibility between love of the local – the *petite patrie* – and that of the country – the *grande patrie*. Because thus someone from Toulouse might ardently regret that their town once became French, that so many beautiful Romanesque churches were destroyed to make way for a mediocre, imported Gothic style, and that the Inquisition halted the spiritual flowering, and they can promise themselves even more ardently that this same town should become German.

The same applies to the external. If the country is considered to be a vital milieu, it only needs to be protected from external influences as far as is necessary to remain so, and not absolutely. The state ceases to be the absolute ruler by divine right over the territories for which it is responsible; a reasonable and restricted authority exercised by international bodies to deal with essential problems of an international dimension would cease to seem like betrayal. Milieus for the circulation of ideas could be created, vaster than France and encompassing it, or connecting some French territories to non-French territories. Would it not be natural, for example, that in a certain area Brittany, Wales, Cornwall and Ireland should feel like parts of one same milieu?

But again, the more people are attached to these non-national milieus, the more they want to preserve national freedom because such cross-border relations do not take place for vanquished populations. That is why cultural exchanges between Mediterranean countries were incomparably more intense and more vibrant before, as opposed to after, the Roman conquest, whereas all these countries, reduced to the unfortunate condition of provinces, fell into a dull uniformity. Exchange only takes place if each participant preserves its own genius, and that is not possible without freedom.

Generally speaking, while the existence of a large number of life-giving milieus is recognized, with one's country constituting only one of these, even so, when the country is in danger of disappearing, all the obligations implied by loyalty to all these environments converge in the single obligation to help one's country. Because the members of a population subjugated by a foreign state are deprived of all of these milieus at once, and not only of their national milieu. And so, when a nation finds itself threatened to this extent, the obligation to join the army becomes the sole expression of all a person's loyalties here below. This is true even for conscientious objectors if they are offered an option equivalent to fighting.

Once this is recognized, certain changes should result in attitudes to war in the case of the nation being under threat. First of all, the distinction between soldiers and civilians, which the pressure of events has already almost obliterated, must be abolished altogether. That was the main cause of the reaction after 1918. Each individual owes their country the totality of their strength, their resources, and even their life, until the danger is over. It is desirable that the suffering and the danger should be spread across all categories of the population, young and old, men and women, well and sick, within the bounds of the technical possibilities, and even a little beyond. Finally, honour is so closely linked to the fulfilment of this obligation, and external pressure is so contrary to honour, that those who so wish should be exempt from this obligation; as a result, they would forfeit their nationality, and furthermore, either be expelled and prohibited from ever returning to the country or be subjected to continual humiliations as a way of publicly branding them as being without honour. It is shocking that the lack of honour should be punished in the same way as theft or murder. Those who do not want to defend their country must lose, not their life or their freedom, but purely and simply their country.

If the country is in such a state that for many this is an inconsequential punishment, then the military code will also prove to be ineffective. We cannot ignore this.

If the obligation to serve in the army includes at certain moments all earthly loyalties, similarly the state has a duty at all times to preserve every milieu, both inside and outside the territory, from which a proportion of the population, small or large, draws life for the soul.

The state's most obvious duty is to effectively guarantee the country's security at all times. Security does not mean the absence of danger because danger is ever present in the world, but it does mean a reasonable chance of getting out of difficulty in the event of a crisis. But that is only the state's most basic duty. If it does no more than that, then it does nothing because if that is all it does, it cannot even succeed at that.

Its duty is to make the country a reality to the highest possible degree. It was not a reality for many French people in 1939. It became one again through privation. It must remain so in possession, and for that, it must truly be a source of life, it must truly be a soil of rootedness. It must also be a favourable environment for participation and faithful attachment to all types of milieu other than itself.

Today, as the French are rediscovering a sense of France as a reality, they are also more conscious than ever of local differences. The division of France into separate sections, the censorship of correspondence which restricts exchanges of thought to a small area, is partially to blame, and paradoxically the forced intermingling of the population has also played a large part. Today people feel much more continuously and acutely than before that they are Breton, Provençal, Parisian or a native of Lorraine. This sentiment contains a hint of hostility that needs to be eliminated; furthermore, it is also urgent to eliminate xenophobia. But this sentiment in itself should not be discouraged – on the contrary. It would be disastrous to declare that it is inimical to patriotism. In the current state of distress, disarray, solitude and uprootedness in which the French find themselves, all loyalties, all attachments should be preserved as all-too-rare and infinitely precious treasures, to be watered like ailing plants.

Little does it matter that the Vichy government has promoted a regionalist doctrine. Its only error is not to have implemented it. Far from advocating the opposite to its injunctions in everything, we should adopt many of the thoughts put out by the propaganda of the National Revolution but turn them into realities.

In the same way, the French in their isolation have come to believe that France is a small country and that locked up inside it they are suffocating and need something more. The idea of Europe, of European unity, played a large part in the success of the collaborationist propaganda at first. This sentiment too should be widely encouraged and nurtured. It would be disastrous to see this idea as being opposed to patriotism.

And finally, circles of ideas and debate (*milieux d'idées*) that are not part of the machinery of government should also be widely encouraged because this is the sole condition that means they are not corpses. This applies to the trade unions, if they are not overwhelmed with daily responsibilities in economic organization. It applies to Protestant and Catholic Christian milieus, and more particularly organizations such as the JOC (Young Christian Workers).[107] But a state that allowed itself to be influenced even very slightly by the wishes of the clergy would most certainly kill them. This is true of the associations that arose after the defeat, some official – the *Chantiers de Jeunesse* and *Compagnons* – others clandestinely, in other words, the Resistance groups.[108] The official organizations had some life despite their official nature, thanks to an exceptional combination of factors. But if their official role were to be maintained, they would die. The others were born out of the struggle against the state, and if we were to give in to the temptation to give them an official existence within public life, that would ravage them morally to a terrible degree.

On the other hand, if milieus of this kind are outside public life, they cease to exist. So they must not be part of it, but they must not be outside it either. A process to ensure this could be, for example, for the state to frequently appoint people chosen from these milieus for special missions, on a temporary basis. But this would require on the one hand for the state itself to choose those people, and on the other that all their comrades should take pride in their being selected. Such a method could become an institution.

Once again, differences should be encouraged while trying to prevent animosity. Never can the ferment of ideas do any harm to a country like ours. It is mental inertia that is deadly.

The duty that behoves the state to provide the people with something that is truly a country cannot be a condition for the military obligation that behoves the entire population in the event of a threat to the nation. Because if the state fails in its duty, if the country is weakened, nevertheless, for as long as national independence survives, there is the hope of resurrection. If we look closely, we will see in the past of every country, very surprising peaks and troughs, sometimes quite close together. But if the country is conquered by a foreign army, there is no longer any hope, except that of a rapid liberation. When there is nothing else, hope alone is worth dying for.

And so, although the country is a fact, and as such subject to external conditions, to happenstance, the obligation to come to its aid in the event of mortal danger is still unconditional. But it is clear that in fact the population will be all the keener to defend it if the reality of the country has been made more tangible.

The notion of country thus defined is incompatible with the current understanding of the country's history, with the current understanding of national glory, and above all with the way people currently speak of the Empire.

France possesses an empire, and consequently whatever the stance taken with regard to principles, it poses problems that are very complex and very different from one locality to another. But we should not confuse them. First of all there is a question of principle, and less specific still, a question of sentiment. On the whole, should a Frenchman be happy that France has an empire, and think and talk about it with joy and pride, in the tones of a legitimate owner?

Yes, if this Frenchman is a patriot in the mould of Richelieu, Louis XIV or Maurras. No, if Christian inspiration and the thinking of 1789 are indissolubly blended into the very substance of his patriotism. It could be said that any other nation was entitled to carve out an empire for itself, but not France, for the same reason that made the temporal sovereignty of the pope a scandal in the eyes of Christianity. When one assumes, as France did in 1789, the role of thinking for the world, of defining justice for the world, one does not become the owner of human flesh. Even if it is true that had we not done so, others would have snatched up those afflicted souls and treated them even worse. That is not a legitimate reason; ultimately, the total harm would have been less. Reasons of this sort are generally bad. A priest does not become the owner of a brothel on the basis that a pimp would have treated the women worse. France should not have sacrificed self-respect out of compassion. And in any case, it did not do so. No one would dare to seriously argue that France set out to conquer those populations to prevent others from abusing them, particularly because to a large extent, in the nineteenth century, it was France that took the initiative of making colonial adventures fashionable again.

Among the peoples placed under submission by France, some feel very keenly how scandalous it is that France did that. Their rancour towards us is aggravated by a deeply painful bitterness and bewilderment.

It is possible that today France will have to choose between attachment to its empire and the need to have a soul once more. More generally, France must choose between having a soul and the Roman, or Corneille-style notion of *grandeur*.

If it chooses badly, if we ourselves push France to choose badly, which is only too likely, it will have neither one nor the other, but only the most horrendous affliction, which the country will suffer in astonishment, without anyone being able to identify the cause. And all those who are capable of speaking, of holding a pen, will forever bear the responsibility for a crime.

Bernanos understood and said that Hitlerism was the return of pagan Rome. But had he forgotten, have we forgotten, how great an influence Rome has had on our history, our culture, and still today on our thinking? If, out of horror of a certain form of evil, we have taken the terrible resolve to wage war, with all its attendant atrocities, can we be excused if we wage a less ruthless war against that same form of evil within our own souls? If we are attracted by heroic, Corneille-style *grandeur*, Germany can well attract us too because the German soldiers are certainly 'heroes'. In the present confusion of thinking and feelings around the idea of patriotism, do we have any guarantee that the sacrifice of a French soldier in Africa is inspired by a purer notion of sacrifice that that of a German soldier in Russia? At present, we do not. If we are not conscious of the terrible responsibility this entails, we cannot be innocent amid this unleashing of crimes across the world.

If there is one point on which we should despise everything and brave everything for the love of truth, it is this. We are all united in the name of patriotism. What are we, what contempt do we not deserve, if, within our notion of the country, there is the slightest trace of a lie?

But if our patriotism is not inspired by Corneille-type sentiments, what motive will replace them?

There is one that is no less powerful, is absolutely pure, and fully responds to the present circumstances. And that is compassion for one's country. There is a glorious advocate: Joan of Arc used to say that she felt pity for the kingdom of France.

But we can cite an infinitely higher authority. In the Gospels, we cannot find the slightest hint that Christ felt anything resembling love towards Jerusalem or Judaea, other than the love that goes with compassion. He never showed any kind of attachment to his country. But he expressed compassion more than once. He wept over the city on foreseeing, as it was easy to do at the time, the destruction that would soon befall it. He spoke to it as to a person. 'Jerusalem, Jerusalem, how often I have longed [to gather your children together].'[109] Even bearing his cross, he again expressed the pity he felt.

Let us not imagine that compassion for one's country excludes a lust for war. It spurred the Carthaginians to one of the most prodigious exploits in history. Defeated and reduced to almost nothing by Scipio Africanus, they subsequently endured for fifty years a process of demoralization compared with which France's capitulation is as nothing. They were exposed to all the humiliations inflicted on them by the Numidians with no recourse, and, having renounced by treaty the freedom to go to war, they implored Rome in vain for permission to defend themselves. When they finally did so without Rome's authorization, their army was annihilated. They then had to beg the Romans for forgiveness. They agreed to hand over three hundred children of the nobility and all their weapons. Then their envoys were given the order to evacuate the city completely, and for ever, so that it could be razed. They erupted in cries of indignation, and then tears. 'They ceased their reproaches and began to bewail, with fresh lamentations, their own fate and that of their wives and children, calling them by name and also their country, as though she could hear their cries like a human being.'[110] Then they begged the Romans, if they wanted to harm them, to spare that city, those stones, monuments and temples, which had done no wrong, and instead to exterminate the entire population; they said that this choice would be less shameful for the Romans and infinitely preferable for the people of Carthage. The Romans remained intransigent. The city rose up, even though it had no resources, and it took Scipio Africanus, at the head of a vast army, three whole years to conquer the city and destroy it.

There is a warmth in this poignant feeling of tenderness towards a beautiful, precious, fragile and perishable thing that

THE NEED FOR ROOTS

is different from that of national greatness. The energy inspiring it is absolutely pure. It is very intense. Is a man not easily capable of heroism when it comes to protecting his children or his elderly parents, to whom no prestige of greatness is attached? An absolutely pure love of one's country has an affinity with the feelings inspired in a man by his young children, his elderly parents or the wife he loves. The thought of weakness can ignite love as can that of strength, but the flame is pure in a very different way. Compassion for vulnerability is always bound up with love for true beauty because we feel acutely that truly beautiful things should be guaranteed eternal life but are not.

It is possible to love France for the glory that seems to guarantee it an extended life far into time and space. Or it can be loved like a thing which, being earthly, can be destroyed, and is therefore all the more precious.

These are two distinct types of love; perhaps, probably, incompatible, even though language confuses them. Those whose heart is made to feel the latter type can, by dint of habit, use the language that is only suited to the former.

Only the latter is justifiable for a Christian because it alone is tinged with Christian humility. It alone belongs to the type of love that can be called charity. We should not think that this love can only have as its object an afflicted country. Happiness is as much an object for compassion as affliction because it is earthly – in other words, incomplete, fragile and ephemeral. What is more, sadly there is always a certain degree of affliction in the life of a country.

Nor should we believe that such a love would be likely to ignore or neglect what there is of genuine and pure greatness in France's past, present and future aspirations. Quite the contrary. The more good we can discern in the being that is the object of compassion, the more tender, the more poignant it is, and it disposes us to discern the good. When a Christian imagines Christ on the Cross, their compassion is not diminished by the thought of perfection, nor vice-versa. But on the other hand, such a love can have its eyes open to the injustices, cruelties, errors, lies, crimes and disgraces contained in the past, the present and the country's desires, without dissimulation or reticence, and without being diminished by it; the love is simply rendered more painful. For compassion, crime itself is a reason not to move away, but to go closer, to share, not the guilt, but the shame. Men's crimes did not diminish Christ's compassion. Compassion is alert to good and evil and finds reasons to love in both. It is the only love here below that is true and just.

It is at present the only love that is fitting for the French. If the events we have just experienced are not enough to warn us that we must change our way of loving our country, what lesson will it teach us? What more will it take to gain our attention than a sledgehammer blow on the head?

Compassion for our country is the only feeling that does not ring false at present, that is appropriate for the state in which the souls and bodies of the French find themselves, that has both the humility and dignity fitting for affliction, and also the simplicity affliction demands above all else. To evoke France's historic greatness right now, its past and future glories and the brilliance surrounding its existence, is not possible without a sort of inner tension that makes the tone somewhat forced. Nothing akin to vainglory can be fitting for the afflicted.

For the French who are suffering, such an evocation comes into the category of compensations. To seek compensations in times of affliction is evil. If this evocation is repeated too often, if it is provided as the sole source of comfort, it can do boundless harm. The French are avid for greatness. But it is not Roman-style greatness that the afflicted need. Either it feels to them like a mockery, or it poisons their soul, as was the case in Germany.

For France, compassion is not a compensation but a spiritualization of the suffering the country has undergone; it can transform even the most physical suffering, such as cold and hunger. He who is cold and hungry and is tempted feel self-pity can instead, through his own weakened flesh, direct his pity towards France. That very cold and hunger then channel the love of France through the body deep into the soul. And this compassion can cross borders unhindered, spread to all afflicted countries, to all countries without exception because all human populations are subject to the wretchedness of our condition.

Whereas vainglory in national greatness is exclusive by nature and non-transferable, compassion is universal by nature. It is only more virtual for things that are distant and foreign, and more real, more physical, more freighted with blood, tears and effective energy for things that are close.

National vainglory is far removed from day-to-day life. In France, it can only find expression in the Resistance, but many either have not had the opportunity to take part in the Resistance, or do not devote all their time to it. Compassion for France is just as powerful a motive for resistance action, but in addition it can find uninterrupted expression day to day, on all sorts of occasions, even the most ordinary, through a sense of fraternity in relations between the French. Fraternity grows easily in compassion for a misfortune which, while inflicting its share of affliction on each one, threatens something much more precious than individual wellbeing. National pride, either in prosperity or in affliction, is incapable of arousing true, warm fraternity. There was none among the ancient Romans. They were oblivious to genuinely tender feelings.

Patriotism inspired by compassion gives the poorest section of the people a privileged moral place. National greatness is only a stimulus among the lower social orders at times when everyone can hope for the glory of the country and at the same time for a personal share in that glory, as large as they can wish for. This was the case at the start of Napoleon's reign. Any little fellow, born in any district, was entitled to carry in his heart any dream of a future; no ambition was so great as to be ludicrous. People knew that not all ambitions would be fulfilled, but each one had a chance, and many could be partially fulfilled. A unique document from the time states that Napoleon's popularity was due less to the devotion of the French to his person than to the possibilities that he offered them of advancement, the opportunity to carve a career. That is precisely the sentiment that appears in *The Red and the Black*.[111] The Romantics were children who were bored because they no longer had the possibility of unfettered social advancement. They sought literary glory as a replacement product.

But this stimulus only exists in troubled times. It cannot be said that it ever addresses the people as such; every man of the people who experiences it dreams of breaking away from the people, breaking out of the anonymity that defines the condition of the people. When this ambition is widespread, it is the effect of a troubled social condition and the cause of worse upheavals, since social stability hamstrings this ambition. Although it is a stimulus, it cannot be said that it is healthy, either for people's souls or for the country. It is possible that this stimulus plays a large part in the current resistance movement because on the question of France's future, the illusion is easily entertained, and, as to people's personal futures, anyone, if they have proved themselves in the midst of danger, can expect anything in the state of latent revolution in which the country finds itself. But if this is the case, it represents a terrible danger for the reconstruction period, and it is urgent to find another stimulus.

In a period of social stability, when without exception those who are anonymous more or less remain so, when they do not even dream of escaping their condition, the people cannot feel at home in a patriotism founded on pride and the lustre of glory. They feel as ill at ease as in the salons of Versailles, which are an expression of it. Glory is the contrary of anonymity. If to military glories we add literary, scientific and other achievements, the people will continue to feel alienated. The knowledge that some of those Frenchmen covered in glory are from the people will not provide any reassurance in periods of stability; because they have escaped their condition, they have ceased to be of the people.

Conversely, if the country is presented to them as a beautiful and precious thing which is on the one hand imperfect, and on the other very fragile and vulnerable and must be cherished and preserved, they will justifiably feel closer to it than the other social classes. Because the people have a monopoly on one form of knowledge, perhaps the most important of all, that of the reality of affliction. As a result, they feel much more keenly how precious are the things that deserve protection from it, how each of us is obliged to cherish these things and safeguard them. Melodrama reflects this state of popular sensitivity. Why it is such a poor literary form is a question worth studying. But far from being a false genre, it is very close, in a way, to reality.

If such a relationship were to be established between the people and the country, they would no longer experience their own suffering as crimes committed by the country against them, but as ills suffered by the country in them. There is a vast difference. But in another sense, this difference is slight, and it would take little to overcome it. But that little would have to come from another world.

This supposes a disconnection between the country and the state. That is possible if Corneille-style *grandeur* is abolished. But that would result in anarchy if by way of compensation the state did not find a means of earning additional esteem on its own.

To do this, the state must definitely not return to former methods of parliamentary life and inter-party strife. But most important perhaps is the complete overhaul of the police. Circumstances appear favourable. It would be useful to study the British police. In any case it is to be hoped that the liberation of the country will lead to the disbanding of the police, apart from those who personally fought against the enemy. They must be replaced by men who are respected by the public, and, since today, unfortunately, money and qualifications are the main source of that respect, police officers and inspectors should be required to have a relatively high level of education, and those top-level qualifications should be correspondingly well remunerated. Even if the fashion for *Grandes Écoles* continues in France – which may not be desirable – there would need to be an elite police college with a competitive entrance exam.[112] These are crude methods, but something of this kind is essential. Furthermore, and much more importantly, there should be no more social categories like 'prostitute' or 'ex-convict' that have an official existence like cattle handed over for the police to treat as they please, providing them with both victims and accomplices; a dual contamination is then inevitable, the contact discredits both parties. Both categories should be abolished by law.

The crime of dishonesty towards the state by public figures should be punished more severely than armed robbery.

In its administrative function, the state should appear as the custodian of the country's assets – a good custodian on the whole that can reasonably be expected to be more bad than good in general because its task is difficult and carried out in morally unfavourable conditions. Obedience is nevertheless obligatory, not because the state has the right to command, but because it is essential for the preservation and repose of the country. People must obey the state, whatever it is, rather like affectionate children left in the care of an incompetent governess while their parents are away, obeying her all the same out of love for their parents. If the state is not incompetent, so much the better; furthermore, the pressure of public opinion should always act as an incentive to push the state to rise above incompetence. But whether it is incompetent or not, the obligation of obedience is the same.

Admittedly, this obligation is not boundless, but it can have no limits other than a rebellion by the conscience. No criterion can be given for this limit; it is even impossible for everyone to set one for themselves once and for all. When someone feels they can no longer obey, they disobey. But at any rate, one necessary although not sufficient condition for them to be able to disobey without committing a crime, is for them to be driven by an obligation so compelling that it makes them scorn all risks without exception. If someone is inclined to disobey, but is stopped by the excessive danger, they cannot be forgiven either for having thought of disobeying or for not having done so. Furthermore, each time someone is not rigorously obliged to disobey, they are rigorously obliged to obey. A country cannot have freedom if it is not recognized that disobeying the public authorities, whenever it does not stem from a compelling sense of duty, is more shameful than theft. In other words, public order must be held as more sacred than private property. The authorities can promote this way of seeing through teaching and through appropriate measures that would need to be devised.

But only compassion for the country, the concerned and

tender preoccupation to preserve it from affliction, can give to peace, and especially to civil peace, what civil or foreign war unfortunately possesses of itself – something exalting, touching, poetic and sacred. This compassion alone can enable us to rediscover the long-lost sentiment, so rarely felt during the course of history, that Théophile [de Viau] expressed in the beautiful line '*La sainte majesté des lois*' – the holy majesty of laws.

The era when Théophile [de Viau] wrote those words is perhaps the last era when this sentiment was profoundly felt in France. Then came Richelieu, then the Fronde, then Louis XIV, and then the rest. Montesquieu tried and failed to re-instil it in the public through a book.[113] The people of 1789 claimed they felt it, but they could not have felt it deep in their hearts, otherwise the country would not have slid so easily into war, both civil and foreign.

Since then, even our language has become unfit to express it. And yet that is the sentiment we try to evoke – or its paler replica – when we speak of legitimacy. But naming a sentiment is not sufficient to arouse it. And that is a fundamental truth that we forget too readily.

Why lie to ourselves? In 1939, before the war, under the regime of decree-laws, already republican legitimacy no longer existed. It had vanished like Villon's youth '*qui son partement m'a celé*' (the time that's vanished furtively), noiselessly, without warning that it was going, and without anyone making a gesture or saying a word to stop it.[114] As for the sentiment of legitimacy, it was utterly dead. That it should reappear now in the thoughts of exiles, that it should occupy a certain place, alongside other sentiments that are in fact incompatible with it, in the dreams of healing of a sick people, means nothing, or very little. If it was non-existent in 1939, how could it be effective, immediately after years of routine disobedience?

Furthermore, the 1875 Constitution cannot be a basis of legitimacy after sinking into indifference or even general contempt in 1940, after being abandoned by the people of France. Because the people of France have abandoned it. Neither the resistance groups nor the French in London can do anything about this. If a glimmer of regret was expressed, it was not by a section of the people, but by parliamentarians, whose profession is to keep alive an interest in the republican institutions that has died everywhere else. Once again, little does it matter that much later, it resurfaced to some extent. At present, hunger imbues the Third Republic with all the poetry of an era when there was bread. It is a fugitive poetry. Besides, at the same time the repugnance felt for several years that reached its peak in 1940 persists. (The Third Republic was in fact criticized in a document officially emanating from London; since then, it can hardly be taken as a basis of legitimacy.)

Nevertheless, it is certain that insofar as the things of Vichy will disappear, insofar as revolutionary, possibly Communist, institutions will not emerge, there will be a return to the structures of the Third Republic. But purely because there will be a vacuum, and something will be needed to fill it. That is necessity, not legitimacy. For the people, this corresponds not to loyalty, but to a glum resignation. Meanwhile, the date 1789 stirs up an echo that is profound in a different way, but which corresponds only to an inspiration and not to institutions.

Given that there has been a break in continuity in our recent history, legitimacy can no longer have a historical nature; it must stem from the eternal source of all legitimacy. Those who put themselves forward to govern the country must officially recognize certain obligations responding to the people's essential aspirations, permanently etched deep in their souls. The people need to be able to trust their word and their capabilities and be given the means to demonstrate this. And the people must feel that in accepting them, they commit to obeying them.

Since the country needs the people to be obedient towards the public authorities, that is therefore a sacred obligation. It confers the same sacred character on the public authorities themselves because they are the object of this obligation. This is not idolatry towards the state associated with Roman-style patriotism: it is the opposite. The state is sacred, not like an idol, but like liturgical objects or the altar stones, or the baptism water and suchlike. Everyone knows that they are only matter. But pieces of matter are considered sacred because they serve a sacred purpose. That is the kind of majesty that is fitting for the state.

If the powers that be are not able to fill the people of France with a similar inspiration, they will have the choice only between disorder and idolatry. Idolatry can take the form of Communism. That is most likely what will happen. It can also take the form of nationalism. Then its object would probably be the duo, so characteristic of our time, comprising the man acclaimed as leader and the rigid machinery of the state. But, on the one hand, publicity can create leaders and on the other, if circumstances place a man of genuine worth in such a position, he rapidly becomes prisoner to his role as idol. To put it another way, in modern language, the lack of a pure inspiration will leave the French people with no other options than disorder, Communism or fascism.

There are people, for example in America, who are wondering whether the French in London are not leaning towards fascism. That is to frame the question very badly. The intentions in themselves have very little importance, except when they are heading directly towards evil, because for evil there are always resources within reach. But good intentions only count if they are matched by the corresponding resources. Saint Peter had no intention of denying Jesus, but he did so because he did not possess within him the grace that would have enabled him to refrain. And even the energy, the categorical tone he used to assert the opposite intention contributed to depriving him of that grace. That is one example that is worth remembering in all the trials life puts before us.

The question is to know whether the French in London possess the necessary means to stop the people of France from sliding into fascism, and at the same time prevent them from falling either into Communism or into disorder. Fascism, Communism and disorder being merely the barely distinguishable expressions of a single evil, it is a matter of knowing whether they have a remedy for this evil.

If they do not have it, their *raison d'être*, which is to maintain France in the war, is annihilated by victory, which will then plunge them back among the mass of their compatriots. If they do have it, they should already have begun to apply it liberally and effectively well before victory. Because a treatment of this kind cannot be started in the midst of the nervous disorders that will accompany – in each individual person and in the masses – the country's liberation. Even less can it be started once people's nerves have calmed down, should appeasement come about one day. Then it will be much too late, and any treatment will then be out of the question.

The important thing then is not that they affirm in front of the foreigner their right to govern France; the same is true for a doctor, the important thing is not to affirm his right to treat a patient. The key thing is to have diagnosed the disease, decided on a treatment, chosen the medication and made sure it is available to the patient. When a doctor can do all that, not without risk of error, but with a reasonable chance of having got it right, then, if people want to prevent him from doing his job and put in his place a charlatan, it is his duty to fight that with all his strength. But if, in a place where there are no doctors, several ignoramuses busy themselves around a patient for whom the state requests the most precise, the most enlightened care, what does it matter in whose hands they end up dying or being saved purely by chance? Without a doubt it is best for them to be in the hands of those who love them. But those who love them will not inflict on them the misery of a battle raging at their bedside unless they have a method capable of saving them.[115]

The problem of finding a method to inspire a people is completely new. Plato alludes to it in *Politics* and elsewhere. There were probably teachings on this subject within the secret body of knowledge of pre-Roman antiquity, which has been entirely lost. Perhaps the Knights Templar and the early Freemasons were still discussing this problem. Unless I am mistaken, Montesquieu ignored it. Rousseau, who was a powerful thinker in his day, acknowledged its existence very clearly, but did not go any further. The people of 1789 do not seem to have suspected its existence. In 1793, without having taken the trouble to pose it, even less to explore it, hasty solutions were improvised: festivals of the Supreme Being, the Feast of the Goddess Reason.

These were ridiculous and odious. During the nineteenth century, the intellectual level had sunk well below the level at which such questions are asked.

Nowadays, people have investigated and analysed the question of propaganda. Hitler, in particular, made a lasting contribution to human thought on the subject. But it is in fact an entirely different matter. Propaganda does not aim to inspire; it closes off and blocks all orifices through which inspiration might enter. It inflates the entire soul with fanaticism. Its processes cannot be applied to the opposite purpose, nor is it a matter of reversing the methods adopted; the causal relationship is not so straightforward.

Nor should we think that the inspiration of a people is a mystery particular to God alone and for which therefore there can be no method. The highest and most perfect degree of mystical contemplation is infinitely more mysterious, yet Saint John of the Cross wrote treatises on the means to achieve it, treatises of a scientific precision far superior to the writings of the psychologists and educators of our era. If he felt compelled to do this, he was probably correct because he was certainly competent. The beauty of his work is sufficient evidence of its authenticity. To be honest, since the mists of antiquity, long before Christianity, and until the second half of the Renaissance, it was universally recognized that there is method in spiritual matters and in everything connected with the good of the soul. The increasingly methodical hold that humans have exerted over matter since the sixteenth century has made them believe that matters of the soul are either arbitrary or governed by some magic whereby intentions and words have an immediate effect.

This is not the case. Everything in creation is dependent on method, including the points of intersection between this world and the next. This is implied in the word *Logos*, which means 'relation' even more than 'word'. The method simply differs when the domain of application differs. The higher we go, the more rigorous and precise it becomes. It would be very strange if the order of material things reflected more divine wisdom than the order of spiritual things. The contrary should be true.

It is unfortunate for us that this question, on which, if I am correct, there is no guidance, should be the one that we so urgently need to resolve today. This on pain not so much of dying out but of never having existed.

Furthermore, if Plato, for example, had formulated a generic solution, it would not be enough for us to study it to get ourselves out of trouble. History is of little help concerning our predicament. It does not refer us to any country that has been in a situation even remotely resembling the one in which France is likely to find itself in the event of a German defeat. Besides, we cannot even anticipate what that situation will be. We only know that it will be unprecedented. And so, even if we knew how to breathe inspiration into a country, we still would not know how to proceed in the case of France today.

On the other hand, since this is a practical problem, knowledge of a general solution is not essential for a specific case. When a machine stops, a worker, foreman or engineer can have an idea of how to get it running again without having an overall knowledge of machine repairs. The first thing to do in such a case is to look at the machine. But, to look at it constructively requires having in mind the very notion of mechanical connections.

In the same way, looking at France's changing situation day by day, we need to have in our minds a notion of public action as a mode of educating the country.

It is not enough to have glimpsed this idea, considered it attentively, then grasped it. It needs to be permanently instilled in the soul, so that it is present even when attention is focused elsewhere.

It requires even greater effort on our part in that it is an entirely new idea. Since the Renaissance, public activity has never been conceived in this way, but only as a means of establishing a form of power seen as desirable in relation to one thing or another.

Education – whether aimed at children or adults, individuals or a people, or even oneself – consists in creating motives. It is the job of teaching to impart what is beneficial, what is obligatory and what is good. Education deals with the motives for effective action because an action is never executed in the absence of motives capable of galvanizing the necessary energy.

To desire to lead human creatures – oneself or anyone else – towards good, by simply showing the way, without having made the effort to ensure the corresponding motives are there, is like stepping on the accelerator to make a car with an empty petrol tank move forward.

Or it is like trying to light an oil lamp without having first put in any oil. This mistake was criticized in a well-known work, read, reread and cited for twenty centuries.[116] All the same, the same action is still committed.

It is quite easy to categorize the means of education contained in public action.

Firstly, fear and hope, prompted by threats and promises.

Suggestion.

The expression – either official or otherwise approved by an official authority – of some of the thoughts which before being articulated were genuinely in the hearts of the masses, or in the hearts of certain active elements of the nation.

Example.

The methods of action themselves and the organizations forged to take action.

The first means is the crudest, and it is always deployed. The second is universally employed today; it is the one that Hitler has so brilliantly implemented.

The other three are ignored.

We must try to conceive of them in relation to the three successive forms that our public action is likely to take. The present form; the act of taking power at the moment of the country's liberation; the provisional exercise of power during the ensuing months.

Right now, we only have two intermediaries, the radio and the underground movement. For the French masses, the radio is almost the only one.

The third of the five successive processes should in no way be confused with the second. The suggestion is, as Hitler saw, a stranglehold. It is a constraint. The main source of its efficacy is repetition on the one hand, and on the other the strength of the group from which it emanates or that it plans to conquer.

The efficacy of the third process is of a completely different kind. It is founded on the impenetrable structure of human nature.

It can so happen that a thought, sometimes internally formulated, sometimes unformulated, secretly preoccupies the soul, yet only has a weak effect on it.

If we hear that thought expressed outside ourselves, by someone else, someone whose words people listen to, its power is increased a hundredfold and on occasion this can provoke an internal transformation.

It can also so happen that, whether we realize it or not, we need to hear certain words, which, if they are spoken out loud and come from a place from which we naturally expect good, inject comfort, energy and something akin to food.

In private life, these two functions of speech are fulfilled by friends or natural guides, although very rarely in fact.

But there are circumstances when public crises acquire so much more importance in everyone's private life than their own preoccupations that many unspoken thoughts and needs are found to be the same in almost every human being composing a people.

This creates the possibility of action, which, while having as its object an entire people, remains essentially a personal not a collective action. Far from stifling resources hidden deep within each soul, as any collective action inevitably does, due to the nature of things, this kind of action, no matter how lofty its aims, awakens and arouses them and enables them to grow.

But who can carry out such an action?

Under normal circumstances, there can be no place from which it can be conducted. Major obstacles prevent it from being enacted by a government, other than to a partial and minor degree. Further obstacles form a similar impediment to for it to be executed other than by the state.

But in this respect, the circumstances in which France currently finds itself are wonderfully, providentially favourable.

In many other respects, it has been disastrous that France did not, like other countries, have a regular government in London. But in this respect, it is exceptionally fortunate; and again, it is also fortunate that the North African affair did not lead to the transformation of the National Committee into a regular government.

The hatred of the state, which has been latent, hidden and very deep-seated in France since Charles VI, prevents words coming directly from the government from being heard by every Frenchman as the voice of a friend.

On the other hand, during an action of this kind, words must have an official character to be truly effective.

The leaders of the French Resistance are somewhat comparable to a government insofar as their words have exactly the necessary degree of officialdom.

The movement has more or less retained its original nature, that of a revolt that sprang from the depths of a few loyal and completely isolated souls, so that the words emanating from it will sound to every Frenchman like the intimate, warm and affectionate voice of a friend.

Above all else, General de Gaulle, surrounded by those who have followed him, is a symbol. The symbol of France's loyalty to itself, concentrated for a moment almost solely in him; most importantly it is the symbol of everything in human beings that rejects the base adoration of force.

In France, everything that is said in his name has the authority that attaches to a symbol. Subsequently, whoever speaks in his name can, at will and according to what they feel is preferable at a given moment, draw inspiration from the feelings and thoughts fomenting in the minds of the French, or at a higher level, and in that case as high as they like; nothing prevents them from sometimes drawing inspiration from the region beyond the skies. While it would be inappropriate for words issued by a government, tainted of necessity by every base deed associated with the exercise of power, conversely, it would be appropriate for words to come from a symbol representing that which is considered by all to be the highest.

A government that uses words and thoughts that are too elevated for it, far from reflecting some of their lustre, discredits them and makes itself look ridiculous. This happened with the principles of 1789 and the slogan 'Liberté, Égalité, Fraternité' during the Third Republic. That is what happened to the words, often lofty in themselves, proclaimed by the so-called National Revolution. In the latter case, admittedly, the disgrace of betrayal led to discredit with lightning speed. But almost certainly it would have happened anyway, although much less quickly.

The French exiles currently in London have, for a short while perhaps, the extraordinary privilege of being to a large extent symbolic, so enabled to promote the most ambitious inspirations without discredit, and without any impropriety on their part.

So, in consequence of the very unreality affecting it from the outset – due to the basic isolation of those who launched it – the exile movement can draw, if it is alert, on a much greater profusion of reality.

'[. . .] for my strength is made perfect in weakness', according to Saint Paul.[117]

It is a singular blindness that caused, in a situation full of such wonderful possibilities, the desire to sink to the banal, vulgar situation of a government of exiles. It is fortunate that this desire has not been satisfied.

Overseas, moreover, the advantages of the situation are analogous.

Since 1789, France has in fact held a unique position among nations. That is something recent, for 1789 is not so long ago. From the end of the fourteenth century, a period of ferocious repression wrought upon Flemish and French cities by [Charles VI's uncles, as regents] until 1789, other countries saw France's politics as essentially represented by tyranny and absolutism on the one hand, and the servility of its subjects on the other.[118] When du Bellay wrote: 'France, mother of arts, of arms, and of laws,' the last word was an exaggeration, as Montesquieu plainly showed, and as Retz before him had explained with brilliant clarity. Since the death of Charles VI there had been no longer any rule of law in France. From 1715 to 1789, France followed England's example with a fervour charged with humility. Amidst so many enslaved populations only the English then seemed worthy of the name of citizens. But after 1792, when France, having stirred the hearts of the oppressed, found itself engaged in a war against England, it became the focus for the prestige associated with ideas of justice and liberty. The result for the French people during the following century was the type of exaltation that other peoples had not known, but which spread to them and influenced them.

The French Revolution corresponded, unfortunately, to such a violent break with the past across the entire European continent that a tradition dating back to 1789 was in practice the equivalent of an ancient tradition.

The [Franco-German] war of 1870 showed what France had become in the eyes of the world. In this war, the French were the aggressors, despite the Ems telegram ruse; such a ruse is itself proof that the aggression came from the French side.[119] The Germans, internally divided, still shattered by the memory of Napoleon, were anticipating a French invasion. They were greatly surprised to be able to march into France as easily as a knife going through butter. But they were even more surprised to find themselves the object of horror in the eyes of Europe, when their only wrongdoing was to have defended themselves successfully. But the defeated country was France and, despite Napoleon, and because of 1789, it was sufficient for the victors to inspire horror.

The private diary of the Crown Prince Frederick reveals what a painful shock this opprobrium was to the best of the Germans, who could not understand it.

Perhaps this is the origin of the Germans' inferiority complex, the seemingly contradictory mixture of a bad conscience and the feeling that they have suffered an injustice, and their fierce reaction. In any case, from then on, in the European consciousness, the Prussian took the place of the stereotypical German – the utterly inoffensive, daydreaming, blue-eyed musician, *gutmütig* (or bluff), pipe-smoking and beer-drinking fellow who could still be encountered in Balzac's novels. And increasingly Germany continued to live up to its new image.

France suffered scarcely less moral damage. Some admired

the way the country built itself up again after 1871. But they did not see the price it had paid. France had become realistic. It had ceased to believe in itself. The massacre of the Commune, so shocking for its ferocity and the numbers killed, gave the workers a permanent feeling of being pariahs, excluded from the nation, and, among the bourgeoisie, as a result of a guilty conscience, a degree of physical fear of the workers. This became evident again in June 1936. The fall of France in June 1940 is in some way a direct effect of the civil war of May 1871, so brief and so bloody, which continued covertly for almost three-quarters of a century. From then on, the bond between the youth of the *Grandes Écoles* and the people, a bond from which all French ideas of the nineteenth century had drawn a sort of sustenance, became a mere memory. On the other hand, the humiliation of defeat steered the thinking of the bourgeois youth, as a reaction, towards the most mediocre conception of national greatness. Obsessed by the conquest it had suffered and that had diminished it, France no longer felt capable of a vocation more elevated than that of conquest.

And so, France became a nation like the rest, bent only on carving out its portion of yellow and black flesh across the world and of establishing its hegemony in Europe.

After a life of such intense elation, sinking to such a low level could only happen if there was a state of profound disquiet. The lowest point of this disquiet came in June 1940.

It must be said, because it is true, that after the disaster, France's initial reaction was to repeat its own past, its recent past. This was not a result of Vichy's propaganda. On the contrary, it was what initially gave the so-called National Revolution a semblance of success.[120] This was a justified and healthy reaction. The only aspect of the disaster that could be seen as a good thing was the possibility of replicating a past of which it had been the culmination. A past in which France had done nothing but claim the privileges of a mission it had denied because it no longer believed in such a mission.[121]

Overseas, France's collapse only aroused sympathy in places where the spirit of 1789 had made its mark.

France's brief annihilation as a nation could enable it to

regain its place among the nations and become – what it had been and what it had long been expected to become again – an inspiration. For France to regain its past greatness in the world – a greatness so vital for the health of the country's inner life – it had to become an inspiration, before becoming a nation once more by defeating its enemies. Later this would probably be impossible, for several reasons.

There too, the French government in exile in London is in the best situation imaginable, if it knows how to make the best of it. It is just as official as necessary to speak in the name of a country. Not having any governmental authority over the French, however nominal or fictitious, entirely reliant on free consent, it has something of a spiritual power. Unalloyed loyalty in the darkest hours, blood freely spilled every day in its name, give it the right to liberally use the finest words in the language. It is exactly where it needs to be to make the world hear the language of France. A language that derives its authority not from power, which has been destroyed by defeat, nor from glory, which has been eradicated by shame, but above all from a sophistication in its thinking commensurate with the present tragedy, and from a spiritual tradition etched in peoples' hearts.

This movement's twofold mission is easy to define: firstly, to help France to find in the depths of its affliction an inspiration in keeping with its genius and with the present needs of a population in distress. And secondly, once this inspiration is regained, or at least glimpsed, to spread it throughout the world.

If France pursues this dual mission, many things of a less ambitious order will follow. If France pursues other things first, these will not be accomplished.

Of course, it is not a question of a verbal inspiration. All real inspiration passes through the muscles and is expressed in actions. Today the actions of the French can only be those that help drive out the enemy.

And yet it would not be fair to think that the sole mission of the French organization in London is to raise the potential intensity of the French population's energy to its highest degree in the struggle against the enemy.

Its mission is to help France recover an authentic inspiration which, thanks to its very authenticity, naturally stimulates the effort and heroism required to liberate the country.

This does not amount to the same thing.

Because it is necessary to accomplish a mission of such an elevated order, crude and effective techniques comprising threats, promises and suggestions will not suffice.

On the contrary, the use of words echoing the unspoken thoughts and needs of the human beings who constitute the French people – now that is a process that is wonderfully suited to the task to be accomplished, on condition that it is appropriately implemented.

For this to happen first of all requires a receiving body within France. In other words, people whose primary task, whose primary concern, is to identify those unspoken thoughts and unspoken needs, and to convey them to London.

What is essential for this task is a passionate interest in human beings, whoever they are, and in their souls, an ability to put oneself in their shoes and to be alert to signs of unspoken thoughts, a certain intuitive sense of the history that is unfurling, and the faculty to express delicate nuances and complex relations in writing.

Given the extent and complexity of the subject to be observed, there should be many such observers, but on a practical level, that is impossible. At the very least, it is urgent to use in this way anyone who can be employed thus, without exception.

On the assumption that there is in France a receiving body – inadequate though it is bound to be, but real – the second operation, the most important by far, takes place in London. It is that of the choice to be made; it is that which is likely to forge the country's soul.

Knowledge of the words likely to resonate with the French, as if echoing something that is already in their hearts – that knowledge is purely factual knowledge. It contains no indication of a good, and politics, like all human activity, is one directed towards a good.

The state of the French people's hearts is nothing other than a fact. In principle that is neither a good nor an evil; in actual fact it is a combination of good and evil, in proportions that can vary greatly.

That is an evident truth, but one which it is good to reiterate because the sentimentality naturally associated with exile could make us forget that.

Among all the words likely to resonate in the hearts of the French, it is important to choose those for which finding an echo is a good thing, and to say and repeat those words and stifle the others, so as to result in the extinction of that which it is beneficial to abolish.

What will be the selection criteria?

There are two that come to mind. One, the good, in the spiritual sense of the word. The other, usefulness. That is to say, of course, usefulness in relation to the war and to France's national interests.

As regards the first criterion, first of all there is a premise to be analysed. It needs to be weighed up very carefully, at great length, in our souls and our consciences, and then be adopted or rejected once and for all.

A Christian cannot but adopt it.

It is the premise that what is spiritually good is good in all ways, in all respects, at all times, in all places, in all circumstances.

That is Jesus' message when he says: 'Grapes are not gathered from thorns or figs from thistles. So every good tree bears good fruit, but the bad tree bears bad fruit. A good tree cannot produce bad fruit, nor can a bad tree produce good fruit.'[122]

This is the meaning of these words: above the earthly, carnal realm, where ordinarily our thoughts dwell, and which contains everywhere an inextricable mixture of good and evil, there is another spiritual realm, where good is only good, and even in the lower realm, only produces good; where evil is only evil and only produces evil.

It is a direct consequence of belief in God. Absolute good is not only the best of all good – then it would be a relative good – but the only total good, which contains in it to an eminent degree all the goods, including those sought by the people who turn away from it.

All pure good that derives directly from it has an analogous property.

And so, among the list of echoes in the hearts of the French likely to be aroused from London, first we must choose all that is purely and authentically good, with no consideration for expediency, with no other criterion than authenticity; and all this must be relayed to them, often tirelessly, through words that are as simple and stark as possible.

Naturally, everything that is solely evil, hatred, baseness, must likewise be rejected, with no consideration for expediency.

There remain the average motives, which are inferior to spiritual good without being of themselves necessarily bad, and for which the question of expediency arises.

For each of these, it is necessary to examine, completely if possible, really delving into every aspect of the issue, all the effects it is likely to produce in such-and-such respect, in such-and-such potential set of circumstances.

Failure to take this precaution could inadvertently cause the undesired outcome rather than that desired.

For example, after 1918, the pacifists thought they had to appeal to people's yearning for security and comfort to be more easily heard. They hoped thus to gain enough influence to determine the country's foreign policy. They planned in this case to lead it in a direction that guaranteed peace.

They failed to ask themselves what effects the motives stirred up and encouraged by them would have in the event that once they had achieved influence, albeit extensive, that influence was not sufficient to put them in charge of foreign policy.

If only they had asked themselves the question, the reply would have appeared immediately and clearly. In such a case, the motives thus stirred up could neither prevent nor delay war, but only see it won by the most aggressive side, the most bellicose, and discredit love of peace itself for a long time.

Let it be said in passing, the nature itself of the democratic institutions, as we understand it, is a perpetual invitation to this sort of criminal and lethal negligence.

To avoid committing it, for each motive we should ask ourselves what effects it might produce in this or that milieu, and in what others? It may produce effects in such-and-such a domain, but in what others? Such-and-such a situation might arise, but what others? For each one, what effects is it likely to cause in each milieu, in each sphere, now, later and even later? In what ways will each of these potential effects be beneficial, and in what ways harmful? What is the likelihood of each possibility?

Each of these points and all these points taken together must be given careful consideration. Any inclination towards making a choice should be suspended for a while before coming to a decision and running the risk, as with all human decisions, of making a mistake.

Once the choice is made, it needs to be put to the test and, of course, the recording system in France must try gradually to identify the results.

But the verbal expression is only a beginning. Action is a much more powerful tool for sculpting souls.

It has a dual attribute with regard to motives. First of all, a motive is only truly real in the mind when it has prompted an action executed by the body.

It is not enough to encourage such-or-such motives already present or embryonic in the hearts of the French, and to count on people to translate their own motives into actions.

It further requires, from London, in the greatest possible measure, as continually as is possible, with as many details as possible, and through all appropriate means, radio and others, to give directions on actions to be taken.

A soldier talking about his own behaviour during a campaign said: 'I obeyed all the orders but I felt that it would have been impossible for me and beyond my courage to face a danger voluntarily if I had not been given orders.'

This observation contains a very profound truth. An order is an incredibly effective stimulus. It contains within it, in certain circumstances, the driving force that is crucial for the action to be undertaken.

Let it be said in passing, studying what constitutes these circumstances, what defines them and what are the variations, and drawing up a complete list would be to acquire a key to the solution of the most essential and urgent problems of war and of politics.

The clearly acknowledged and necessary responsibility of precise and very strict obligations pushes a person towards danger in the same way as an order. It only arises once engaged in action and through the effect of the specific circumstances of the action. The ability to recognize it is all the greater when the information is clear; it depends even more on intellectual integrity – an infinitely precious virtue that prevents people from lying to themselves to avoid discomfort.

There are three types of people capable of exposing themselves to danger without the incentive of an order or a precise responsibility. There are those who have a great deal of natural courage, a temperament to a large extent that knows no fear, and an imagination that is little inclined to nightmares. These people often face danger lightly, in an adventurous spirit, paying little heed to choosing danger. Secondly, there are those for whom bravery is difficult, but who summon the energy to face it in impure motives; the desire for a medal, vengeance or hatred are examples of this kind of motivation; there are a great many others, very different depending on character and circumstances. And lastly, there are those who obey a direct and specific order coming from God.

This last case is not as rare as people might think because when it does occur, it is often secret – even for the person concerned – and because those to whom this applies are sometimes people who think they do not believe in God. And although not as rare as is generally thought, unfortunately it is not frequent.

The other two categories correspond to a bravery which, although often spectacular and honoured in the name of heroism, is vastly inferior in human merit to that of a soldier who obeys his superiors' orders.

The French Movement in London is as official as is necessary for its directives to have the authority of orders, without however tarnishing the pure, lucid headiness that goes hand in hand with the willingness to sacrifice.

This gives the Movement vast possibilities and responsibilities.

The more actions that are carried out in France based on its orders, that is people acting under its orders, the better chances France will have of regaining a soul that will lead to a triumphant comeback from the war – triumphant not only militarily, but also spiritually – and a reconstruction of the country in peacetime.

In addition to the quantity of actions, the question of choice is crucial.

It is crucial in several respects, some of which are so exalted and of such great importance that the compartmentalization that places this domain entirely in the hands of conspiracy engineers should be seen as disastrous.

In a very general manner, in every type of domain, it is inevitable that evil will prevail wherever technology is entirely or almost entirely sovereign.

Technicians always tend to make themselves sovereign because they are aware that they know their business, and that it is entirely justifiable on their part. The blame for the resulting evil which is the inevitable outcome lies solely with those who have given them free rein. When they are given free rein, it is because the clear and very precise conception of the specific goal to which a particular technology must be subordinate has not always been borne in mind.

The stated direction given by London to the action being carried out in France must fulfil several aims.

The most obvious is the immediate military objective, with regard to intelligence and sabotage.

In this respect, the French in London can only be intermediaries between the needs of England and the good will of the French in France.

The extreme importance of these things is obvious, given that it is becoming increasingly clear that communications rather than battles will decide the outcome of the war. The locomotives-sabotage pairing is symmetrical with that of boat-submarine. The destruction of locomotives is equivalent to that of submarines. The relationship between these two types of destruction is that between attack and defence.

Disrupting production is no less essential.

The volume, the amount, of our influence on the action carried out in France depends chiefly on the material resources made available to us by the English. Our influence on France, that we have and, more, importantly that we can gain, may be very valuable to the English. So there is a reciprocal need, but ours is much greater, at least in the immediate, and all too often that is the only one taken into account.

In this situation, if we do not have relations with the English that are not only good, but also warm, truly friendly and close, that is intolerable and must cease. Wherever human relations are not what they should be, both sides are generally at fault. But it is always much more useful to think of one's own shortcomings and curb them. Furthermore, our need is much greater, at least our immediate need. Besides, we are émigrés taken in by them, and we have a debt of gratitude. And lastly, the English are not reputed to be good at stepping back and putting themselves in the place of another. Their best attributes, their particular function on this planet, are almost incompatible with doing so. Unfortunately, this ability is in fact almost as rare in us, but it belongs by the nature of things to what is called France's vocation. For all these reasons, it is up to us to make an effort to build appropriately warm relations; for our part we must ensure that a sincere wish for understanding, devoid of course of any hint of servility, breaks through their reserve and reaches the real capacity for friendship beneath.

In major world events, personal feelings play a part, the full extent of which can never be discerned. The fact that there is or isn't a friendship between two men, between two human milieus, can in some cases be decisive for the destiny of the human race.

That is entirely understandable. A truth only ever appears in the mind of a particular human being. How will they communicate it? If they try to present it, no one will listen to them because others, not knowing this truth, will not recognize it as such. They will not know the truth of what they are being told, and will not pay it sufficient attention to realize it because they will have no reason to make the effort to do so.

But friendship, admiration, fondness, or any other sympathetic feeling will make them naturally disposed to paying a certain degree of attention. Someone who has something new to say – because no attention is necessary for platitudes – may only be listened to initially by those who love them.

And so, the circulation of truths depends entirely on the state of people's feelings; and that applies to every kind of truth.

With exiles who do not forget their country – and those who do are lost – their hearts are so irresistibly turned towards their afflicted homeland that they have a limited reservoir of affection for the country in which they are living. This friendship cannot truly take root and blossom in their hearts unless they do themselves a sort of violence. But this violence is an obligation.

The French in London have no more imperative obligation towards the French people, who are looking to them, than to ensure that there is a genuine, vibrant, close and effective friendship between them and the English elite.

In addition to the strategic usefulness, there are still other considerations that must impact on the choice of actions. They are even more important, but take second place because the strategic usefulness is a condition for the action to be concrete. Its absence leads to confusion, not action, and the indirect virtue of action, which gives it its main value, is also absent.

This indirect virtue, once again, is twofold.

Action confers the fullness of reality on the motives that have produced it. The expression of these motives, understood from the outside, only confers a half-reality on them. Action possesses an entirely different virtue.

Many different feelings can co-exist in the heart. The choice of those which must, having been identified in the hearts of the French people, be brought into the degree of existence that is conferred to them by official expression, is already limited by material necessities. If, for example, every evening a fifteen-minute address to the French people is given, and if the message has to be repeated frequently because of jamming – and in any case, repetition is an educational necessity – only a limited number of things can be said.

As soon as we move into the realm of action, the restrictions are even tighter. A new choice has to be implemented, based on the criteria already outlined.

We need to examine how a motive is converted to action. The same action can be produced by a particular motive, or another, or yet another, or by a combination. Conversely, another motive may be unlikely to produce it.

To encourage people not only to carry out a particular action, but also to do so prompted by a particular motive, the best and perhaps the only method seems to consist of the established connection through speech. That is to say that every time an action is recommended over the radio, this advice must be reinforced by the expression of one or several motives. Each time the advice is repeated, the motive must be reiterated.

It is true that the precise instructions are communicated by a means other than the radio. But they should always be reinforced by radio encouragements, with the same purpose, designated only so far as caution permits, minus the exact details but plus the motives.

Action has a second virtue in the domain of motives. It not only concretises motives that previously existed in a semi-ghost-like state. It also stirs motives and sentiments which did not previously exist at all.

This occurs each time that either the influence or the pressure of circumstances pushes action beyond the sum of energy contained in the motive that produced the action.

This mechanism – which it is essential to understand both for the conduct of our own lives and for action on people – is just as likely to lead to good or to evil.

For instance, it often happens that a chronically sick family member, affectionately cared for out of a sincere love, ends up arousing in their loved ones a secret, unavowed hostility because they have been obliged to devote more energy to the invalid than their affection contained.

Among the common people where such obligations added to the usual fatigues are so weighty, the result is sometimes a seeming lack of sensitivity, or even cruelty, which is incomprehensible from the outside. That is why, as Gringoire once charitably observed, the case of child martyrs is more frequent among the common people than elsewhere.

This mechanism's possibilities for producing good are well illustrated by a wonderful Buddhist story.

Buddhist tradition tells how Buddha made a vow to take with him to heaven anyone who could say his name with the desire to be saved by him. On this tradition rests the practice known as Reciting the Buddha name. It consists of repeating a certain number of times a few Sanskrit, Chinese or Japanese syllables that mean 'Hail Buddha of Infinite Light'.

A young Buddhist monk was worried about eternal salvation for his father, an elderly miser who thought only of money. The prior of the monastery had the old man brought to him and promised him a coin each time he recited the Buddha name; if he came to him in the evening to tell him how much he was owed, he would be paid. Delighted, the old man devoted every possible moment to this practice. He came to the monastery to receive his payment every evening. Without warning, he stopped appearing. After a week, the prior sent the young man to ask after his father. He found out that the old man was so absorbed by the recitation of the Buddha name that he could no longer count how many times he did so, and that was what was stopping him from going to claim his money. The prior told the young monk to do nothing, but to wait. Some time later, the old man arrived at the monastery with shining eyes and said he had had an illumination.

It is to phenomena of this kind that the following precept of Christ alludes: 'Lay up for yourselves treasures in heaven [. . .] For where your treasure is, there your heart will be also.'[123]

This means that there are actions that have the virtue of transporting some of the love that is found in a man's heart from Earth to heaven.

A miser is not a miser when he begins to accumulate. He is probably stimulated by the thought of the pleasures that money can buy. But the efforts and privations he demands of himself each day create a drive. When the sacrifice far outweighs the initial impulse, the treasure, the object of the sacrifice, becomes an end in itself, and he subordinates his own person to it. The obsession of the collector relies on a similar mechanism. There are countless other examples.

And so, when the sacrifices made to achieve an object far outweigh the impulse that prompted them, the result with regard to that object is either a movement of repulsion, or a new and more intense type of dedication that has nothing to do with the initial impulse. In the second case, there is good or evil depending on the nature of the object.

If in the case of the sick family member there is often repulsion, it is because this kind of effort has no future; nothing external rewards the internal accumulation of fatigue. The miser, on the other hand, sees his treasure grow.

There are also situations, combinations of characters, such that on the contrary, a sick family member inspires a fanatical attachment. On studying all this sufficiently, it might be possible to identify laws.

But even a summary knowledge of these phenomena can give us practical rules.

To avoid the repulsion effect, we must pre-empt possible motive fatigue. Every so often, we must give an official stamp to new motives for the same actions, motives echoing sentiments that might have taken root spontaneously deep in people's hearts.

Above all we must ensure that the transfer mechanism that attaches the miser to his treasure operates in a way that produces good and not evil; avoid, or in any case reduce to the bare minimum, all the evil that could thus be aroused.

It is easy to understand how.

The mechanism in question consists of the following: an action that has been carried out with effort for reasons external to itself, becomes of itself the object of attachment. The result is good or evil depending on whether the action in itself is good or evil.

If someone kills German soldiers to serve France and then after a while develops a taste for killing human beings, clearly that is bad.

If someone helps workers fleeing from being sent to Germany to serve France and then after a while develops a taste for helping the unfortunate, clearly that is good.

Not all cases are so straightforward, but all can be analysed in this way.

All things being equal, modes of action should always be chosen that contain within them a drive towards good. The same is necessary very often when all things are not in fact equal. It is necessary not only for the good, which would be enough, but also for the usefulness.

Evil, much more than good, is an effective motive, but once pure good has become an effective motive, it is the source of an inexhaustible and unwavering drive, which is never the case with evil.

It is easy for someone to become a double agent out of patriotism, better to serve their country by deceiving the enemy. But if efforts spent on this activity are greater than the impulse of the patriotic motive, and if they subsequently acquire a taste for the activity itself, there will almost inevitably come a point when they no longer know which country they are serving and which one they are deceiving, and they will be prepared to serve or deceive anyone.

Conversely, if someone is driven to actions that lead to a growing love of a good higher than that of the country, the soul acquires that mettle that creates martyrs, and the country benefits from it.

Faith is more realist than realist politics. Someone who does not have certainty does not have faith.

And so, each of the modes of action that comprise illegal resistance in France needs to be very carefully analysed and weighed up, and every aspect of the question examined each time.

Attentive scrutiny on the spot, carried out solely from this point of view, is indispensable.

Nor is it excluded that we may need to invent new forms of action, taking into account both these considerations and immediate goals.

(For example, build immediately a vast conspiracy to *destroy official documents* relating to state control of individuals. This destruction can be through very varied methods – fires, etc.– and would have huge immediate and long-term benefits.)

The organization that co-ordinates these actions constitutes a degree of reality even greater than action. When such an organization has not been created artificially but has grown like a plant out of day-to-day necessities and at the same time has been shaped by patient vigilance focused clearly on a good, then that is perhaps the highest possible degree of reality.

There are organizations in France. But there are also – which is of even greater interest – embryos, seeds, the first signs of burgeoning organizations.

They must be examined, watched in situ, and the authority in London used as a tool to shape them discreetly and patiently, like a sculptor who intuits the form contained within the block of marble and carves it out.

This shaping must be guided both by immediate and non-immediate considerations.

All that has been said previously about words and action applies here too.

An organization that crystallizes and captures the words spoken officially, translates the inspiration behind them into its own words and implements them in co-ordinated actions for which it acts as a guarantor of ever-increasing effectiveness, an organization that is a living, warm milieu exuding intimacy, fraternity and affection – that is the humus in which the afflicted French, uprooted by the disaster, can live and find their salvation in both war and peace.

This must be done now. After the victory, in the inevitable unleashing of individual appetites for wellbeing or for power, it will be utterly impossible to start anything.

It must be done immediately. It is extremely urgent. To miss the moment would be almost as reprehensible as a crime.

In the depths of affliction, France's sole source of salvation and greatness is to renew contact with its genius. That must be done now, right away, while the affliction is still crushing, while France has a future possibility of making real the first glimmer of awareness of its regained genius, by expressing it through fighting action.

After victory, this possibility will be gone, and peace will not offer an equivalent. Because it is infinitely harder to imagine, to conceive of, a peace action than a war action. To pass through a peace action, an inspiration must already have a high degree of consciousness, of light, of realism. This will only be the case for France, when the moment of peace comes, if the final period of the war has produced that effect. The war must be the teacher that develops and nurtures inspiration. For that, a profound, authentic inspiration, a true light, must appear in the midst of war.

France must once again be fully present in the war and participate in the victory at the cost of spilling its blood, but that will not be enough. This could happen in the shadows, and the real benefit then will be feeble.

Furthermore, its fighting energy must be fed by nothing else but its true genius, salvaged from the depths of affliction, albeit with a degree of consciousness that is inevitably weak after such darkness.

The war itself can then turn it into a flame.

Because of the political and military circumstances themselves, the true mission of the Free French Movement in London is spiritual before being political and military.

It could be defined as being the country's spiritual guide.

*

The mode of political action outlined here requires each choice to be preceded by the simultaneous consideration of several very different factors. That involves a high degree of attention, of a similar order to that demanded by creative thinking in art and science.

But why should politics, which determines the destiny of peoples and has justice as its object, require less attention than art and science, whose object is beauty and truth?

Politics has a very close affinity with the arts such as poetry, music and architecture.

Simultaneous composition on several levels is the law of artistic creation and that is what constitutes its difficulty.

In the arrangement of words and the choice of each word, a poet must simultaneously navigate at least five or six levels of composition. Versification rules – the number of syllables and rhymes – in the chosen poetry form; the grammatical coordination of the words; their logical coordination in developing the ideas; the purely musical succession of the sounds contained in the syllables; the material rhythm so to speak created by the breaks and pauses, the length of each syllable and each group of syllables; the mood imbuing each word as a result of the suggestive possibilities it contains, and changes of mood as the words follow on from one another; the psychological rhythm created by the length of the words reflecting a particular atmosphere or thought movement; the effects of repetition and novelty; and probably other things too; and a unique intuition of beauty giving unity to the whole.

Inspiration is a tension of the faculties of the soul that makes possible the degree of attention that is indispensable for multi-layered composition.

Someone who is not capable of such attention will develop that capacity one day if they persist with humility, perseverance and patience, and if they are driven by a steadfast and fierce desire.

If they are not possessed by such a desire, it is not indispensable for them to write poetry.

Politics too is an art governed by multi-layered composition. Anyone who finds themselves with political responsibility, if they have in them a hunger and thirst for justice, must wish to develop that capacity for multi-layered composition, and subsequently must develop it over time.

Except that today, time is pressing. The needs are urgent.

The method of political action outlined here goes beyond the possibilities of human intelligence, at least insofar as those possibilities are known. But that is precisely the cost. We should not ask ourselves if we are or are not capable of applying it. The answer will always be no. It should be conceived in a perfectly clear manner, thought about for a long time and often, and etched forever in the place in the soul where thoughts take root; it should be present in all decisions. Then perhaps there is a likelihood that the decisions, although imperfect, will be good.

Someone who writes poetry with the desire to create poems as beautiful as those of Racine will never write a beautiful line. Even less if they do not even have that hope.

To produce poetry in which some beauty resides requires having desired to equal, through the arrangement of the words, the pure, divine beauty that Plato said is found beyond the skies.

One of the fundamental truths of Christianity is that progress towards a lesser perfection is not produced by the desire for a lesser perfection. Only the desire for perfection has the virtue of destroying part of the evil that sullies the soul. Hence Christ's command: 'You are to be perfect, as your heavenly Father is perfect.'[124]

Just as human language is far from divine beauty, so humans' sense and intellectual faculties are far from the truth, and so the necessities of social life are far from justice. It is therefore not possible that politics should not require just as much creative inventiveness as art and science.

That is why nearly all conflicts of political opinions and arguments are as alien to politics as the clash of aesthetic opinions in the cafés of Montparnasse is to art. The politician on the one hand, like the artist on the other, can only find in this a certain stimulant, which must be taken in a very low dose.

Politics is almost never seen as an art of a very high kind. But that is because, for centuries, people have been accustomed to considering it solely, or at any rate, chiefly, as the technique for acquiring and then holding on to power.

But power is not an end. By nature, by essence, by definition, it constitutes exclusively a means. Power is to politics what a piano is to musical composition. A composer who needs a piano to create their melodies will be hamstrung if they are in a village where there is no piano. But if one is found for them, then they must compose.

Afflicted as we are, we have confused the making of a piano with the composition of a sonata.

*

An educational method does not amount to much if it is not inspired by the conception of a certain human perfection. When it comes to the education of a people, this idea must be that of a civilization. We should not seek it in the past, which contains only imperfection. Even less in our dreams of the future, which are of necessity as mediocre as we are, and consequently far inferior to the past. We should seek the inspiration for such an education, and the method itself, among the truths eternally inscribed in the nature of things.

Below are some indications on this subject.

There are four obstacles in particular between us and a civilization that may have some value. Our false conception of greatness; the deterioration of our sense of justice; our idolatry of money and the absence within us of any religious inspiration. I can say 'we' without any hesitation because at present it is doubtful whether a single human being on Earth is free of this flaw, and more doubtful still whether there is a single one among the white race. But if there are some, as is to be hoped despite everything, they are hidden.

Our conception of greatness is the most serious flaw and the one we are least conscious of. At least as a flaw in us; in our enemies, it shocks us, but, despite the warning contained in Jesus's words about the straw and the beam, it does not occur to us to recognize it as applying to us.[125]

Our conception of greatness is the very same that inspired Hitler's entire life. When we condemn it without the slightest inclination to look at ourselves, it must make the angels weep or laugh, if there are angels who are interested in our propaganda.

Apparently, as soon as Tripolitania was occupied, a stop was put to the fascist teaching of history. That is very good. But it would be interesting to know, in what, for antiquity, fascist teaching differed from that of the French Republic. The difference must have been slight because the great authority on ancient history of republican France, Jérôme Carcopino, gave lectures in Rome on Ancient Rome and Gaul which were entirely appropriate to give in that city, where they were very well received.[126]

Today, the French in London are somewhat critical of Mr Carcopino, but not because of his historical ideas. Another Sorbonne historian said in January 1940 to someone who had written something quite harsh about the Romans: 'If Italy sides against us, you will have been right.' This is not good enough as a criterion of historical judgement.

The defeated often benefit from a sentimentality that is sometimes even unjust, but only those who are temporarily defeated. Affliction is of enormous prestige so long as it affects the strong. The affliction of the weak is not even worthy of attention or can even arouse repulsion. When Christians had become unshakeably convinced that Jesus, although he had been crucified, was then resuscitated and would soon return in glory to reward his followers and punish all the others, they no longer feared any ordeal. But before, when Jesus was simply a completely pure being, as soon as he was affected by affliction, they abandoned him. Those who loved him the most could not find in their hearts the strength to run risks for him. Ordeals are above courage when, in order to confront them, there is not the incentive of revenge. Revenge does not need to be personal; a Jesuit martyred in China is supported by the temporal greatness of the Church, even though he cannot expect any help from it for himself. Here below, there is no other force than force. That could serve as an axiom. As for strength that is not earthly, contact with it cannot be bought at a lesser price than the passage through a sort of death.

Here below, there is no other force than force, and it is that force that imbues sentiments with strength, including compassion. There are countless examples. Why, after 1918, were the pacifists so much more moved by Germany than by Austria? Why did the need for paid holidays seem to be an axiom of clear-cut obviousness to so many people in 1936 and not in 1935? Why do so many more people take an interest in factory workers rather than farm workers? And so on.

The same applies to history. We admire the heroic resistance of the defeated when time brings a certain revenge, not otherwise. We have no compassion for the things that are totally destroyed. Who has compassion for Jericho, Gaza,

Tyre, Sidon, Carthage, Numantia, Greek Sicily or pre-Columbian Peru?

But, people will object, how can we mourn the disappearance of things about which we know virtually nothing? We know nothing of them because they have disappeared. Those who destroyed them did not feel duty-bound to become the custodians of their culture.

Generally speaking, the gravest errors, the ones that distort all thinking, destroy the soul and cause it to stray from the true and the good, are indiscernible. Because they are caused by the fact that some things escape our attention. If they escape our attention, how can we pay attention to them, no matter how hard we try? That is why truth is essentially a supernatural good.

The same is true of history. The defeated escape attention. It is the seat of a Darwinian process that is even more merciless than the principle that governs animal and plant life. The defeated vanish. They are nothing.

The Romans are said to have civilized Gaul. It had no art before Gallo-Roman art, no ideas before the Gauls had the privilege of reading the philosophical writings of Cicero, and so on.

We know almost nothing about Gaul, but the scant information we have is proof enough that all that is a lie.

Gallic art is unlikely to form the subject of theses by our archaeologists because the material was wood. But the city of Bourges was such a pure marvel of beauty that the Gauls lost their final campaign because they lacked the courage to destroy it themselves. Of course, Caesar razed it, and at the same time massacred 40,000 human beings who were inside the city.

We know through Caesar that the Druids' studies lasted for twenty years and consisted of learning by heart poems about gods and the universe. And so at any rate, Gallic poetry contained numerous religious and metaphysical poems that formed the subject of twenty years' study. Compared to the incredible richness suggested by this factor alone, Latin poetry looks somewhat paltry, despite Lucretius.

Diogenes Laertius says that Greek wisdom was traditionally

attributed to several foreign sources, including the Druids of Gaul. Other writings show that Druid thought was close to that of the Pythagoreans.

And so, this people had a wealth of sacred poetry but only the works of Plato provide a clue to its inspiration.

All that was lost when the Romans exterminated all the Druids, for the crime of patriotism.

Admittedly the Romans put an end to the practice of human sacrifices which they claimed was widespread in Gaul. We know nothing about what these were, about the manner and spirit in which they were made, whether it was a means of executing criminals or a killing of innocents and, in this latter case, whether it was consensual or not. The Romans' testimony is very vague and cannot be accepted without caution. But what we know with certainty, is that the Romans instigated in Gaul and elsewhere the killing of thousands of innocents, not to honour the gods, but to entertain the crowds. It was the Roman institution par excellence, the one they took everywhere with them – they whom we presume to consider as civilizers.

Nevertheless, if it were to be said publicly that pre-Roman Gaul was far more civilized than Rome, that would sound ridiculous.

That is simply a typical example. Although Gaul was succeeded on the same soil by a nation that is ours, although both in France and elsewhere patriotism has a strong tendency to hark back to the past, although the few surviving documents constitute indisputable evidence, the defeat of the Gauls is an insurmountable obstacle to our recognizing the elevated spiritual quality of that destroyed civilization.

There have however been some attempts to do so, such as that by Camille Jullian.[127] But because the land of Troy has never been home to a nation, no one has ever taken the trouble to identify the truth that is blatantly obvious in *The Iliad*, in Herodotus or in Aeschylus' *Agamemnon*. In other words, Troy had reached a level of civilization, culture and spirituality far superior to those who unjustly attacked and destroyed it, and its disappearance was a catastrophe in the history of humanity.

Before June 1940, to encourage patriotism, the French press was full of articles comparing the Franco-German conflict to the Trojan war. It was claimed that this war was a battle between civilization and barbarism, the barbarians being the Trojans. But there is not the slightest justification for this inaccuracy, except that Troy was defeated.

If we are unable to stop ourselves from making this mistake when it comes to the Greeks, who were haunted by remorse for the crime committed and testified themselves on behalf of their victims, how much more so in the case of other nations, which invariably denigrate those they have killed?

History is based on documents. Professional integrity prevents a historian from considering baseless theories. It appears very reasonable, but, in reality, there is no substance. Since there are omissions in the documents, balanced thought requires that baseless theories be borne in mind, so long as it is on that understanding and that there are several for each point.

All the more reason for reading between the lines in documents and transporting oneself fully into the events described, totally forgetting oneself and letting one's attention dwell at length on significant small things in order to grasp their full significance.

But respect for documentary evidence and for the professionalism of the historian do not predispose the mind to this kind of exercise. The so-called historical mind does not pierce the paper to find flesh and blood. It consists of a subordination of thought to the document.

But, in the nature of things, documents are produced by the powerful, the victors. And so history is no other than a compilation of statements made by the murderers in relation to their victims and to themselves.

Informed in this manner, the so-called tribunal of history is unable to judge in any other way than that of Aesop's fable 'The Plague Among the Beasts'.[128]

On the Romans, we have absolutely nothing other than the writings of the Romans themselves and of their Greek slaves. The latter, the afflicted, have said quite a lot despite their servile reticence, if only we took the trouble to read them closely. But why would anyone bother? There is no motive to make the effort. It is not the Carthaginians who award the prizes of the Académie Française or professorships at the Sorbonne.

Similarly, why would we take the trouble to dispute the information given by the Hebrews about the populations of Canaan, which they exterminated or enslaved? It is not the people of Jericho who put forward nominations to the Institut catholique.[129]

We know from one of the biographies of Hitler that a book that had a profound influence on him in his youth was a tenth-rate book on Sulla.[130] What does it matter that the book was tenth-rate? It reflected the attitude of the so-called elite. Who would write about Sulla with contempt? If Hitler had wanted the kind of greatness that he saw glorified in this book and everywhere, there was no mistake on his part. It is indeed that greatness that he has attained, the one we kow-tow to as soon as we look back towards the past.

We confine ourselves to the base submission of the spirit in its regard; we have not, like Hitler, attempted to seize it with both hands. But, in this regard, he is better than us. If we recognize something as being a good, we must want to seize it. Not to do so is cowardly.

Let us imagine this wretched, deracinated youth wandering the streets of Vienna, avid for greatness. It was a good thing on his part to be avid for greatness. Whose fault is it if he didn't identify any other means of achieving that greatness than through crime? Since the common people have been able to read and oral traditions have been lost, those who are able to wield the pen are the ones who provide the public with ideas of greatness and examples illustrating them.

The author of that mediocre book on Sulla, all those who, in writing about Sulla or about Rome had helped create the atmosphere in which this book was written, more generally all those who, having the authoritativeness to wield words or the pen, contributed to the prevailing atmosphere of thought in which the adolescent Hitler grew up – they are all perhaps guiltier than Hitler of the crimes he commits. Most are dead, but those who are alive today are no different from their predecessors and cannot be rendered more innocent thanks to an accident of birth date.

People speak of punishing Hitler. But he cannot be punished. He wanted just one thing and he has it: and that is to go down in history. Whether he is killed, tortured, locked up or humiliated, history will always be there to protect his spirit against the ravages of suffering and death. What will be inflicted on him will inevitably be historical death, historical ravages, in fact, history. Just as, for the person who has attained the perfect love of God, any event is a good coming from God, so it is for this idolater of history: everything that comes from history must be good. What is more, he has a far greater advantage because the pure love of God resides in the centre of the soul; it leaves the person's sensibility exposed to blows; it is not a suit of armour. Idolatry is an armour; it stops pain from entering the soul. Whatever is inflicted on Hitler, it will not stop him from feeling that he is a glorious being. Above all, it will not prevent, in twenty, fifty, one hundred or two hundred years, a solitary, starstruck little boy – German or otherwise – from thinking that Hitler was a glorious being who had from beginning to end a grand destiny, and from wishing with all his heart for a similar destiny. In that case, woe betide his contemporaries.

The only punishment capable of penalizing Hitler and of deterring little boys avid for glory in future centuries from following his example is a transformation of the meaning of greatness so complete that Hitler is divested of it.

It is an illusion due to the blindness of national hatreds to believe it is possible to divest Hitler of greatness without a total transformation of the understanding of what greatness is in the minds of the people of today. And to achieve this transformation, a person must have accomplished it within themselves. Each of us can, right now, begin Hitler's punishment within our own hearts, by modifying our sense of what greatness should be. That is far from easy because it goes against a powerful and pervasive social pressure which is that of the prevailing atmosphere. To achieve this, a person must exclude themselves spiritually from society. That is why Plato said that the ability to identify good exists only in predestined beings who have been directly taught by God.

It makes no sense to explore the similarities and differences between Hitler and Napoleon. The only question that is of interest is to know whether the one can be justifiably divested of greatness without divesting the other, whether their claims to admiration are analogous or fundamentally different. And if, after posing the question clearly and confronting it squarely and at length, we allow ourselves to slip into lies, we are lost.

Marcus Aurelius said more or less the same thing in connection with Alexander and Caesar: if they were not just, nothing forces me to imitate them.[131] Likewise, nothing forces us to admire them.

Nothing forces us, except the sovereign influence of force.

Is it possible to admire without loving? And if admiration is love, how can we dare love anything other than good?

It would be easy to make a pact with oneself only to admire in history the actions and lives through which the spirit of truth, justice and love shines, and, far below, those within which it is possible to discern a real sense of this spirit at work.

That would exclude, for example, Saint Louis himself because of the regrettable advice he gave to his friends to plunge their swords into the belly of anyone who spoke words tainted with heresy or unbelief in their presence.

Admittedly, people will say in his defence that that was the spirit of his time, which, being seven centuries before our own, was proportionately fanatical. That is a lie. Shortly before Saint Louis, the Catholics of Béziers, far from plunging their swords into the bodies of their town's heretics, all died rather than deliver them up. The Church has forgotten to include them among the ranks of martyrs – a rank it bestows on inquisitors put to death by their victims. Over the past three centuries, lovers of tolerance, enlightenment and secularism have barely honoured this memory either; such a heroic form of virtue which they flatly call tolerance would have been awkward for them.

But even if it were true, even if the cruelty of fanaticism did govern all mediaeval souls, the only conclusion to be drawn would be that there is nothing to admire or love in that era. That would not put Saint Louis one millimetre closer to good. The spirit of truth, justice and love has absolutely nothing to do with an era; it is eternal; evil is the distance that separates actions and thoughts from it; tenth-century cruelty is just as cruel as twentieth-century cruelty, no more and no less. To discern cruelty, we must take into account the circumstances, the variable meanings attached to actions and words and the symbolic language specific to each milieu, but once an action has been recognized as indisputably cruel, whatever the place and date, it is appalling.

We would inevitably feel it if we loved as ourselves all the afflicted who, two or three thousand years ago, suffered the cruelty of their fellow human beings.

We would not then be able to write, as Mr Carcopino does, that slavery became gentle in Rome under the Empire, given that it rarely involved a punishment any harsher than the rod.

The modern superstition regarding progress is a by-product of the lie through which Christianity became the official Roman religion; it is connected to the destruction of the spiritual treasures of the countries that were conquered by Rome, to the dissimulation of the perfect continuity between those spiritual treasures and Christianity, to a historical conception of the Redemption, which makes it a temporal and not an eternal operation. Later the idea of progress became secularized; now it is the poison of our times. In stating that inhumanity was a great and good thing in the fourteenth century, but an aberration in the nineteenth, how could a young boy of the twentieth century, who enjoyed reading about history, not think: 'Now the era when humaneness was a virtue is over and the era of inhumanity is back'? Why should history not be cyclical rather than a continuum? The dogma of progress dishonours good by making it a matter of fashion.

Moreover, it is only because the historical spirit consists of believing the word of murderers that this dogma seems to correspond so perfectly to the facts. When at times horror manages to break through the thick carapace of a reader of Livy, they say to themselves 'Those were the customs of the day.' But it is clear from the Greek historians that the brutality of the Romans horrified and numbed their contemporaries just as that of the Germans does today.

Unless I am mistaken, among all the facts relating to the Romans that can be found in ancient history, there is only one example of a perfectly pure good. Under the triumvirate, during the proscriptions, the consular figures, the consuls and the praetors whose names were on the list kissed the knees of their own slaves and implored their help, calling them their masters and saviours; for Roman pride could not endure affliction. The slaves, rightly, rebuffed them. There were very few exceptions. But one Roman, without having had to demean himself, was hidden by his slaves in his own house. Soldiers who had seen him enter tortured the slaves to force them to hand over their master. The slaves suffered without giving in. But the master, from his hiding place, could see the torture. He could not bear the sight and handed himself over to the soldiers, who immediately slew him.

If forced to choose between several destinies, anyone who has a heart would choose either to be that slave-master, rather than a Scipio, Caesar, Cicero, Augustus or Virgil, or even one of the Gracchi.

This is an example of what it is legitimate to admire. There are few things that are perfectly pure in history. Most of them relate to people whose names have disappeared, like that Roman, like the citizens of Béziers in the early thirteenth century. If we were to look for names that are synonymous with purity, we would find few. In Greek history, we could perhaps only cite Aristides, Dio, Plato's friend, and Agis, the young socialist king of Sparta, killed at the age of twenty. In the history of France, would we find any names other than Joan of Arc? It is unlikely.

But little does that matter. Why should we have to admire many things? Most importantly, we should only admire what we can admire with all our soul. Who can admire Alexander with all their soul, unless their soul is base?

There are people who suggest abolishing the teaching of history. Agreed, it would be good to abolish the absurd custom of

learning lessons from history, apart from as limited a framework as possible of dates and milestones, and to apply to
history the same kind of scrutiny as to literature. But abolishing
the study of history would be disastrous. There is no homeland
without history. The United States is all too clear an illustration
of a people deprived of the dimension of time.

Others suggest teaching history by downplaying wars. That
would be to lie. We know all too well today – and it is equally
true of the past –, that nothing is more important for peoples
than war. We must speak about war as much or more than we
do, but we must speak about it differently.

There is no other process for learning about the human heart
than the study of history combined with life experience, in such
a way as they shed light on each other. We have a duty to feed
the minds of adolescents and people with this sustenance. But
it must be a sustenance of truth. Not only should the facts be
correct, as far as it is possible to verify, but they must be presented in their true perspective in relation to good and evil.

History is a web of baseness and cruelty among which a few
drops of purity very occasionally glimmer. If it is thus, it is first
of all because there is little purity among human beings; then
because most of this little purity is, and remains, hidden. We
must seek, if we can, indirect testimonies. Norman churches
and Gregorian chant were only able to appear among populations where there was a great deal more purity than in the
following centuries.

To love France, we need to feel it has a past, but we must not
love the historical shell of that past. We must love the part that
is mute, anonymous, vanished.

It is utterly false to think that some providential mechanism
passes the best of an era on to posterity. In the nature of things,
it is false greatness that is passed on. There is a providential
mechanism, but it operates solely in such a way as to mix a
little authentic greatness with a great deal of false greatness; it
is up to us to make the distinction. Otherwise, we would be
lost.

The transmission of false greatness through the centuries is
not specific to history. It is a general law. It also governs

literature and the arts, for example. There is a certain dominance of literary talent over the centuries that echoes the dominance of political talent in space; they are dominances of the same kind, also temporal, also belonging to the domain of matter and force, equally base. They can also be an object of trade and commerce.

[The Italian poet] Ludovico Ariosto was not embarrassed to say to his master, the Duke of Este, in his [epic] poem *Orlando Furioso*, something tantamount to: 'I am in your power during my lifetime, and it depends on you whether I am rich or poor. But your name is in my power in the future, and it depends on me whether in three hundred years' time people speak well or ill of you, or not at all. It is in our interests to get along. Give me favour and wealth, and I will sing your praises.'[132]

Virgil had too great a sense of propriety to expose publicly a transaction of this kind. But in fact, that is exactly the deal that took place between Augustus and him. His poetry is often delightful to read, but despite that, he and his peers should be called something other than poets. Poetry is not for sale. God would be unjust if the *Aeneid*, which was composed under these conditions, were of equal value to the *Iliad*. But God is just, and the *Aeneid* is far removed from this equality.

It is not only in the study of history but in all the subjects taught to children that good is despised, and once they are adult, in the food offered to their minds, they find only reasons for this contempt to harden.

It is clear that talent has nothing to do with morality; this is a truth that has become commonplace among children and adults. However, in all areas, only talent is seen as admirable by both children and adults. In all the manifestations of talent in whatever form, they see displayed with impudence the lack of virtues they are recommended to practise. What can they conclude, other than that virtue signals mediocrity? This conviction has become so deeply embedded that the word 'virtue', once so full of meaning, has now become laughable, likewise 'honesty' and 'good'. The English are closer to the past than other countries; in the same vein, today there is no word in the French language to translate 'good' or 'wicked'.

How can a child who sees cruelty and ambition glorified in the history books, selfishness, pride, vanity and ambition trumpeted in literature, and in science lessons all the discoveries that have turned human life upside-down, without any account being taken of the method of the discovery or the effect of the upheaval; how will that child learn to admire what is good? Everything that attempts to counter this general tendency, for example praising Pasteur, rings false. In the atmosphere of false greatness, it is hopeless to want to salvage the truth. We must scorn false greatness.

Granted, talent has no connection with morality, but the fact is that there is no greatness in talent. It is false to say there are no links between perfect beauty, perfect truth and perfect justice; there are more than links, there is a mysterious unity because good is whole.

There is a point of greatness where the creative genius of beauty, the revelatory genius of truth, heroism and saintliness are indistinguishable. Already, approaching this point, we see the greatnesses tending to merge. In Giotto's paintings, we cannot separate the genius of the artist from the Franciscan spirit, nor in the paintings and poems of the Zen sect in China can we distinguish the genius of the painter or poet from the state of mystic enlightenment nor, when Velázquez depicts kings and beggars, the genius of the painter from the ardent and impartial love that pierces the depths of the soul. The *Iliad* and the tragedies of Aeschylus and of Sophocles bear the unmistakeable hallmark of poets in the state of holiness. From the purely poetic point of view, without taking account of anything else, it is infinitely preferable to have composed Saint Francis of Assisi's 'Canticle of the Sun', that jewel of perfect beauty, rather than Victor Hugo's entire oeuvre. Racine wrote the only work of all French literature that can almost sit alongside the great Greek masterpieces, at the time when his soul was undergoing a religious conversion. He was far from a state of holiness when he wrote his other plays, which do not contain that heartrending beauty. A tragedy like *King Lear* is the direct fruit of the pure spirit of love. Norman churches and Gregorian chant are suffused with holiness. Monteverdi, Bach and Mozart were pure beings in their lives as in their works.

THE NEED FOR ROOTS

If there are geniuses in whom genius is so pure that it is clearly very close to the greatness particular to the most perfect of saints, why waste time admiring others? We can use others and draw from them knowledge and pleasure, but why love them? Why give one's heart to anything other than good?

In French literature there is an identifiable thread of purity. In poetry, we should start with François Villon, the first, the greatest. We know nothing of his flaws, nor even if he had any, but the purity of his soul is evident through his heartrending portrayal of affliction. The last, or almost last, is Racine because of *Phaedra* and the *Spiritual Canticles*. In between, we could mention Maurice Scève, Théodore-Agrippa d'Aubigné and Théophile de Viau, who were three great poets and men of a rare spirituality. In the nineteenth century, all the poets were more or less men of letters, which shamefully sullies poetry; at least Lamartine and Vigny truly aspired to something pure and authentic. There is a little true poetry in Gérard de Nerval. At the close of the century, Mallarmé was admired as much as a kind of saint as for being a poet, and these were two indistinguishable greatnesses in him. Mallarmé is a true poet.

In prose, there is perhaps a mysterious purity in Rabelais, where actually, everything is mysterious. This certainly applies to Montaigne, despite his many shortcomings, because he was always inhabited by the presence of a pure being, without which he would probably have remained mediocre, that person being Étienne de La Boétie.[133] In the seventeenth century, we could cite Descartes, Retz, Port-Royal and especially Molière. In the eighteenth, Montesquieu and Rousseau. That is perhaps all.

Assuming there is some accuracy in this list, it does not mean that people should not read the others, but they should read them without believing that they will find the spirit of France in them. The spirit of France resides only in what is pure.

People are completely right to say that it is a Christian and Hellenic genius. That is why, in the education and the culture of the French, it would be justifiable to devote much less attention to things that are specifically French, and more to Roman art, Gregorian chant, liturgical poetry and art, to poetry, the prose of the Greeks of the good period. There we can drink abundantly of beauty that is absolutely pure in every respect.

It is unfortunate that Greek is seen as an elite subject for specialists. If we stopped making the study of Greek secondary to that of Latin, and if only we sought to make a child capable of reading a simple Greek text with a translation alongside it easily and with pleasure, we could disseminate a slight knowledge of Greek very widely, even outside secondary school. Every moderately gifted child would be able to enter into direct contact with the civilization from which we have drawn the very concepts of beauty, truth and justice.

Never will the love of good necessary for the country's salvation be kindled in the population's hearts so long as people believe that in any area, greatness can be the result of anything other than good.

That is why Jesus said: 'Every good tree bears good fruit, but a bad tree bears bad fruit.'[134] Either a perfectly beautiful work of art is a bad fruit, or the inspiration that has produced it is close to holiness.

If pure good were never capable of producing here below real greatness in art, in science, in theoretical speculation, in public action, if in all these domains there were only false greatness, if in all these domains everything were contemptible and consequently reprehensible, there would be no hope for secular life. There would be no possible illumination of this world by the other.

But this is not the case, which is why it is vital to distinguish real greatness from false, and to uphold only the real as an object of love. Real greatness is the good fruit that grows on the good tree, and the good tree is a disposition of the soul bordering on holiness. The other so-called greatnesses must be analysed coldly, the way natural curiosities are examined. If effectively the division into the two categories contains errors, it is still essential to embed the principle itself of making the distinction deep in our hearts.

The modern conception of science is to blame for the present-day atrocities, as are those of history and art; it too must be transformed before we can hope to see the dawn of a better civilization.

This is all the more crucial because, although science is strictly a matter for experts, science and scientists enjoy tremendous universal prestige, and in non-totalitarian states this prestige is far greater than anything else. In France, when the war broke out, it was perhaps even the only form of prestige that remained; nothing else was accorded any respect. In the atmosphere of the Palais de la Découverte in 1937, there was something that was both promotional and quasi-religious in the crudest sense of the word. Science, combined with technology, which is simply its application, is the only thing that can make us proud to be westerners, people of the white race, modern people.[135]

When a missionary persuades a Polynesian to abandon their ancestral beliefs about the creation of the world, which are so poetic and so beautiful, in favour of those of Genesis, suffused with a very similar poetry, that missionary draws their persuasive powers from their consciousness of their superiority as a white person, a consciousness based on science. And yet science is as foreign to them personally as it is to the Polynesian because science is foreign to anyone who is not an expert. Genesis is even more foreign. A village elementary-school teacher who makes fun of the parish priest, and whose attitude discourages the children from going to mass, draws his persuasive powers from his consciousness of his superiority as a modern man over a mediaeval dogma, a consciousness based on science. And yet, considering how limited his possibilities are for verifying it, Einstein's theory has as little foundation and flies in the face of common sense just as the Christian tradition does with regard to the conception and birth of Christ.

In France, people doubt everything, they respect nothing. There are people who scorn religion, the country, the state, the courts, property, art – in other words, everything. But their contempt stops at science. The crudest scientism has no adepts more passionate than the anarchists. Le Dantec is their guru.[136] It inspired the Bonnot Gang, and the man who was considered the biggest hero by his comrades was nicknamed 'Raymond la Science'.[137] At the other extreme are priests and monks so immersed in religious life that they are contemptuous of all secular values, but their scorn stops at science. In all the arguments pitting religion against science, there is on the side of the Church an almost comical intellectual inferiority because it derives not from the power of its arguments, which are generally very mediocre, but purely from an inferiority complex.

When it comes to the prestigious status of science, today there are no unbelievers. This gives not only scientists, but also philosophers and writers, insofar as they write about science, a responsibility equal to that of the priests in the thirteenth century. Both are human beings supported by society, so they have the leisure to research, find and communicate what is truth. In the twentieth century as in the thirteenth, the bread provided for this purpose is probably, unfortunately, bread wasted, or perhaps worse.

The Church in the thirteenth century had Jesus, but it also had the Inquisition. Science in the twentieth century does not have an Inquisition, but nor does it have Jesus or any equivalent.

The task taken on today by the scientists and by all who write on science-related matters is of such magnitude that, like the historians and even more so, they are perhaps more to blame for Hitler's crimes than Hitler himself.

This is what is written in a section of *Mein Kampf*:

Man must not fall into the error of thinking that he was ever meant to become lord and master of Nature. A lopsided education has helped to encourage that illusion. Man must realize that a fundamental law of necessity reigns throughout the whole realm of Nature and that his existence is subject to the law of eternal struggle and strife. He will then feel that there cannot be a separate law for mankind in a world in which planets and suns follow their orbits, where moons and planets trace their destined paths, where the strong are always the masters of the weak and where those subject to such laws must obey them or be destroyed.[138]

These words faultlessly express the only conclusion that can reasonably be drawn from the conception of the world contained in our science. Hitler's entire life is purely the implementation of this conclusion. Who can blame him for having implemented what he believed he recognized as true? Those who carry within them the foundations of the same belief but have not become aware of it or translated it into actions, have only avoided being criminals for lack of a certain type of courage which he possesses.

Once again, it is unjust to accuse the lost adolescent, the wretched, spiritually starved vagabond, but it is rather those who fed him lies who are guilty. And those who fed him lies were our elders, whom we resemble.

In the calamity of our era, the executioners and the victims are both, above all, the unwilling bearers of a testimony to the appalling morass at the bottom of which we lie.

To have the right to punish the guilty, we must first of all cleanse ourselves of their crime, sheltering in all sorts of disguises within our own souls. But if we succeed in doing this, once accomplished, we will no longer have any desire to punish; and if we think we have a duty to do so, we will do so as little as possible and with extreme sadness.

Hitler very clearly saw the absurdity of the eighteenth-century idea that still has currency today and which, in fact, already has its roots in Descartes. For two or three centuries, people had believed that force alone ruled over all natural phenomena and at the same time that people could and must base their mutual relations on justice, recognized through reason. That is a flagrant absurdity. It is not conceivable that the entire universe should be totally subject to the rule of force and that human beings can be exempt from it, when we are made of flesh and blood and our ideas fluctuate according to sensory perceptions.

There is only one choice. Either we must see a principle other that force at work in the universe, or we must recognize force as the sole and sovereign ruler over human relations too.

In the first case, we find ourselves in radical opposition to modern science as founded by Galileo, Descartes and others and followed in the eighteenth century especially by Newton, and in the nineteenth and twentieth centuries. In the second case, we find ourselves in radical opposition to the humanism of the Renaissance, which triumphed in 1789 and acted as the inspiration for the entire Third Republic in a considerably weakened form.

The philosophy that inspired the secular spirit and radical politics is based both on this science and on this humanism, which are clearly incompatible. We cannot therefore say that Hitler's victory of 1940 over France was the victory of a lie over a truth. An incoherent lie was defeated by a coherent lie. That is why, at the same time, spirits faltered as well as weapons.

During the past few centuries, we have confusedly felt the contradiction between science and humanism, even though we have never had the intellectual courage to confront it. We tried to resolve it without having first of all subjected it to analysis. This intellectual dishonesty is always punished by the commission of errors.

Utilitarianism was the fruit of these attempts. It is the supposition of a wonderful little mechanism by means of which force, entering into the sphere of human relations, becomes an automatic producer of justice.

The economic liberalism of the nineteenth-century bourgeoisie rests entirely on the belief in such a mechanism. The only restriction was that, to have the property of being an automatic producer of justice, force must take the form of money, to the exclusion of all use either of arms or of political power.

Marxism is no other than the belief in such a mechanism. In Marxism, force is called history; it takes the form of the class struggle; justice is consigned to a future which must be preceded by a sort of apocalyptic disaster.

And Hitler too, after his moment of intellectual courage and clear-sightedness, fell into the belief in this little mechanism. But he needed a completely new model. However, he had neither the desire for nor the capability of original thinking, bar a few flashes of brilliant intuition. So he borrowed his model from the people who continuously obsessed him through the repulsion they inspired in him. He simply chose as his device the notion of the chosen race, the race destined to make everything bend to it, and then to establish among his slaves the kind of justice that is suited to slavery.

To all these seemingly diverse conceptions which ultimately are so similar, there is only one drawback – the same for all of them. It is that they are lies.

Force is not a machine for automatically creating justice. It is a blind mechanism which randomly has just or unjust effects, but on the basis of probability, almost always unjust. The passage of time makes no difference; it does not increase the tiny proportion of chance effects that are just.

If force is absolutely sovereign, justice is absolutely unreal. But it is not. We know it experimentally. Deep in people's hearts, it is real. The structure of a human heart is a reality among the realities of this universe, in the same way as the trajectory of a star.

It is not within human power to totally exclude every kind of justice from the purpose they assign to their actions. The Nazis themselves were not able to do so. Were it humanly possible, they of all people would doubtless have been able to do this.

(Let it be said in passing that their conception of the just order that should ultimately result from their victories is based on the idea that, for all those who are slaves by nature, servitude is both the most just and the most fortunate condition. Now this is the very thinking of Aristotle, his main argument for justifying slavery. Although Saint Thomas [Aquinas] did not approve of slavery, he considered Aristotle to be the greatest authority on all subjects accessible to human reason, including justice. Consequently, the existence in contemporary Christianity of a Thomist current constitutes a bond of complicity – among many others, unfortunately – between the Nazis and their opponents. Because even though we reject this Aristotelian idea, we are inevitably led in our ignorance to accept others which are at its root. A man who takes the trouble of developing an apology for slavery does not love justice. The century in which he lives has nothing to do with it. To accept as authoritative the ideas of a man who does not love justice is an offence against justice, inevitably punished by the deterioration of discernment. Even though Saint Thomas committed this offence, nothing obliges us to repeat it.)

If justice is indelible in the human heart, it has a reality in this world. Then it is science that is wrong.

Not science, to be precise, but modern science. The Greeks had a science that is the foundation of our own. It included arithmetic, geometry and algebra in a particular form, astronomy, mechanics, physics and biology. The volume of accumulated knowledge was naturally much less. But for its scientific nature, in the sense of the word as we understand it, according to the criteria we consider valid, this science was equal to, and surpassed, ours. It was more exact, more precise and more rigorous. The use of demonstration and of experimentation were both conceived in the utmost lucidity.

If this is not generally acknowledged, it is solely because the subject itself is little known. Unless they are driven by a particular vocation, few people will think of immersing themselves in the atmosphere of Greek science as if in a current and living thing. Those who have done so had no difficulty in recognizing the truth.

Mathematicians who are approaching their forties today have recognized that after a long waning of the scientific brain in the development of mathematics, there is now a return to the rigour so crucial for scientists, thanks to the use of methods that are almost identical to those of the Greek geometricians.

Greek science did not produce many technical applications; this is not because it was insensitive to them, but because Greek scientists did not want them. Obviously very backward compared to ourselves – unsurprisingly for people of 2,500 years ago – the Greeks feared the effect of technical inventions that might be put to use by tyrants and conquerors. So, instead of making public the largest possible number of technical discoveries and selling them to the highest bidder, they kept the ones they did make strictly secret and for their own amusement, and in all likelihood remained poor. But Archimedes did once put his technical know-how into practice to defend his country. He implemented it himself, without revealing any secrets to anyone. The account of the feats he accomplished is still today mostly incomprehensible to us. He was so successful that the Romans were only able to enter Syracuse at the price of a semi-betrayal.

Now this science, as scientific as ours or more so, was absolutely not materialistic. Furthermore, it was not a profane discipline. The Greeks regarded it as a religious discipline.

The Romans killed Archimedes. Shortly afterwards, they killed Greece, as the Germans would have killed France, were it not for Britain. Greek science vanished completely. Nothing of it survived in Roman civilization. If the memory of it was passed on in the Middle Ages, it was with so-called Gnostic thought, in select circles of the initiated. Even in this case, it seems there was only preservation and not creative continuation, except perhaps in the field of alchemy, of which we know little.

Be that as it may, in the public domain, Greek science was only revived at the beginning of the sixteenth century (unless the date is erroneous), in Italy and in France. It very quickly flourished and invaded every aspect of European life. Today, nearly all our thinking, customs, reactions and general behaviour bear an imprint of either its spirit or its applications.

This is true especially of intellectuals, even if they are not what we call 'scientists', and even more of the workers, who spend their lives in an artificial world made up of scientific applications.

But, as in some fairy tales, this science reawakened after a sleep of nearly two thousand years, was no longer the same. It had been changed. It was something different, something that was absolutely incompatible with any religious spirit.

That is why today, religion is a Sunday-morning affair. The rest of the week is ruled by the spirit of science.

Non-believers, whose entire week is dominated by science, have a triumphant sense of internal unity. But they are wrong because their morality is no less in contradiction with science than the religion of the others. Hitler saw that clearly. He convinced many others to see it too, everywhere where there is a tangible presence or the threat of the SS, and even beyond.

Today there is almost nothing but adhesion without reservation to a totalitarian system, brown, red or other, that can give, so to speak, a solid illusion of internal unity. That is why it is such a powerful temptation for so many lost souls.

For Christians, the absolute incompatibility between the spirit of religion and the spirit of science, which both have their devotees, lodges a permanent dull, unacknowledged disquiet in the soul. It may be almost imperceptible; it is variously perceptible as the case may be; it is, of course, nearly always unacknowledged. It prevents internal cohesion. It prevents Christian enlightenment from permeating all thoughts. Through an indirect effect of its continuous presence, at every moment of their lives, the most fervent Christians carry judgements and opinions in which, unbeknown to them, criteria are applied that are contrary to the spirit of Christianity. But the most damaging consequence of this disquiet is to make it impossible for virtue and intellectual integrity to be exercised fully.

The modern-day lack of religious belief among the common people can be explained almost entirely by the incompatibility between science and religion. This phenomenon began when populations started being urbanized, living in an artificial universe, the crystallization of science. In Russia, the transformation was accelerated by a propaganda which relied almost entirely on the spirit of science and technology to uproot faith. Everywhere, once urban dwellers stopped being religious, the rural populations, made vulnerable due to their sense of inferiority with regard to the towns, followed suit, albeit to a lesser degree.

Due to the very fact of the desertion of the churches by the common people, religion was automatically situated on the right and became a bourgeois affair, a matter for reactionaries. Because the fact is, an established religion is obliged to rely on churchgoers. It cannot rely on those who remain outside. Admittedly, from before this abandonment, the clergy's servility towards the temporal powers made it commit serious errors. But these would have been rectifiable had it not been for this abandonment. If these errors were partially to blame for this desertion, it was only in a very small way. It is almost solely science that has emptied the churches.

If a section of the bourgeoisie has been less perturbed in its piety than the working class, it is first of all because it had a less ongoing and less physical contact with the applications of science. But it is above all because it did not have faith. Someone who does not have faith, cannot lose it. Apart from a few exceptions, for the bourgeoisie, the practice of religion was a matter of social conventions. The scientific conception of the world does not prevent the upholding of social conventions.

And so, with the exception of a few shining examples, Christianity is in fact a social convention bound up with the interests of those who exploit the people.

It is not surprising then that there is such a paltry number at present waging the struggle against today's form of evil.

All the more so because, even in milieus, in hearts, where religious life is sincere and intense, too often it has at its very centre a principle of impurity due to an absence of the spirit of truth. The existence of science gives Christians a bad conscience. Few of them dare be certain that, were they to go back to the beginning and consider all the questions, eliminating all preferences in a spirit of absolutely impartial analysis, the Christian dogma would appear to them as being manifestly and totally the truth. This uncertainty should loosen their ties to religion; this is not the case because religious life gives them something they need. They feel in a confused way themselves that they are bound to religion by a need. But the need is not a legitimate bond between humans and God. As Plato said, there is a vast distance between the nature of necessity and that of good. God gives Himself to man freely and excessively, but humans must not wish to receive. They must give themselves totally, unconditionally, and for the sole reason that after having wandered from illusion to illusion in the uninterrupted search for good, they are certain of having found the truth in turning to God.

Dostoevsky committed the most terrible blasphemy when he said: 'If someone proved to me that Christ is outside the truth and that in reality the truth were outside of Christ, then I should prefer to remain with Christ rather than with the truth.'[139] Christ said: 'I am the truth.' He also said that he was bread and wine. But he added: 'I am the true bread, the true wine,'[140] that is to say the bread that is only the truth, the wine that is only the truth. One must desire them first of all as truth, and only then as food.

People must have completely forgotten these things, since they were able to take Bergson for a Christian – Bergson who believed he saw in the energy of the mystics the ultimate expression of that *élan vital* which he idolized.[141] Whereas what is marvellous about mystics and saints, is not that they have more life, a more intense life than others, but that in them the truth has become life. In this world, life, Bergson's *élan vital*, is nothing but lies, and death alone is true. Because life makes us believe what we need to believe in order to live. This servitude has been established as a doctrine under the name of pragmatism, and Bergson's philosophy is a form of pragmatism. But those who, despite being of flesh and blood, have internally crossed a boundary equivalent to death, receive on the other side another life, which is not primarily life, but which is primarily truth; truth become living. True like death and living like life. A life, in the words of Grimm's fairy tale, as white as snow and red as blood. And that is the breath of truth, the divine Spirit.

Pascal had already committed the crime of a lack of probity in the search for God. His mind having been formed by the practice of science, he did not dare hope that in giving that mind free rein, it would recognize in Christian dogma a certainty. And nor did he dare run the risk of having to do without Christianity. He embarked on an intellectual quest by deciding in advance where it should lead him. To avoid all danger of ending up elsewhere, he submitted himself to a conscious and deliberate suggestion, and then sought evidence. In the field of probabilities, indications, he glimpsed some very powerful things. But as to actual evidence, he only produced scant examples, the argument of the wager,[142] the prophecies, the miracles. The worst thing for him is that he never attained certainty. He never received faith, and that was because he had sought to procure it.

Most of those who turn to Christianity, or who, having been born into it and never left, embrace it with true sincerity and fervour, are pushed and then sustained by a need of the heart. They would not be able to do without religion. At least, not without it causing some sort of deterioration in them. But for religious feeling to derive from the spirit of truth, we must be fully prepared to abandon our religion, even if we were to lose all reason to live, in the event that it were anything other than the truth. Only in this frame of mind is it possible to identify where there is truth or not in religion. Otherwise, we do not dare even to ask the question in all its rigour.

God must not be a reason for living for a human heart, as treasure is for the miser. Harpagon and Grandet both loved their treasure; they would have allowed themselves to be killed for it; they would have died of grief because of it; they would have accomplished feats of bravery and strength for it.[143] It is possible to love God in this way. But we must not. Or rather, this type of love is only permitted to a certain part of the soul because it is not open to any other, but it must remain submissive to and given over to the part of the soul that is worth more.

It can be said without fear of exaggeration that today, the spirit of truth is almost absent from religious life.

This can be seen, for instance, in the nature of the arguments put forward in favour of Christianity. Some are like advertisements for cure-alls like 'Pink' pills.[144] That applies to Bergson and to everything inspired by him. In Bergson, faith is presented like a superior kind of 'Pink' pill which provides an extraordinary degree of vitality. The same applies to the historical argument. It consists of saying: 'You see how mediocre humanity was before Christ. Christ came, and look how subsequently human beings, despite their weaknesses, were on the whole something good!' That is absolutely contrary to the truth. But even if it were true, it is to reduce apologetics to the level of 'before and after' advertisements for pharmaceutical products. It is to measure the efficacy of Christ's Passion which, although it is not fictitious, is necessarily infinite, through a historical, temporal and human effect, which, were it even real – which it is not – would necessarily be finite.

Pragmatism has invaded and tainted the very conception of faith.

If the spirit of truth is almost absent from religious life, it would be odd for it to be present in secular life. That would be the reversal of an eternal hierarchy. But that is not how it is.

Scientists demand that the public accord the same religious reverence to science as is owed to the truth, and the public believes them. But people are being deceived. Science is not a fruit of the spirit of truth, and that is clear as soon as we pay attention. Because scientific research, as it has been understood from the sixteenth century until today, cannot have as its motive the love of truth.

That involves a criterion whose application is universal and certain. In order to appreciate a particular thing, this consists of trying to identify the proportion of good contained not in the thing itself, but in the motives behind the effort that have produced it. For however much good is in the motive, so much good will be in the thing itself, and not more. Christ's words about the trees and the fruits guarantee that.

It is true that God alone can see the motives concealed in people's hearts. But the conception that governs an activity, a conception that generally is not secret, is compatible with some motivations and not with others. There are some that it necessarily excludes, in the nature of things.

And so, it is a question of conducting an analysis that enables us to appreciate the result of a particular human activity by examining the motives compatible with the conception governing it.

This analysis results in a method for improving human beings – peoples and individuals, starting with the self – by modifying conceptions so as to draw on the purest motives.

The certainty that any conception incompatible with truly pure motives is itself marred by error is the first article of faith. Faith is first and foremost the certainty that good is one. To believe that there are several distinct and mutually independent goods, such as truth, beauty and morality – that is the sin of polytheism, and not simply allowing the imagination to play with Apollo and Diana.

By applying this method to analysing the science of the past three or four centuries, we have to acknowledge that the beautiful name of truth is infinitely superior to it. Given the effort that scientists make day after day for the entire duration of their lives, they cannot be motivated by the desire to possess truth. Because what they acquire is simply knowledge, and knowledge is not in itself an object of desire.

A child learns a geography lesson to achieve good marks, or out of obedience to orders, or to please their parents, or because they find a poetry in distant countries and in their names. If none of these motives exists, the child will not learn the lesson.

If at a certain moment he or she doesn't know the capital of Brazil, and if the following moment they learn it, they have acquired new knowledge. But they are no closer to the truth than before. In some cases, the acquisition of knowledge helps get closer to the truth, but in others it does not. How do we discern between them?

If a man catches the woman he loves and in whom he had placed all his trust in the act of infidelity, he comes into brutal contact with the truth. If he learns that a woman he does not know, whose name he is hearing for the first time, in a town he does not know any better, has been unfaithful to her husband, that does not change his relationship to the truth at all.

This example is the key. The acquisition of knowledge brings us closer to the truth when it is knowledge of what we love, and not in any other instance.

Love of the truth is an inaccurate term. The truth is not an object of love. It is not an object. What we love is something that exists, that can be thought, and as a result can be the occasion of truth or error. A truth is always the truth of something. Truth is the radiance of reality. The object of love is not truth, but reality. To desire the truth is to desire a direct contact with reality. To desire a contact with reality is to love it. We only desire the truth so as to love in truth. We desire to know the truth of what we love. Instead of talking about love of the truth, it is better to speak of a spirit of truth in love.

Genuine, pure love always desires above all else to remain wholly in the truth, unconditionally, whatever it may be. All other kinds of love desire satisfactions above all else, and therefore lead to error and falsehood. Genuine, pure love is of itself the spirit of truth. It is the Holy Spirit. The Greek word that we translate as 'spirit' literally means fiery breath, and in antiquity it meant the notion that science today calls energy. What we translate as 'spirit of truth' means the energy of truth, truth as an active force. Pure love is this active force, love that does not want, at any price, in any circumstances, either falsehood or error.

For this love to have been the motive of the scientist in their exhausting research endeavour, they must have had something to love. It would require their conception of the object of their study to contain a good. However, the contrary takes place. Since the Renaissance – more exactly, since the second half of the Renaissance – the conception itself of science is that of a discipline whose object is placed outside good and evil, outside good especially; it is considered without any connection either to good or to evil, but more particularly without any connection to good. Science only studies the facts as such, and mathematicians themselves regard mathematical relations as facts of the mind. Facts, force and matter, in isolation, considered in themselves, with no connection to anything else – there is nothing there that human thought can love.

That being so, the acquisition of new knowledge is not a sufficient stimulus for scientists' endeavours. They need others.

First of all they have the stimulus found in hunting, sport or games. Mathematicians can often be heard comparing their specialism to a chess game. Some compare it to activities requiring intuition, psychological insight, because they say that you have to guess in advance what mathematical conceptions will prove either sterile or fruitful if adopted. That again is gameplaying, almost a game of chance. Very few scientists go deeply enough into the subject for their hearts to be captivated by beauty. There is one mathematician who readily compares mathematics to a sculpture carved from a particularly hard stone. People who present themselves to the public as high priests of the truth singularly defile the role they assume in comparing themselves to chess players; the comparison with a sculptor is more honourable. But if someone's vocation is to be a sculptor, it is better to be a sculptor than a mathematician. On closer analysis, in the present-day conception of science, this comparison makes no sense. It is the very muddled fore-shadowing of another conception.

Technology accounts for so much of science's prestige that one might suppose that the thought of its applications is a powerful stimulus for scientists. In actual fact, the stimulus is not the thought of the applications, it is the prestige itself that the applications confer on science. Like politicians who are intoxicated with the thought of making history, scientists are intoxicated by feeling they are part of something big. Big in the sense of false greatness – a greatness independent of any consideration of good.

At the same time, some scientists, those whose research is chiefly theoretical, while having a taste of this intoxication, are proud to say they are indifferent to technical applications. That way they enjoy two benefits that are incompatible in practice, but compatible in the sphere of illusion – which is always an extremely agreeable situation. They are among those who shape human destiny, and so their indifference to that destiny reduces humanity to the proportions of a race of ants; they are like gods. They do not realize that in the present-day conception of science, if technical applications are removed, there is nothing left that can be regarded as a good. The skill of a game like chess is something of no value. Without technical applications, the public would not be interested in science, and if the public were not interested in science, those who pursue a scientific career would have chosen something else. They have no right to the detached attitude they assume. But although it is not justified, it is a stimulus.

Conversely, for others, the thought of technical applications acts as a stimulus. But they are sensitive only to the importance, not to the good or the evil of these applications. A scientist who feels they are on the brink of making a discovery likely to radically disrupt human life puts all their energy into achieving this. It seems they never, or hardly ever, stop to think about the likely effects of this upheaval in terms of good and evil, or abandon their research if evil seems the most likely outcome. Such heroism seems impossible even; and yet it should be a given. But here again, false greatness dominates, that which is defined in terms of quantity and not of good.

Ultimately, scientists are continually spurred on by social motives which are almost inadmissible, so petty are they; they do not play an obviously important role but are extremely powerful. Anyone who saw the French forsake their country so easily in June 1940, and then, a few months later, before hunger really started to bite, display prodigious endurance, braving exhaustion and the cold for hours to get hold of an egg, cannot ignore the incredible energy of petty motives.

The primary social motive of scientists is purely and simply professional duty. Scientists are people who are paid to produce science; they are expected to produce and they feel obliged to produce science. But that is not incentive enough. Career advancement, professorships, rewards of all kinds, honours and money, international receptions, colleagues' esteem or admiration, reputation, fame, titles – all these count for a great deal.

Scientists' behaviour is the best evidence. In the fifteenth and sixteenth centuries, scientists set each other challenges. When they published their discoveries, they deliberately omitted links in the chain of proof, or they re-jigged the order, to prevent their peers from understanding completely; that way they protected themselves from the danger that a rival might claim to have made the discovery before them. Descartes himself admits to having done that in his *Geometry*. That proves that he was not a philosopher in the sense that Pythagoras and Plato understood the word, that is a lover of divine wisdom. Since the demise of Ancient Greece, there have been no philosophers.

Nowadays, as soon as a scientist finds something, before even having tried and tested its validity, they rush to send advance notification of a report to establish first claim. A case like that of Gauss is perhaps unique in our science.[145] He left manuscripts detailing the most wonderful discoveries lying in the bottom of a drawer, then, when someone developed something sensational, he would casually remark: 'That is all exact, I discovered it fifteen years ago, but one can go much further and posit such-or-such a theorem.' But he was also a genius of the first order. Perhaps there have been a few like him, a tiny handful, during the past three or four centuries; what science meant to them has remained their secret. Lesser stimuli occupy a very large place in the day-to-day endeavours of all the others.

Nowadays, the ease of communications across the world in peace time and a specialization pushed to the limits have resulted in the experts in each specialism, who are each other's sole public, making up the equivalent of a village. Gossip circulates continuously; everyone knows everyone else, has either sympathy or antipathy towards them. Generations and nationalities rub shoulders; private affairs, politics and professional rivalries play an important part. As a result, the collective opinion of this village is bound to be tainted, but it constitutes the only form of control over the scientist because neither the lay person nor scientists from other specialisms are acquainted with their work. The force of social stimuli subjects scientists' thinking to this collective opinion; they want its approval. What public opinion accepts is accepted in science, and what it does not accept is excluded. There is no impartial judge, since each specialist, by virtue of being a specialist, has a stake.

It can be argued that the fecundity of a theory is an objective criterion. But this criterion only applies among those who are accepted. A theory that is rejected by the collective opinion of the village of scientists is automatically sterile because no one seeks to develop it further. This applies especially to physics, where the research and control resources themselves are a monopoly in the hands of a very closed milieu. If people had not become infatuated with the quantum theory when Max Planck first introduced it, even though or perhaps because it was absurd, because they were tired of reason – no one would ever have known that it was fecund. At the time when people became infatuated with it, there was no evidence that made it possible to foresee that it would be. And so there is a Darwinian process in science. Theories spring up as if by chance, and it is the fittest that survive. Such a science can perhaps be a form of the *élan vital*, but not a form of the quest for the truth.

The general public itself cannot be, and is not, unaware that science, like any product of a collective opinion, is subject to fashion. Scientists speak often enough of outmoded theories. It would be a scandal if we were not too stupefied to be conscious of any scandal at all. How can people have a religious reverence for something that is subject to fashion? Africans who worship fetishes are greatly superior to us; they are infinitely less idolatrous than we are. They have a religious respect for a piece of carved wood that is beautiful, and on which beauty confers an eternal quality.

We truly suffer from the disease of idolatry; it is so deep-rooted that it removes from Christians the faculty of bearing witness to the truth. No dialogue of the deaf can be anything like as comical as the argument between modern thinking and the Church. In putting forward arguments against the Christian faith in the name of scientific thinking, non-believers choose truths that constitute indirectly or even directly manifest proofs of that faith. Christians never notice this, and they try, weakly, with a bad conscience, with a deplorable lack of intellectual probity, to deny these truths. Their blindness is the punishment for the crime of idolatry.

No less comical is the confusion of idol-worshippers when they seek to express their enthusiasm. They look for something to praise but find nothing. It is easy to praise applications, except that applications are technology, not science. What is there to praise in science itself? More precisely, given that science resides in humans, what is there to praise in scientists? That is not easy to identify. When people want to hold up a scientist for public admiration, they always choose Pasteur, at least in France. He serves as a cover for the idolatry of science in the same way as Joan of Arc does for nationalist idolatry.

He is chosen because he did a great deal to relieve people's physical ailments. But if the intention of achieving this was not the dominant motive for his endeavours, then his success should be seen as mere coincidence. If it was the prime motive, the admiration we owe him has nothing to do with the greatness of science – it is a practical virtue; if that is the case, Pasteur should be ranked in the same category as a nurse who is devoted to the point of heroism and he would only be distinguished from her by the scope of the results.

Since the spirit of truth is absent from the motives of science, it cannot be present in science. And if we had hoped on the other hand to find it to a higher degree in philosophy and literature, we would be disappointed.

Are there many books or articles that give the impression that the author, first before sitting down to write and then before delivering the book for publication, asked themselves with genuine concern: 'Am I in the truth?' Are there many readers who, before opening a book, ask themselves with genuine concern: 'Am I going to find truth here?' If all those whose profession is to think – priests, vicars, philosophers, writers, scientists, teachers of all kinds – were given as of now the choice between two destinies: either sinking immediately and definitively into idiocy, in the literal sense of the word, with all the humiliations such a fall entails and retaining only enough lucidity to feel all the bitterness of it, or a sudden and prodigious expansion of their intellectual faculties, which would guarantee them immediate international renown and posthumous glory for thousands of years but with the drawback that their thinking would always lie a little outside the truth, can we believe that given such a choice, many of them would feel even the slightest hesitation?

These days, the spirit of truth is almost absent both from religion and from science and from all thinking. The terrible evils against which we are struggling, without even appreciating how tragic they are, derive entirely from this. 'The spirit of vanity and falsehood, fatal forerunner of the fall of kings', to quote Racine, is no longer the monopoly of royalty.[146] It extends to all classes of the population; it grips entire nations and sends them into a frenzy.

The remedy is to bring the spirit of truth back among us, and first of all into religion and science, which implies that they become reconciled.

The spirit of truth can reside in science on condition that the scientist is motivated by love of the object that is the material of their study. This object is the universe in which we live. What can we love in it, if not its beauty? The true definition of science is that it is the study of the beauty of the world.

As soon as we put our minds to the question, it is obvious. Matter and blind force are not the object of science. Thought cannot reach them; they flee before it. The scientist's thinking never goes beyond relations that weave matter and force into an invisible, intangible and unalterable network of order and harmony. 'Heaven's net is vast,' says Lao Tzu, 'though its meshes are wide, it lets nothing slip through.'[147]

How could human thought have as its object anything other than thought? This difficulty is so well known in knowledge theory that it is no longer discussed since it is considered trite. But there is an answer, which is that human thought is thought too. The scientist's aim is to unite their own mind with the mysterious wisdom eternally inscribed in the universe. In that case, how could there be opposition or even differentiation between the spirit of science and that of religion? Scientific investigation is simply a form of religious contemplation.

That was certainly true in ancient Greece. So, what has happened since? How is it that when the Roman sword felled this science, it was essentially religious in spirit, but when it reawakened after its long slumber, it was materialistic? What event occurred in the meantime?

A transformation happened within religion. I am not referring to the advent of Christianity. Early Christianity, as is still to be found in the New Testament, and especially in the Gospels, was, like the Mystery religions of antiquity, perfectly capable of being the central inspiration for a perfectly rigorous science. But Christianity underwent a transformation, probably linked to its becoming the official Roman religion.

After this transformation, Christian thought, except a few rare mystics who were always exposed to the danger of being condemned, no longer admitted any other conception of divine Providence than that of a personal Providence.

This conception is found in the Gospels, where God is referred to as the Father. But they also contain the idea of an impersonal Providence that is in one sense almost like a mechanism. 'That ye may be the children of your Father which is in heaven: for he maketh his sun to rise on the evil and on the good, and sendeth rain on the just and on the unjust. [. . .] Be ye therefore perfect, even as your Father which is in heaven is perfect' (Matthew, 5:45; 5:48).

And so it is the blind impartiality of inert matter, that relentless regularity of the order of the world that is completely indifferent to human qualities – and therefore so often accused of injustice – that is held up as a model of perfection for the human soul. It is an idea of such profundity that even today we are not capable of grasping it; contemporary Christianity has completely lost it.

All the parables about the seed echo the idea of an impersonal Providence. Grace descends from God into all beings; what it becomes there depends on what they are. Where it truly enters, the fruits it bears are the result of a process similar to a mechanism, and which, like a mechanism, takes place over time. The virtue of patience, or to translate the Greek word more precisely, of *attente immobile* (motionless waiting), relates to this necessity of duration.[148]

God's non-intervention in the operation of grace is expressed as clearly as is possible: 'So is the kingdom of God, as if a man should cast seed into the ground; and should sleep, and rise night and day, and the seed should spring and grow up, he knoweth not how. For the Earth bringeth forth fruit of herself; first the blade, then the ear, after that the full corn in the ear' (Mark 4:26).

Everything relating to asking also resembles something like a mechanism. Any real desire for a pure good, once a certain degree of intensity is reached, causes the good in question to descend. If this does not happen, either the desire is not real, or it is too weak, or the desired good is imperfect, or it is mingled with evil. When the conditions are fulfilled, God never refuses. Like the germination of grace, it is a process that is accomplished over time. That is why Christ tells us to be persistent. The comparisons he uses also suggest a mechanism. It is a psychological mechanism that forces the judge to satisfy the widow: 'Yet because this widow troubleth me, I will avenge her, lest by her continual coming she weary me' (Luke 18:5), and the man who has gone to bed to open the door to his friend: 'Though he will not rise and give him, because he is his friend, yet because of his importunity he will rise and give him as many as he needeth' (Luke 11:8). If we exercise any sort of constraint on God, it can only be a mechanism instituted by God. Supernatural mechanisms are at least as rigorous as the law of gravity, but natural mechanisms are the conditions for the production of events as such, without any consideration of value. And supernatural mechanisms are the conditions for the production of pure good as such.

This is confirmed by the practical experience of the saints. It was said that they found they could sometimes, by dint of desire, cause more good to descend on a soul than that soul itself desired. This confirms that good descends from heaven to Earth only insofar as certain conditions are in fact fulfilled on Earth.

The entire works of St John of the Cross are nothing more than a rigorously scientific study of supernatural mechanisms. And this applies to Plato's philosophy too.

Even judgment, in the Gospels, appears as something impersonal: 'He that believeth in him is not condemned: but he that believeth not is condemned already [...] And this is the condemnation [...] For every one that doeth evil hateth the light [...] But he that doeth truth cometh to the light' (John 3:18–21). 'As I hear, I judge: and my judgment is just' (John 5:30). 'And if any man hear my words, and believe not, I judge him not: for I came not to judge the world, but to save the world. He that rejecteth me, and receiveth not my words, hath one that judgeth him: the word that I have spoken, the same shall judge him in the last day.'[149]

In the story of the labourers of the eleventh hour, the vineyard owner appears to be acting on a whim.[150] But if we pay close attention, it is the contrary. He paid each man the same wage because he had no change. Saint Paul defines the wage: 'I shall know even as I am known.'[151] There are no degrees. Likewise there are no degrees in the act that entitles the labourer to a wage. You are called: you go running or you do not. It is not within anyone's power to anticipate the call, even by a second.

The moment does not count; nor is account taken of the quantity or the quality of the work in the vineyard. People spend or do not spend time in eternity depending on whether they have agreed or refused.

'For whosoever exalteth himself shall be abased; and he that humbleth himself shall be exalted.'[152] This evokes a set of scales, as if the earthly part of the soul were on one side and the divine on the other. A Good Friday hymn also compares the Cross to scales. 'They have received their reward.'[153] God therefore only has the power to reward efforts that are without reward here below, efforts accomplished in the void; the void attracts grace. Efforts carried out in the void constitute the operation that Christ calls 'laying up treasures in heaven'.

Even though the Gospels have only conveyed to us a small part of Christ's teachings, we could find in them what could be termed a supernatural physics of the human soul. Like any scientific doctrine, it contains only things that are clearly intelligible and empirically verifiable. But the verification consists in the march towards perfection, and consequently we must take the word of those who have achieved it. But we do believe, without verification, the word of the scientists when they tell us of what is going on in their laboratories, even though we do not know whether they love the truth. It would be more appropriate to believe the word of the saints, at least those who are authentic, because it is certain that they love the truth absolutely.

The question of miracles does not create a conflict between religion and science because it is badly framed. In order to frame it accurately, we need to define what a miracle is. In saying that it is an event that defies the laws of nature, we are saying something utterly devoid of meaning. We do not know the laws of nature. We can only make suppositions about them. If these suppositions are contradicted by the facts, it is because our supposition was at least partially wrong. To say that a miracle results from God's will is no less absurd. Of all the events that occur, we have no reason to claim that some rather than others are determined by God's will. Generally speaking, we only know that everything that happens, without exception, is in keeping with the will of God as Creator, and that everything that contains at least a scrap of good derives from the supernatural inspiration of God as absolute good. But when a saint performs a miracle, what is good is the saintliness, not the miracle.

A miracle is a physical phenomenon for which the prior conditions require a total abandonment of the soul, either to good or to evil.

We have to say either to good or to evil because there are diabolical miracles. 'For false Christs and false prophets shall rise, and shall shew signs and wonders, to seduce, if it were possible, even the elect' (Mark 13:22). 'Many will say to me in that day, Lord, Lord, have we not prophesied in thy name? And in thy name have cast out devils? and in thy name done many wonderful works? And then will I profess unto them, I never knew you: depart from me, ye that work iniquity' (Matthew 7:22–3).[154]

It is in no way contrary to the laws of nature that there are physical phenomena that accompany a total abandonment of the soul to good or to evil, which only occur in such a case. It would be contrary to the laws of nature if it were otherwise. Because there is a physical state that corresponds to each state of the human soul. Salt tears correspond to grief, so why should there not be, in certain states of mystical ecstasy, a levitation of the body above the ground, as has been described? The fact may be true or not; little does it matter. What is certain is that, if mystical ecstasy is something real in the soul, there must be corresponding phenomena in the body that do not appear when the soul is in a different state. The connection between mystical ecstasy and these phenomena is constituted by a mechanism similar to the one that associates tears with grief. We know nothing of the former mechanism, but we know no more of the latter.

The only supernatural fact here below is saintliness itself and that which is close to it; it is the fact that the divine commandments become, in those who love God, a motive, an active force – fuel, in the literal sense, like petrol in a car. If three steps are accomplished with no other motive than the wish to obey God, those three steps are miraculous; they are also miraculous whether they are executed on the ground or on water. Except that if they are executed on the ground, nothing extraordinary appears.

Reportedly stories of walking on the water and resurrection of the dead are frequent in India to the extent that no one, other than gawkers, would bother to go and watch such an act. At any rate, accounts of such feats are certainly very common. They were very common too in Ancient Greece during its decline, as testified by Lucian.[155] This singularly diminishes the apologetical value of miracles for Christianity.

A Hindu anecdote tells of an ascetic who returned to see his family after fourteen years of solitude. His brother asked him what he had acquired. He led him to the river and walked across it before his eyes. The brother called the ferryman, crossed in a boat, paid a few coins and said to the sadhu: 'Is it worth having made fourteen years' effort to acquire what I can buy for a few paisa?' That is the common-sense attitude.

As for the accuracy of the extraordinary feats recounted in the Gospels, we can confirm or deny none of them except randomly, and the question is of no interest. It is certain that Christ possessed certain special powers; how could we doubt it, since we can verify that Hindu and Tibetan holy men possess such powers? Knowing precisely how accurate each particular anecdote is would be of no use to us.

Christ's powers constituted not a proof, but a link in the chain of a demonstration. They were the certain sign that Christ was someone apart from ordinary humanity, among those who have given themselves either to good or to evil. These powers did not indicate which of the two. But that was easy to determine, thanks to Christ's manifest perfection, the purity of his life, the perfect beauty of his words, and the fact that he exercised his powers only for acts of compassion. The result was only that he was a saint. But when those who were certain he was a saint heard him say that he was the Son of God, they may have hesitated as to the meaning of those words, but they were bound to believe that they contained a truth. Because when a saint says such things, he can neither be lying nor be wrong. We too are bound to believe everything that Christ said, except where we can assume an inaccurate transcription; and what reinforces the proof is beauty. When it is a matter of good, beauty is a rigorous and certain proof, moreover there can be none other. It is utterly impossible for there to be any other.

Christ said: 'If I had not done among them the works which no one else did, they would have no sin.' But he also said: 'If I had not come and spoken to them, they would have no sin, but now they have no excuse for their sin.'[156] Elsewhere he speaks of his 'good works'.[157] The deeds and words are spoken of in the same breath. The sole purpose of the exceptional character of the deeds was to attract attention. Once attention is attracted, there can be no other proof than beauty, purity and perfection.

The words addressed to Thomas: 'Blessed are they that have not seen, and yet have believed' cannot apply to those who believe in the resurrection without having seen it.[158] That would be praising credulity, not faith. Everywhere there are old women who will readily believe every story of the dead resuscitated. Surely those who are called blessed are those who have no need of the resurrection in order to believe, and for whom perfection and the Cross are the proofs.

And so, from the religious point of view, miracles are secondary; and from the scientific point of view, they come naturally into the scientific conception of the world. As for the idea of proving God's existence through the violation of the laws of nature, it would have probably seemed monstrous to the early Christians. It could only emerge from our sick minds, which believe that the fixed order of the world can provide the atheists with legitimate arguments.

The succession of world events also appears in the Gospels, as if regulated by an impersonal Providence similar to a mechanism in one sense at least. Christ said to his disciples: 'Behold the fowls of the air: for they sow not, neither do they reap, nor gather into barns; yet your heavenly Father feedeth them. [. . .] Consider the lilies of the field, how they grow; they toil not, neither do they spin: and yet I say unto you, that even Solomon in all his glory was not arrayed like one of these. [. . .] Are not two sparrows sold for a farthing? and one of them shall not fall on the ground without your Father.'¹⁵⁹ This means that God's solicitude towards the saints is of the same kind as that which He bestows on the birds and the lilies. The laws of nature govern the way in which the sap rises in plants and blossoms into flowers, in which the birds find food; and these laws operate in such a way that beauty is produced. The laws of nature also providentially operate so that, among human creatures, the resolution to seek first the kingdom and justice of the heavenly Father does not automatically lead to death.

We can also say, if we wish, that God watches over every bird, every flower and every saint; it comes down to the same thing. The relationship between the whole and the parts is specific to human intelligence. As regards events as such, whether we consider the universe as a whole, or as one of its parts, carved out as we wish in space, in time, in any classification; or another part, or another, or a collection of parts; in short, however we use notions of the whole and parts, conformity with the will of God remains invariable. There is as much conformity with the will of God in a leaf that falls unseen as in the Flood. As regards events, the notion of conformity with the will of God is the same as the notion of reality.

When it comes to good and evil, there can be conformity or nonconformity with the will of God depending on the relationship to good and evil. Faith in Providence consists of being certain that the universe in its totality is in conformity with the will of God, not only in the primary sense, but also in the secondary, in other words, in this universe, good prevails over evil. This can only mean the universe in its totality because unfortunately we cannot doubt that there is evil in particular things. Thus, the object of this certainty is an eternal and universal provision constituting the basis for the invariable order of the world. Divine Providence is never represented otherwise, if I am not mistaken, either in the sacred texts of the Chinese, the Indians or the Greeks, or in the Gospels.

But when the Christian religion was officially adopted by the Roman Empire, this impersonal aspect of God and divine

Providence was sidelined. God was turned into an understudy for the emperor. The operation was made easy by the Judaic dimension from which Christianity had not been able to purify itself due to its historical origin. In the texts pre-dating the exile, Jehovah's judicial relationship with the Hebrews was that of a master to his slaves. They were the slaves of Pharaoh; Jehovah, having saved them from the hands of the Pharaoh, inherited his rights. They were his property and he ruled over them as any man rules over his slaves, except that he had at his disposal a broader range of rewards and punishments. He ordered them indifferently to do good or evil, mostly evil, and in both cases, they merely needed to obey. It mattered little that they were maintained in obedience by the vilest motives, so long as the orders were executed.

Such a conception was precisely in tune with the Romans' hearts and minds; slavery had permeated and degraded all human relations. They debased the most beautiful things. They dishonoured supplicants by forcing them to lie. They dishonoured gratitude by considering it as a softened form of slavery; according to their thinking, a person receiving a benefit forfeited some of their freedom in exchange. If it was a great benefit, it was customary for the recipient to tell the benefactor that they were their slave. They dishonoured love: for them, being in love was either to acquire the person they loved as a chattel, or, if that was not possible, to submit servilely to them to obtain carnal pleasures, even if they had to share that person with ten others. They dishonoured their country in conceiving of patriotism as the desire to reduce all people who were not their compatriots to slavery. But it would be briefer to list what they did not dishonour. We would probably find nothing.

Another thing they dishonoured was sovereignty. The ancient conception of legitimate sovereignty, as far as we can surmise, seems to have been extremely beautiful. We can only surmise because it didn't exist among the Greeks. But it is probably the conception that survived in Spain until the seventeenth century, and, to a much lesser degree, in England up until today.

After a brutal and unjust exile and having single-handedly

conquered more extensive territories than the land where he was born, El Cid obtained the favour of an audience with the king.[160] The moment he caught sight of him from a distance, he alighted from his horse, threw himself on his hands and knees and kissed the ground. In Lope de Vega's play, *The Star of Seville,* the king wants to prevent an assassin from being sentenced to death because the murder had secretly been commanded by him; he summons separately each of the three judges to let them know his orders. Each one, kneels before the king and assures him of their total submission. After which, as soon as they come together in court, they unanimously sentence the murderer to death. To the king, who demands an explanation, they reply: 'Give us your orders as subjects, but as chief alcaldes, ask not unjust things, for then we bear our wands; as vassals we're without them.'[161]

This conception is that of unconditional, total, submission, but accorded only to a legitimate authority, with no regard either for power or possibilities of prosperity or affliction, reward or punishment. It is exactly the same conception as that of obedience to the superior in monastic orders. A king thus obeyed truly was a representation of God for his subjects, like a prior for his monks. This was not thanks to an illusion that would have made him appear divine, but solely through the effect of a convention believed to be divinely approved. It was pure religious respect absolutely free from idolatry. The same conception of legitimate authority was replicated from the king down, from top to bottom of the social scale. The whole of public life was thus infused with the religious virtue of obedience, like that of a Benedictine monastery in the heyday.

In the eras we are acquainted with, we find this conception among the Arabs, as observed by T. E. Lawrence;[162] it could still be found in Spain until that afflicted country had to suffer Louis XIV's grandson and thus lost its soul in the lands of the south of the Loire until they were conquered by France and even after, because this inspiration is still evident in Théophile de Viau. For a long time, French royalty veered between this conception and that of the Romans, but it chose the Roman conception, and that is why there can be no question of reviving it in France. We would be only too happy if there were for us some possibility of a truly legitimate royalty.

A number of indications lead us to conclude that the Spanish conception of legitimate royalty was that of the oriental monarchies of antiquity. But all too often, it was wounded. The Assyrians did it a lot of damage. Alexander too – that product of Aristotle's teachings, and who was never refuted by his master. The Hebrews, those fugitive slaves, never knew it. Nor most likely did the Romans – a handful of adventurers united by need.

What took its place in Rome, was the relationship between master and slave. Cicero already admitted with shame that he considered himself as being half Caesar's slave. Apart from Augustus, the emperor was regarded as the master of all the inhabitants of the Roman Empire, in the sense of a slave owner.

People do not imagine that the affliction they find natural to inflict on others can be inflicted on them. But when this actually happens, to their horror, they find it natural; deep in their hearts they cannot find any resource for indignation and resistance against a treatment that they themselves never shrank from inflicting. This is how it is at least when the circumstances are such that, even for the imagination, nothing can serve as external support, when the only resource is that hidden in the heart. If past crimes have destroyed these resources, they are utterly weakened and will accept any degree of humiliation. It is on this mechanism of the human heart that the law of reciprocity relies; the law is expressed in the Apocalypse by the words: 'He that leadeth into slavery shall go into slavery.'[163]

That was how many French people, having found it completely natural to speak of collaboration to the oppressed indigenous peoples of the French colonies, continued to use this word without any difficulty when speaking to their German masters.

Likewise, the Romans, seeing slavery as the fundamental institution of society, were unable to find it in their hearts to say no to a man who claimed to have ownership rights over them, and had successfully upheld this claim through force of arms. Nor could they say no to his heirs, whose property they became through the inheritance laws. Hence all the cowardices, the enumeration of which sickened [the historian] Tacitus, especially since he had played his part in them. They committed suicide on being commanded to do so. Otherwise, slaves did not kill themselves – that would be to rob the master. When Caligula ate, he had senators standing behind him wearing tunics, which for slaves in Rome was the hallmark of debasement. At banquets he would absent himself for a quarter of an hour to take a noblewoman into his private apartments, and then would bring her back, red-faced and dishevelled to the guests, among them her husband. But those people had always found it completely natural to treat not only their slaves thus, but also the colonised populations of the provinces.

And so, in the cult of the emperor, the institution of slavery was made divine. Millions of slaves dedicated an idolatrous cult to their owners.

That is what determined the Romans' attitude in religious matters. They were said to have been tolerant. Effectively, they tolerated all religious practices devoid of any spiritual content. It is likely that Hitler, were he so inclined, could tolerate theosophy without any risk. The Romans could easily tolerate the cult of Mithras, a false orientalism for snobs and idle women.

There were two exceptions to their tolerance. Firstly, they could not naturally suffer that just about anyone could claim the right of ownership over their slaves. Hence their hostility towards Jehovah. The Jews were their property and could not have another owner, either human or divine. It was simply a matter of a dispute between slave owners. Finally, the Romans, out of their concern for prestige, and to demonstrate concretely that they were the masters, slaughtered almost the entire human herd, the ownership of which was under dispute.

The other exception was related to spiritual life. The Romans could not tolerate anything that was rich in spiritual content. The love of God is a dangerous fire; contact with it could damage their vile deification of slavery. And so they ruthlessly destroyed spiritual life in all its forms. They mercilessly persecuted the Pythagoreans and all the philosophers affiliated to authentic traditions. Let it be said in passing, it is extremely mysterious how a hiatus once allowed a genuine Stoic of Greek not Roman inspiration to ascend the throne; and the mystery is all the greater since he treated the Christians harshly. They exterminated all the Druids of Gaul; wiped out the Egyptian cults; drowned the worship of Dionysus in blood and heaped ingenious calumnies on it. We know what they did with the Christians initially.

And yet they felt ill at ease in their overly crude idolatry. Like Hitler, they knew the price of an illusory veneer of spirituality. They would have liked to take the outer skin of an authentic religious tradition and apply it to their all-too-visible atheism. Hitler would also greatly like to find or found a religion.

Augustus attempted to woo the clergy of Eleusis. By the time of Alexander's successors, for some unknown reason, the institution of the Eleusinian Mysteries had already declined almost to the point of extinction. The massacres under Sulla, which caused the streets of Athens to run with blood as the waters rose in a flood, could not have done them any good. It is highly dubious whether at the time of the Empire any trace of the authentic tradition survived. Nevertheless, the people of Eleusis refused to be part of the operation.

The Christians agreed to it when they were too weary of being massacred, too disheartened at not seeing the arrival of the triumphant end of the world. That was how the Father of Christ, accommodated to the Roman fashion, became a slave owner and master. Jehovah provided the transition. There was no longer any objection to it. After the destruction of Jerusalem, there was no more ownership dispute between the Roman emperor and Him.

True, the Gospels are full of comparisons drawn from slavery. But in the mouth of Christ, these words are a ruse of love. The slaves are those who wanted with all their hearts to give themselves to God as slaves. And, although that means a gift given in an instant and once and for all, subsequently those slaves do not stop for a single second entreating God to keep them in slavery.

This is incompatible with the Roman conception. If we were the property of God, how could we give ourselves to Him as slaves? He emancipated us due to the fact that He created us. We are outside His kingdom. Our consent alone can, with time, accomplish the opposite operation, and make of ourselves something inert, something analogous to nothingness, where God is the absolute master.

Fortunately, truly Christian inspiration has been preserved by mysticism. But apart from pure mysticism, Roman idolatry tainted everything. Idolatry, because that is the mode of worship, not the name given to the object, which distinguishes idolatry from religion. If a Christian worships God with a heart disposed like that of a Roman pagan in homage to the emperor, that Christian is also idolatrous.

The Roman conception of God still persists today, even in minds such as that of Maritain.

He wrote that the notion of right is even more profound than that of moral obligation because God has a sovereign right over all creatures and has no moral obligation towards them (even though He owes it to Himself to give them what their nature requires).[164]

Neither the notion of obligation nor that of right are appropriate to God, but that of right infinitely less. For the notion of right is much farther removed from pure good. It is a mix of good and evil because the possession of a right implies the possibility of making either a good or a bad usage of it. Conversely, the fulfilment of an obligation is always, unconditionally, a good in every respect. That is why the people of 1789 made such a catastrophic mistake in choosing the concept of right as a founding principle.

A sovereign right is the right of ownership according to the Roman conception or any other that is essentially identical to it. To attribute to God a sovereign right without obligations is to make Him the infinite equivalent of a slave owner in Rome. This only allows for servile devotion. The devotion of a slave for the man who considers him as his property is a base thing. On the other hand, the love that prompts a free person to abandon their body and soul in servitude to that which constitutes the perfect good is the opposite of a servile love.

In the mystic tradition of the Catholic Church, one of the main purposes of the purifications through which the soul must pass is the total abolition of the Roman conception of God. So long as a trace of it remains, union through love is impossible.

But the influence of the mystics was powerless to destroy this conception in the Church as it was destroyed in their own souls because the Church needed it as the Empire had needed it. The Church needed it to exert its temporal domination. Consequently, the separation of power into spiritual and temporal power, so often referred to in connection with the Middle Ages, is more complex than it might seem. Obedience to the king according to the classic Spanish conception is something infinitely purer and more religious than obedience to a Church armed with the Inquisition and proposing a conception of God as slave driver, as was the prevailing notion in the thirteenth century. It is quite possible that, for example, in the thirteenth century in Aragon, the king had a truly spiritual authority, and the Church a truly temporal authority. Be that as it may, the Roman spirit of imperialism and domination never sufficiently relinquished its hold over the Church for it to abolish the Roman conception of God.

As a result, the conception of Providence became unrecognizable. It is so blatantly absurd that it is mind-numbing. The true mysteries of the Faith are absurd too, but in a way that enlightens thought and causes it to produce an abundance of truths that are clear to the intelligence. The other absurdities are perhaps diabolical mysteries. Both are mingled in current Christian thought like the wheat and the tares.

The conception of Providence that corresponds to the Roman-type God is that of a personal intervention by God in the world to adjust certain means for specific ends. It is acknowledged that the order of the world, left to its own devices and without any intervention by God at a particular place, at a particular time and for a particular end could produce effects that did not conform to the will of God. It is accepted that God should practise particular interventions. But it is also accepted that these interventions, whose aim is to correct the effects of causality, are themselves subject to causality. God violates the order of the world to bring about, not what He wants to produce, but causes that will lead to His desired results as an effect.

On reflection, these suppositions correspond exactly to the situation of humans vis-à-vis matter. Humans have particular ends that oblige them to perform particular interventions, which are subject to the law of causality. Let us imagine an important Roman landowner who has vast estates and numerous slaves; then let us expand the estate to the scale of the world. That is the conception of God that in fact dominates part of Christianity, and whose taint perhaps contaminates the whole of Christianity, except the mystics.

If we think of such a landowner living alone, without ever meeting his equals, without any human contact except with his slaves, we wonder how a particular end can emerge in his thinking. He himself does not have any unfulfilled needs. Will he seek the good of his slaves? In that case, he would be going the wrong way about it because in fact the slaves are prey to crime and affliction. If attempts are made to inspire them with noble sentiments by spelling out all the advantages of their lot – as the pro-slave preachers in America most likely did – it only becomes more blatant how limited those advantages are, what a vast gulf there is between the slave master's power and their respective shares of good and bad things. Since this cannot be disguised, the slaves will be told that if they are afflicted, it is their own fault. But this claim, if accepted, does not shed any light on the question of knowing what the landowner's wishes are. It is impossible to represent these wishes other than as whims, some of which are benevolent. In fact, that is how they are represented.

All attempts to identify signs of its owner's benevolence within the structure of the universe are without exception equivalent to Bernardin de Saint-Pierre's observation that [unlike small fruit of a size that can be eaten by one mouth], melons are designed by nature to be sliced and eaten at family meals.[165] These attempts all display the same central absurdity as in the historical considerations regarding the effects of the Incarnation. The good that it is given to humanity to observe in the world is finite, limited. To try and find in it a sign of divine action is to make God himself a finite, limited good. That is blasphemy.

Similar attempts in the analysis of history can be illustrated by an ingenious thought expressed in a Catholic review published in New York, on the latest anniversary of the discovery of America. It said that God had sent Christopher Columbus to America so that several centuries later there would be a country capable of defeating Hitler. That is much worse than Bernardin de Saint-Pierre; it is appalling. God too apparently despises races of colour; the extermination of the populations of America in the sixteenth century seemed to Him a small price to pay for the salvation of the Europeans of the twentieth century, and He could not assure their salvation through less bloody means. One would think that instead of sending Christopher Columbus to America more than four centuries in advance, it would have been simpler to send someone to assassinate Hitler around 1923.

We would be mistaken to think that this is an exceptional degree of stupidity. All providential interpretations of history are necessarily situated on precisely that level. This applies to Bossuet's conception of history.[166] It is both appalling and stupid, equally distasteful to the mind and the heart. It requires an acute sensitivity to the sound of words to consider that courtier and preacher as a great intellect.

When the notion of Providence is introduced into private life, the result is no less ridiculous. When lightning strikes one centimetre away from someone without touching them, they often believe they were saved by Providence. Those who are a kilometre away do not think they owe their life to a divine intervention. It would seem that when the mechanism of the world is about to kill a human being, God asks Himself whether or not He wants to save their life, and if He decides to do so, He gives the mechanism an almost imperceptible helping hand. He can shift the lightning one centimetre to save a life, but not one kilometre, even less purely and simply prevent it from striking. That would appear to be how people think. Otherwise they would say to themselves that Providence intervenes to prevent us from being killed by lightning at every moment of our lives, to the same degree as at the moment when lightning strikes one centimetre away from us. The only moment when Providence does not intervene to prevent such-and-such a human being from being killed by lightning is the very instant when lightning kills them, if that does indeed happen. Everything that does not happen is prevented by God to the same degree. Everything that does happen is permitted by God to the same degree.

The absurd conception of Providence as a personal and particular intervention by God for specific ends is incompatible with true faith. But it is not an obvious incompatibility. It is incompatible with the scientific conception of the world, and here the incompatibility is obvious. The Christians who, under the influence of their education and their surroundings, have this conception of Providence, also have the scientific conception of the world, and that divides their spirit into two completely separate compartments: one for the scientific conception of the world, and the other for the conception of the world as a domain where God's personal Providence is at work. As a result, they can believe neither one nor the other. The latter, incidentally, is unthinkable. Non-believers, unhindered by any religious credence, can easily see that this personal, particular Providence is ridiculous, and faith itself is therefore, in their view, also ridiculous.

The particular designs attributed to God are collages made by us in the more-than-infinite complexity of causal connections. We make these by joining across time certain events with their effects, selected among thousands of others. In saying that these collages correspond to God's will, we are right. But that is true to the same degree and without any exceptions of all the collages that could be made by every kind of human or non-human mind, on any scale of magnitude, across space and time, in the complexity of the universe.

It is not possible to extricate from the space–time continuum an event that would be like an atom, but the imprecision of human language forces us to speak as if it were.

All the events that make up the universe over the total course of time, each of these events, each possible assemblage of several events, each relation between two or more events, between one event and an assemblage of events – all that, to the same degree, has been made possible through the will of God. All of these are particular intentions of God. The sum of all God's particular intentions is the universe itself. Only that which is evil is excluded, and that itself must be excluded not entirely, in every respect, but solely insofar as it is evil. In all other respects, it corresponds to the will of God.

A soldier afflicted by a very painful wound that prevents him from taking part in a battle in which his entire regiment is massacred could believe that God wanted, not to cause him pain, but to save his life. That would be extremely naive and a trap of *amour propre*. God wanted both to cause him pain and to save his life, and to produce all the effects that were in fact produced, but not one over and above another.

There is only one case where it is justifiable to speak of God's particular will, and that is when a particular impulse arises in a person which bears the recognizable hallmark of God's commandments. But then it is a matter of God as a source of inspiration.

The current conception of Providence resembles the school exercise called *explication française*, when it is carried out on a perfectly beautiful poetic text by a poor teacher.[167] The teacher will say: 'The poet has used such-and-such a word to obtain such-and-such effect.' That can only be true for second-, tenth- or fiftieth-rate poetry. In a perfectly beautiful poetic fragment, all the effects, all the resonances, all the evocations likely to be created by the presence of a particular word in a particular place, reflect the poet's inspiration to the same degree, that is to say perfectly. The same applies to all the arts. In that way, the poet imitates God. Poetic inspiration at its peak of perfection is one of the human things that can, by analogy, give an inkling of God's will. The poet is a person, however, in the moments when they attain poetic perfection, they are imbued with an impersonal inspiration. It is in the mediocre moments that the poet's inspiration is personal and then it is not really inspiration. In using poetic inspiration as an image for conceiving of God's will by analogy, we must take the perfect form, not the mediocre.

Divine Providence is not a disruption, an anomaly in the order of the world. It is the order of the world itself. Or rather it is the organizing Principle of this world. It is eternal Wisdom, unique and extending throughout the entire universe in a sovereign network of relations.

That is how it was conceived throughout pre-Roman antiquity. All the parts of the Old Testament that have been penetrated by the universal inspiration of antiquity bring us this conception clothed in an incomparable verbal splendour. But we are blind. We read without understanding.

Brute force is not sovereign here below. It is by nature blind and indeterminate. What is sovereign in this world is determinacy, limits. Eternal Wisdom imprisons this world in a network, a web of determinations. The universe does not fight it. The brute force of matter, which we see as sovereignty, is nothing else in reality than perfect obedience.

That is the guarantee given to humanity, the Ark of the Covenant, the pact, the visible, tangible promise here on Earth, the certain basis of hope. That is the truth that gnaws at our hearts each time we are sensitive to the beauty of the world. That is the truth that explodes with incomparable notes of joy in the beautiful and pure parts of the Old Testament, in Greece among the Pythagoreans and all the sages, in China with Lao Tzu, in the Hindu holy scriptures, in the Egyptian fragments. It is perhaps concealed in countless legends and tales. It will appear in front of us, before our eyes, in our own science, if one day, God opens our eyes as he did with Hagar.[168]

It is discernible in the very words Hitler uses to affirm the contrary misconception: 'in a world in which planets and suns follow their orbits, where moons and planets trace their destined paths, where the strong are always the masters of the weak and where those subject to such laws must obey them or be destroyed.'[169] How could blind force produce circles? It is not weakness that docilely serves force, but force that is subdued by eternal Wisdom.

Hitler and his fanatical youth never felt that in gazing at the stars at night. But did anyone ever attempt to teach it to them? The civilization of which we are so proud did its utmost to conceal it, and as long as something in our souls is capable of being proud of it, we are innocent of none of Hitler's crimes.

In India, a word whose original sense is 'balance' means both the order of the world and justice. Here is a sacred text on this subject, which, in symbolic form, relates both the creation of the world and to human society.

'God, in truth, existed in the beginning, absolutely alone. Being alone, he did not manifest himself. He created a superior form, sovereignty ... That is why there is nothing above sovereignty. That is why on ceremonial occasions the priest is seated above the sovereign ...

'Still, God did not manifest himself. He created the peasant, artisan and merchant class.

'Still he did not manifest himself. He created the servant class.

'Still he did not manifest himself. He created a superior form, Justice. Justice is the sovereignty of sovereignties. That is why there is nothing above Justice. Whoever is without power can be equal to him who has great power by means of Justice, as though by means of some royal authority.

'What is Justice, the same is also Truth. That is why when someone speaks Truth, we say: "He is just." And when someone speaks Justice, we say: "He is true." It is really because Justice and Truth are the same thing.'[170]

A very ancient Hindu stanza runs:

> *That from whence the sun rises,*
> *That wherein the sun sets,*
> *That, the gods have made Justice,*
> *The same today, the same tomorrow.*[171]

Anaximander wrote:

It is out of indeterminateness that things take their birth; and destruction is a return to indeterminateness, which is accomplished by virtue of necessity. For things are subject to chastisement and expiation at one another's hands, because of their injustice, according to the ordering of time.[172]

That is the truth, and not the monstrous conception Hitler drew from the popularization of modern science. Every visible and palpable force is subject to an invisible limit which it shall never cross. In the sea, a wave rises, rises and rises, but at a certain point, even though there is nothing but emptiness, it is halted and forced to subside. In the same way, the German flood was halted, without anybody knowing why, on the shores of the English Channel.

The Pythagoreans used to say that the universe is constituted out of indeterminateness and the principle that determines, limits, halts. It is the latter that is always dominant.

The tradition relating to the rainbow – surely borrowed by Moses from the Egyptians – expresses in the most touching way the trust that the order of the world should inspire in humans:

> And God said, 'Whenever I bring clouds over the Earth and the rainbow appears in the clouds, I will remember my covenant between me and you and all living creatures of every kind. Never again will the waters become a flood to destroy all life.'[173]

The rainbow's beautiful arc is testimony that the phenomena of this world, however terrifying they may be, are all subject to a limit. The magnificent poetry of this text is a reminder to God to exercise His function as a limiting principle.

'You set a boundary that they may not pass, so that they might not again cover the Earth.'[174]

And like the rise and fall of the waves, all the successions of events here on Earth, all being mutually compensated disruptions of balance – births and destructions, increases and decreases – all make us aware of the invisible presence of a system of limits without substance and harder than any diamond. That is why the vicissitudes of things are beautiful, even though they reveal a ruthless necessity. Ruthless, but which is not force, which is the sovereign ruler over all force.

But the idea that truly thrilled the ancients was the notion that what makes the blind force of matter obedient is not another, stronger force. It is love. They thought that matter is obedient to the eternal Wisdom through the virtue of love, which makes it consent to obedience.

In his *Timaeus*, Plato says that divine Providence prevails over necessity by exercising a wise persuasiveness.[175] A Stoic poem from the 3rd century BCE, but whose inspiration has been proven to be much more ancient, speaks thus to God:

> *Truly, this whole universe, spinning around the earth,*
> *Obeys you wherever you lead, and willingly submits to your rule;*
> *Such is the servant you hold in your unconquerable hands,*
> *A double-edged, fiery, ever-living thunderbolt.*[176]

Lightning, that vertical bolt from the sky, is the exchange of love between God and his creation, and that is why Zeus is known as 'the lightning thrower'.

This is the origin of the Stoic conception of *amor fati*, love of the order of the world, which they saw as being central to all virtue. The order of the world must be loved because it is pure obedience to God. Whatever this world bestows or inflicts on us, it does so solely out of obedience. When a friend who has been away for a long time and whose return we eagerly await shakes our hand, it is not important whether the pressure itself is pleasant or unpleasant; if they squeeze too hard and hurt us, we do not even notice it. When the friend speaks, we do not think about whether the sound of their voice is pleasing in itself. The pressure of the hand, the voice – all that is simply the sign for us of a presence, and for that reason is infinitely precious. Similarly, everything that happens to us during our lifetime, being caused by the total obedience of this world to God, puts us in touch with the absolute good constituted by the divine will; in virtue of this, everything without exception, both joys and sorrows, must be greeted with the same inner attitude of love and gratitude.

People who do not know the true good disobey God in that they do not obey Him as is appropriate for a thinking creature, through a consent of thought. But their bodies and souls are entirely subject to the laws of mechanisms that rule sovereignly over physical and psychological matter. The physical and psychological matter in them obeys perfectly; they are perfectly obedient insofar as they are matter, and they are not anything else if they neither possess nor desire the supernatural light which alone elevates humanity above matter. That is why the evil they cause us should be accepted as the evil that makes us inert matter. Apart from the compassion it is appropriate to accord a human mind that is lost and suffering, they should be loved as should inert matter, as being part of the perfectly beautiful order of the universe.

Of course, when the Romans believed they had to dishonour Stoicism by adopting it, they replaced love with an insensitivity based on pride. Hence the prejudice, still common today, that there is a conflict between Stoicism and Christianity, whereas in fact they are sister schools of thought. The names themselves for the Persons of the Trinity – *Logos*, *Pneuma* – are borrowed from the Stoic vocabulary. Knowledge of certain Stoic theories sheds a great deal of light on several perplexing passages of the New Testament. There was an exchange between the two schools of thought because of their affinities. At the centre of both are humility, obedience and love.

But several texts indicate that Stoic philosophy was also that of the entire ancient world, extending to the Far East. All of humanity once lived in the dazzling belief that the universe in which we find ourselves is nothing other than perfect obedience.

The Greeks were thrilled to find a dazzling confirmation in science, and that was the reason for their enthusiasm for the subject.

The operation of intelligence in scientific study makes sovereign necessity over matter appear to the mind as a system of immaterial relations that are without force. Necessity can only be perfectly conceived so long as these relations appear as completely immaterial. They are then only present in thought as a result of superior and pure attention, which starts from a point in the soul not subject to force. That which in the human soul is subject to force, is what finds itself under the influence of needs. We must forget all needs to conceive of relations in their immaterial purity. If we succeed in doing so, we become aware of the interplay of forces through which the satisfaction of needs is granted or refused.

The forces here below are sovereignly determined by necessity, and necessity is made up of relations that are thoughts. Consequently, the force that is sovereign here below is sovereignly governed by thought. Man is a thinking creature; he is on the side that commands force. He is certainly not lord and master over nature, and Hitler was right to say that he is mistaken in believing that he is, but he is the son of the master, the child of the house. Science is the proof of this. A very young child in a wealthy home is under the servants' authority in many things. But when they are on their father's knee and identify with him through love, they have a share in the father's authority.

So long as man tolerates having his mind filled with his own personal thoughts, he is entirely controlled right down to his innermost thoughts by the constraint of needs and the mechanical interplay of forces. If he believes any differently, he is mistaken. But everything changes when, by virtue of a true attention, he empties his mind to allow the thoughts of eternal wisdom to enter. Then he carries within him the very thoughts to which force must submit.

The nature of the relation, and the kind of attention essential for imagining it was, in the eyes of the Greeks, proof that necessity truly is obedience to God. They had another proof, and this was the symbols inscribed in the relations themselves, like the artist's signature on a painting.

Greek symbolism explains the fact that Pythagoras offered up a sacrifice in his joy at having discovered it was possible to draw a right-angled triangle inside a semi-circle.

According to the Greeks, the circle was the image of God because a circle that rotates on its axis is a movement where nothing changes and is complete in itself. For them, the symbol of the circular movement expressed the same truth as that expressed in Christian dogma by the conception of the eternal act that forms the basis for the relations between the Persons of the Trinity.

The geometric mean was in their eyes the representation of divine mediation between God and his creatures. The Pythagoreans' mathematical research centred on finding the geometric means between numbers that are not part of the same geometric progression, for example between one and a non-square number. The right-angled triangle provided the solution. The right-angled triangle is the source of all geometric means. But since it can be drawn inside a semi-circle, the circle can be substituted for it for this purpose. And so, the circle, the geometric representation of God, is the source of the geometric depiction of divine mediation. Such a wonderful discovery warranted a sacrifice.

Geometry then is a double language, which both gives information about the forces active in matter and speaks of the supernatural relations between God and His creatures. It is like those coded characters that appear equally coherent before and after being deciphered.

Interest in the symbol has vanished completely from our science. Even so, it would simply require us to take the trouble to read easily – in some areas of modern mathematics at least, like set theory or integral calculus – symbols that are as clear, beautiful and full of spiritual meaning as that of the circle and of mediation.

The path from modern thinking to ancient wisdom would be short and direct, should we wish to follow it.

In modern philosophy, analyses laying the foundations for a complete theory of sensory perception have appeared almost everywhere in different guises. The fundamental truth that such a theory would reveal is that the reality of objects perceived by the senses does not reside in sensory impressions, but solely in the necessities of which the impressions are the signs.

This perceptible universe in which we are has no other reality than necessity, and necessity is a combination of relations that vanish when they are no longer supported by an exalted and pure attention. This universe around us is thought, materially present in our flesh.

Science, through all its various branches, comprehends mathematical relations or relations similar to mathematical relations through all phenomena. Eternal mathematics, that language with a dual purpose, is the stuff of which the order of the world is woven.

Every phenomenon is a change in the distribution of energy, and consequently is governed by the laws of energy. But there are several types of energy, and they are arranged in a hierarchical order. Mechanical force, gravity or gravitation in the Newtonian sense, which makes us continually feel its pull, is not the highest kind. Intangible, weightless light is an energy that makes the trees and the blades of corn grow, despite gravity. We eat it in corn and fruit, and its presence in us give us the strength to stay upright and work.

Something infinitely tiny, in some conditions, operates in a determining manner. There is no mass so heavy but that a given point is equal to it because a mass does not fall if a single point in it is supported, so long as that point is the centre of gravity. Some chemical transformations only come about if certain almost invisible bacteria are present. Catalysts are imperceptible fragments of matter whose presence is essential for other chemical transformations. Thanks to their presence, other tiny fragments of almost identical composition have a no less decisive power of inhibition; this mechanism is the foundation for the most potent medications discovered recently.[177]

And so it is not only mathematics but the whole of science which, without our thinking to notice it, is a symbolic mirror of supernatural truths.

Modern psychology wants to make the study of the soul into a science. A little more precision would be sufficient to achieve this. The basis should be the concept of psychological matter as expressed by Lavoisier's law and valid for all matter: 'nothing is destroyed, nothing is created'.[178] In other words, changes are either modifications of shape, within which something survives, or displacement, but never simply appearances and disappearances. The notion of limit would need to be introduced, and the principle that in the earthly part of the soul, everything is finite, limited, capable of being exhausted. Lastly, the notion of energy would need to be introduced, by positing that like physical phenomena, psychological phenomena are modifications in the allocation and quality of energy and are governed by the energy laws.

Contemporary attempts to establish a social science would

also be successful, at the price of a little more precision. The basis should be the Platonic idea of the enormous animal or the apocalyptic notion of the Beast. Social science is the study of the enormous animal and must describe in minute detail its anatomy, physiology, natural and conditional reflexes, capacity for being tamed.

The science of the soul and social science are both entirely impossible if the concept of the supernatural is not strictly defined and introduced into science, as a scientific notion, to be handled with extreme precision.

If the human sciences were thus founded, using mathematically rigorous methods and at the same time maintained in connection with religious faith; if in the natural sciences and mathematics symbolic interpretation resumed the place it once had, the unity of the established order in this universe would appear in its supreme clarity.

The order of the world is the beauty of the world. The only difference is the type of attention required, depending on whether we are trying to conceive the necessary relations that comprise it, or to contemplate its radiance.

It is one and the same thing which, with regard to God, is eternal Wisdom, with regard to the universe, perfect obedience, with regard to our love, beauty, with regard to our intelligence, the balance of necessary relations, with regard to our flesh, brute force.

These days, science, history, politics, the organization of labour, even religion insofar as it is sullied by the Roman defilement, offer nothing to human thought other than brute force. This is our civilization. This tree is bearing the fruits it deserves.

The return to truth will reveal, among other things, the truth of physical work.

After freely chosen death, freely chosen physical work is the most perfect form of the virtue of obedience.

The penal nature of work, evoked by the account in Genesis, has been poorly understood for lack of a just notion of punishment.[179] People misread into this text a hint of contempt for work. It is probable that it was transmitted by a very ancient civilization where physical work was honoured above all other activities.

There are several indicators that there was such a civilization, that a very long time ago, physical work was the ultimate religious activity and consequently something sacred. The Mysteries, the religion of all pre-Roman antiquity, were entirely based on symbolic expressions of the salvation of the soul inspired by agriculture. The same symbolism is found in the parables of the Gospels. The role of Hephaestus in Aeschylus' *Prometheus* appears to allude to a religion of blacksmiths. Prometheus himself embodies the non-temporal projection of Christ, a crucified and redemptive God who gave humans the gift of fire; in Greek symbolism, as in the Gospels, fire is the image of the Holy Ghost. Aeschylus, who never says anything arbitrarily, states that the fire given to humans by Prometheus was the personal property of Hephaestus, which seems to suggest that Hephaestus is the personification of it. Hephaestus is a blacksmith God. One can imagine a religion of blacksmiths seeing fire, which makes metal malleable, as mirroring the operation of the Holy Ghost on human nature.

There was perhaps a time when an identical truth was translated into different systems of symbols, and where each system was tailored to certain types of physical work in such a way as to make it the direct expression of faith.

In any case, all the religious traditions of antiquity, including the Old Testament, represent the various trades as being direct teachings of God. Most state that God became flesh for this educational mission. The Egyptians, for example, thought that the incarnation of Osiris had as its object both this practical teaching and redemption through the Passion.

Whatever the truth contained in these extremely mysterious accounts may be, the belief that the trades were taught directly by God implies the recollection of a time when the exercise of the trades was the ultimate sacred activity.

There is no trace of this in Homer, or Hesiod, or in classical Greece, or in the little we know of the other civilizations of antiquity. In Greece, work was considered servile. We cannot know if it was already seen thus before the invasion of the

Hellenes, in the time of the Pelasgi, or whether the Mysteries explicitly preserved in their secret teachings the memory of a time when work was honoured. At the very beginning of the Greek classical era, we see the end of a form of civilization where, except for physical work, all human activities were sacred, where art, poetry, philosophy, science and politics were virtually indistinguishable from religion. A century or two later, through a mechanism that is hard to pinpoint, but in which at all events money played a large part, all these activities had become purely profane and divorced from any spiritual inspiration. The little religion that remained was relegated to places dedicated to worship. Plato, in his day, was a survival from a past that was already distant. The Greek Stoics were a flame that sprang from a spark from that same past and was still alive.

The Romans, an atheist, materialistic nation, destroyed what remained of spiritual life in the territories they occupied by means of extermination; they adopted Christianity only by voiding it of its spiritual content. Under their rule, all human activity was servile, and they ended up removing all reality from the institution of slavery, which paved the way for its disappearance, by reducing all human beings to the condition of slavery.

The so-called Barbarians, many of whom were probably from Thrace and consequently imbued with the spirituality of the Mysteries, took Christianity seriously. The result was that there was almost a Christian civilization. We see the beginnings of it in the eleventh and twelfth centuries. The countries south of the Loire, which were its main hub, were imbued with both Christian and ancient spirituality; if it is true at least that the Albigensians were Manichaeans, and consequently drew not only on Persian thought, but also on Gnostic, Stoic, Pythagorean and Egyptian ideas, the then nascent civilization could have been free of any taint of slavery. The trades would have had a central place in it.

The picture Machiavelli gives of twelfth-century Florence is a model of what modern jargon would call a syndicalist democracy.[180] In Toulouse, the knights and workers fought side by

side against Simon de Montfort to defend their common spiritual treasure. The guilds established during this period of
gestation were religious institutions. One simply needs to look
at a Romanesque church, hear a Gregorian melody, read one or
several perfect troubadour poems, or, better still, the liturgical
texts, in order to see that art was indistinguishable from religious faith, as it was in Greece at its best moment.

But a Christian civilization, where the Christian light would
have illuminated all of life, would only have been possible if the
Roman conception of the subjugation of minds by the Church
had been eradicated. Saint Bernard's relentless and victorious
battle against Abelard shows that this was far from the case.[181]
At the beginning of the thirteenth century, the civilization still
to come was destroyed by the annihilation of its main centre,
that is the countries south of the Loire, by the establishment of
the Inquisition and the stifling of religious thought under the
notion of orthodoxy.

The notion of orthodoxy, in rigorously separating the domain
relating to the wellbeing of souls, which is that of unconditional surrender of thought to an external authority, and the
domain relating to so-called profane matters, where the mind is
free, renders impossible this interpenetration of the religious
and the profane that would be the essence of a Christian civilization. It is in vain that every day, at mass, a little water is
mixed with the wine.

The thirteenth and fourteenth centuries and the beginning of
the fifteenth are the period of the decline of the Middle Ages.
The gradual deterioration and death of a civilization that had
not had the time to be born, the gradual drying up of a simple
seedling.

Around the fifteenth century, came the first Renaissance, which
was like a pale precursor to the resurrection of pre-Roman civilization and the spirit of the twelfth century. Classical Greece,
Pythagoras and Plato were then the object of a religious devotion,
which was in perfect keeping with the Christian faith. But this
attitude was very short-lived.

Soon came the second Renaissance, which tended in the

opposite direction. And this was the origin of what we call our modern civilization.

We are very proud of it, but we are not unaware that it is sick. And we are all in agreement as to the diagnosis of the disease. It is sick from not knowing exactly what place to give to physical labour and to those who perform it.

A lot of thinkers are racking their brains over this question, groping desperately for an answer. They do not know where to start, how to begin or what they should be guided by – and so their efforts are futile.

It is best to reflect on the old story in Genesis, by locating it in its own context, that of ancient thought.

When a human being has excluded themselves from the good by committing a crime, the true punishment consists of their reintegration into the plenitude of good through pain. Nothing is so marvellous as a punishment.

Man has excluded himself from obedience. As punishments, God has chosen work and death. Consequently, work and death, if man consents to suffer them, constitute a vehicle for attaining the supreme good which is obedience to God.

This is luminously clear if, as in antiquity, we see the passiveness of inert matter as the perfect obedience to God, and the beauty of the world as the brilliance of this perfect obedience.

Whatever the mysterious significance of death may be in heaven, here below it is the transformation of a being of quivering flesh and thought, of a being who desires and hates, hopes and fears, wants and does not want, into a little heap of inert matter.

For man, consenting to this transformation is the highest act of total obedience. That is why Saint Paul said of Christ himself, on the subject of the Passion: 'Son though he was, he learned obedience from what he suffered and once made perfect, he became the source of eternal salvation for all who obey him.'[182]

But consenting to death can only be fully real when death comes. It can only be close to plenitude when death is nigh. When the possibility of death is abstract and distant, it is abstract.

Physical work is a daily death.

To work is to put your own being, body and soul, into the circuit of inert matter, to make it an intermediary between one state and another state of a fragment of matter, to make it an instrument. The worker makes their body and soul into an appendage of the tool they are using. The body's movements and the mind's attention depend on the demands of the tool, which itself is adapted to the matter being worked on.

Death and work are things of necessity and not of choice. The world only provides man with food and warmth if he gives himself to the world through his labour. But death and work can be suffered either in an attitude of rebellion of or consent. They can be suffered either in their naked truth or shrouded in lies.

Work does violence to human nature. Sometimes there is an over-abundance of youthful energy that needs an outlet and does not find one; sometimes there is exhaustion, and the will must continually supplement the lack of physical energy, which causes a very great strain. There are a thousand preoccupations, worries, anxieties, a thousand desires, a thousand questions that distract the mind. Monotony leads to contempt, and time weighs with an almost insufferable heaviness.

Human thought dominates time and continuously runs back to the past and forward to the future leaping over any interval; but he who works is subject to time in the same way as inert matter, which moves from one second to the next. It is in this way above all that work does violence to human nature. That is why the workers voice their suffering with the expression 'the hours drag by'.

Consenting to death, when death is present and seen in its nakedness, is an ultimate, instantaneous wrenching away from what each of us calls 'me'. Consenting to work is less violent. But what makes it complete, is that it is repeated each new morning throughout someone's life, day after day, and each day it lasts until the evening, and it begins all over again the next day and often goes on until death. Each morning the worker consents to work for that day and for their entire life. They consent, whether they are sad or happy, worried or desperate for fun, tired or bursting with energy.

Immediately after consenting to death, consenting to the law that makes work essential for the preservation of life is the most perfect act of obedience that it is given to man to fulfil.

It follows that the other human activities, command over men, making technical drawings, art, science, philosophy, and so on, are all inferior to physical work in terms of spiritual significance.

It is easy to define the place that physical work should occupy in a well-ordered social life. It should be its spiritual centre. Political, economic and technical organization, organization, the life of thought should before all else [. . .].[183]

Notes

1 For elaboration and examples of this claim see Simone Weil, 'What is Sacred in Every Human Being?', trans. Eric O. Springsted and Lawrence E. Schmidt, in *Simone Weil: Late Philosophical Writings*: Notre Dame: University of Notre Dame Press, 2015.

2 In moral and legal philosophy, positive rights are distinguished from negative rights on the grounds that they oblige action (positive rights) or inaction (negative rights). Positive rights give the right holder a claim against another person or government for some good, treatment, or service. Negative rights restrict persons or states by prohibiting actions towards the right holder.

3 Extract from *The Book of The Dead*, chapter 125.

4 Matthew 25:35.

5 The phrase 'needs of the soul' (*besoins de l'âme*) appears in Weil's work on syndicalism in the late 1930s. See the 1938 text À propos du syndicalisme 'unique, apolitique, obligatoire' (février–mars, 1938) (OC II 3, pp. 273).

6 This idea is also developed in 'Reflections on the Causes of Liberty and Social Oppression' (1934), in Simone Weil, *Oppression and Liberty*, trans. Arthur Wills and John Petrie, London: Routledge, 2001.

7 Here the 'we' concerned is 'the French'.

8 Annam, or Trung Kỳ, is a part of what is now Vietnam and was established in 1883 as a French protectorate. During Weil's time, the term 'Annam' was used to refer to Vietnam and Vietnamese people were known as Annamites.

9 Georges Guynemer (1894–1917) was a French fighter ace with fifty-four victories during the First World War.

10 Jean Mermoz (1901–1936) was a pioneering aviator.

11 'Opinion' (*l'opinion*) is a significant concept in French political philosophy, including that of Jean-Jacques Rousseau. Rousseau claimed

that opinion is a powerful form of social control. If you want to govern a people's actions you must control *l'opinion*, to shape the standards by which they expect their conduct to be judged.

12 See Simone Weil's 1941 essay 'The Responsibilities of Literature' in *Simone Weil: Late Philosophical Writings*.

13 A reference to André Gide's character Lafcadio, the protagonist in *The Vatican Cellars* who pushes someone off a moving train purely to prove he is capable of committing an act without a rational motive – an *acte gratuit*.

14 This is a reference to the Fall of France in 1940 and subsequent debates concerning the role of literature in the conditions of its possibility. See Weil, 'The Responsibilities of Literature'.

15 See Simone Weil, *On the Abolition of Political Parties*, trans. Simon Leys, New York: New York Review of Books, 2013.

16 *The Book of the Dead,* chapter 125.

17 Unusually, in Weil's manuscript this number is in Arabic rather than roman numerals.

18 The passage cited is from Jacques Maritain's, *Les droits de l'homme et la loi naturelle,* New York: Éditions de la Maison Française, 1942. Maritain was an influential Thomist philosopher, widely admired in de Gaulle's government in exile as an interpreter of the natural law tradition and advocate of rights. For more on Weil's disagreement with Maritain, see the introduction to this volume, pp. xi-xiv.

19 Aristotle, *Politics*, I.6.1255.

20 *Gringoire* was a weekly newspaper founded in 1928 by Horace de Carbuccia. It contained political and literary writings, and aligned itself with the extreme right in the mid-1930s. In addition to making strident attacks against the Popular Front (an interwar alliance of left-wing movements in France), its authors included Henri Béraud, Robert Brasillach, and Philippe Henriot. In Weil's *On the Abolition of Political Parties* (trans. Simon Leys, New York: New York Review of Books, 2013) she identifies this periodical (along with *Marie Claire*) as examples of publications with which it is dishonourable to collaborate. Brasillach's collaboration would become the subject of a high-profile post-war trial, discussed by many writers including Simone de Beauvoir in her essay 'An Eye for an Eye' (1946).

21 This is the starting point of 'Part II' in tripartite editions of *The Need for Roots*. See Introduction, p. xvi.

22 The painter Paul Gaugin (1848–1903) wrote a chronicle of his first trip to Tahiti, *Noa-Noa* (1894), in which he denounced

the French colonial administration and missionaries for their destruction of Maohi culture. Alain Gerbault (1893–1941) was a record-setting French navigator who was first to cross the Atlantic alone from East to West and to sail around the globe alone on his ship, the *Firecrest*. His descriptions of French colonialism in the islands of the South Pacific made a deep impression on Simone Weil. She discusses his 1932 work *L'Évangile du soleil: En marge des traversées* (Paris: Éditions Fasquelle, 1932) in 'À propos de la question colonial dans ses rapports avec le destin du peuple français' (1943), available in English as 'The Colonial Question and the Destiny of the French People,' in *Simone Weil on Colonialism: An Ethic of the Other*, ed. and trans. J. P. Little, Oxford: Rowman & Littlefield, 2003.

23 Georges Bernanos was a prominent Catholic author who had served as a soldier in the First World War. He was the recipient of a well-known letter from Simone Weil in which she describes some of her experiences of the Spanish Civil War, responding to his account of the reign of terror he experienced in Majorca in *Les grands cimitières de la lune* (1938). Here, Weil refers to Georges Bernanos, *Lettre aux Anglais*, a text that circulated in France prior to its publication there in 1946. See Georges Bernanos, *Essais et Écrits de combat*, Paris: Gallimard, Bibliothèque de la Pléiade, 1995, volume II, p. 91.

24 See also Weil's 'Is there a Marxist doctrine?', in *Oppression and Liberty*, trans. Arthur Wills and John Petrie, London: Routledge 2001.

25 On Weil's representation of 'the Hebrews' see 'Israel and the Gentiles', *Pensées Sans Ordre Concernant l'Amour de Dieu*, Paris: Gallimard, 1962, pp. 47–58.

26 See Weil, 'The Great Beast: Reflections on the Origins of Hitlerism' in *Selected Essays: 1934–1943*, trans. Richard Rees, Oxford: Oxford University Press, 1962. '*Quelques réflexions sur les origines de l'Hitlerisme*' OC II 3, p. 168–219.

27 Here Weil is likely alluding to the beginning of part I of Marx and Engels' *Communist Manifesto*.

28 The Tour de France was a system of training created by the trade guilds in which young workers serving their apprenticeship (*compagnons*) set out on a journey around France. These 'journeymen' travelled from city to city, seeking different employments to learn from a wide range of techniques.

29 See also Simone Weil, 'Reflections on the Causes of Liberty and Social Oppression' and 'Is there a Marxist Doctrine?', in Simone

Weil, *Oppression and Liberty*, trans. Arthur Wills and John Petrie, London: Routledge 2001.

30 The discussion of work, affliction, and suffering in the following paragraphs are illuminated by reading Weil's 'Expérience de la vie d'usine' OC II 2, pp. 289–307; and her 'Factory Journal', in *Formative Writings: 1929–1941*, ed. and trans. Dorothy Tuck McFarland and Wilhelmina Van Ness, Amherst, MA: The University of Massachusetts Press, 1987.

31 In June 1936, the Paris metal industry was struck by a wave of factory occupations, which forced employers to introduce more progressive systems of industrial relations. See M. Torigian, 'The Occupation of the Factories: Paris 1936, Flint 1937', *Comparative Studies in Society and History, 41(2)* (1999): 324–47. Weil discusses this in 'La vie et la grève des ouvrières métallos', OC II 2, p. 356.

32 'Dictatorship of the proletariat' is a term coined by Joseph Weydemeyer and adopted by Marx and Engels.

33 Pius XI, in the papal encyclical *Quadragesimo Anno* (15 May 1931), section 146.

34 In 1934 and 1935, under the French government of Pierre-Étienne Flandin, the Banque de France lost 15% of its reserves. When Pierre Laval took office in 1935 his policies led the franc into a new crisis. He attempted to reduce salaries to mitigate unemployment, but this met with resistance from some unions.

35 An organization founded in 1924 by the Belgian Roman Catholic Joseph Cardijn, with the aim of educating working-class youth, encouraging social activism and responsibility among its members from adolescence to early adulthood. The abbreviation JOC lent them the name 'jocistes'. See Weil, 'À Propos des jocistes', *Cahiers du Sud*, April 1941 (OC IV 1, pp. 412–14).

36 The CGT is a national trade union founded in 1895.

37 Weil is alluding to the Chantiers de la jeunesse, founded in 1940 by the Vichy government, and to the Compagnons de France, created by Henry Dhavernas in 1940 and ended in 1944 by the Vichy regime.

38 In Homer's *Iliad* Niobe, queen of Phrygia, is so proud of her dozen children that she compares herself to Leto, the mother of Artemis and Apollo. These twin deities then kill all of her children. See *Iliad*, XXIV, pp. 602–13 and also Weil's 'The Iliad, or the Poem of Force', trans. Mary McCarthy, *Politics*, November 1945, pp. 321–30.

39 Pascal, *Pensées*, L424. Because the manuscript for Pascal's *Pensées* was left unfinished, different editions have proliferated with

different numbering for the fragments. Louis Lafuma respects the provisional classification suggested by the order of MS copies, so in references to the *Pensées* I have provided the Lafuma fragment number.

40 The Collection Budé is an editorial collection of Greek and Latin classical texts, up to the middle of the 6th century (ending with the Emperor Justinian). The nearest equivalent in English is the Loeb Classical Library, but in addition to a facing-page French translation Budé volumes include extensive critical apparatus: introductions, notes, and in some cases detailed commentary.

41 The Compagnons de France was a youth movement created in 1940 by Henry Dhavernas. See above, note 37.

42 In English in the French text.

43 *Confidence* and *Marie Claire* were popular illustrated women's weeklies. The publication of *Confidences* was stopped by Vichy in 1940. *Marie Claire* was among the publications Weil classified as dishonourable. See note 20.

44 In English in the French text.

45 See note 34.

46 A reference to La Fontaine's fable, 'The Cobbler and The Financier', which is based on a story from Horace. See Horace, Macecenas, in *Horace: Satires, Epistles, Ars Poetica*, Loeb edition, London 1942, I.7, 45–95.

47 See note 28.

48 'The French system', also known as Regulationism, was a system of state-controlled prostitution introduced at the beginning of the nineteenth century. State regulated brothels (called '*maisons de tolerance*' or '*maisons closes*') opened in Paris and other major cities throughout the century. They were controlled by a *police des mœurs* (literally 'police of morals'), created for this purpose. Women working in them were required to register with these police and to have bi-weekly examinations for syphilis. The unregistered were subject to arrest and incarceration. Regulationism was attacked by abolitionists from the middle of the nineteenth century onwards; the Republican values of liberty, equality, and fraternity were not extended to prostitutes and the *police des mœurs* were widely suspected of abusing their state power – and many women. During the First World War Regulationism was perpetuated through the creation of military brothels. After the Second World War it was abolished in metropolitan France in 1946, although it remained in force in many colonial contexts.

49 Nicolas-Edme Restif de La Bretonne (1734–1806) was a writer
    whose novels describe the sordid side of eighteenth-century
    French life. Weil requested two of his works from her parents in
    a letter from April 1937: *Le Paysan perverti ou Les Dangers de
    la ville* (1775) and *La Paysanne pervertie* (1784).

50 Pier the Ploughman in the French text.

51 The International Exhibition of Art and Technology in Modern
    Life (Exposition Internationale des Arts et Techniques dans la
    Vie Moderne) was held in Paris from 25 May to 25 November
    1937.

52 Possibly a reference to France's programme of state seculariza-
    tion in the nineteenth and early twentieth centuries (see
    Introduction, p. xx) or more specifically to Victor Cousin's edu-
    cational reform or the 1930s debates about the possibility of a
    'Christian philosophy'.

53 Saint-Sulpice is the name of a significant church in Paris, and of
    a seminary founded nearby by its pastor Jean-Jacques Olier, a
    priest of the French School of Spirituality who also established
    the Sulpicians. Historically, the seminary was a renowned centre
    of ecclesiastical education. Here Weil's implication seems to be
    that Sulpician religion is not 'authentic Christianity'.

54 Jacques Chevalier (1882–1963) was Secretary of State for Public
    Instruction (Minister of Education) in Pétain's government from
    September 1940 to February 1941. In December 1940 it was
    announced that state schools must teach their pupils 'duties
    towards God'. See Jacques Duquesne, *Les Catholiques français
    sous l'Occupation*, Paris: Grasset, 1966, p. 88.

55 John 12:24; see three synoptic versions in Matthew 13:3–9,
    Mark 4:3–9, Luke 8:4–8; Matthew 13:31–2; Mark 4:30–32;
    Luke 13:18–19.

56 The concept of 'attention' is central to Weil's thought. In 'Reflec-
    tions on the Right Use of School Studies' she offers the following
    description: 'Attention consists of suspending our thought, leav-
    ing it detached [*disponible*], empty [*vide*], and ready to be
    penetrated by the object; it means holding in our minds, within
    the reach of this thought, but on the lower level and not in con-
    tact with it, the diverse knowledge we have acquired which we
    are forced to make use of. ... Above all our thought should be
    empty [*vide*], waiting [*en attente*], not seeking anything [*ne rien
    chercher*], but ready to receive in its naked truth the object that
    is to penetrate it.' See 'Reflections on the Right use of School
    Studies with a View to the Love of God' (1942) in *Waiting for*

God, trans. Emma Craufurd, New York: HarperCollins, 2009, pp. 57–65, here p. 62. 'Réflexion sur le bon usage des études scolaires en vue de l'amour de Dieu', OC IV 1, pp. 255–63.

57 In Weil's MS this heading is written in the margins; there is no paragraph space separating the following material from the preceding paragraph.

58 Here Weil may have had in mind the words of historian Alphonse Aulard (1849–1928) who, disappointed by the Republic of the 1880s, exclaimed '*Ah! Que la République était belle sous l'Empire!*'

59 Joseph Ernest Renan (1823–1892) was a French scholar of Semitic languages and civilizations, biblical critic, and historian of religion. He is best known for his influential and pioneering historical works on the historical Jesus (*The Life of Jesus*, 1863), and his political views on nationalism and national identity. Here Weil is referring to '*Qu'est-ce qu'une nation?*' ('What Is a Nation?'), a well-known lecture given at the Sorbonne in 1882.

60 Charles-Louis de Secondat, Baron de La Brède et de Montesquieu (1689–1755) was a French political philosopher whose principal work, *The Spirit of Laws*, was a major contribution to political theory. Among other things, his arguments for the separation of powers (that is, that different bodies should exercise executive, legislative, and judicial powers) had a lasting influence on liberal political theory and the development of the constitution of the Unites States of America.

61 William Shakespeare, *Richard II*, 2.1.

62 See note 23.

63 Jean-Henri Merle d'Aubigné (1794–1872) was a Swiss Protestant minister born into a Huguenot family. He became one of the most popular ecclesiastical historians of the nineteenth century.

64 The Albigensians were members of the heretical Catharistic sect, in Southern France. Their name derives from the city in France where they flourished, Albi. Cathars rejected the teaching of Roman Catholicism and claimed to be the one true Christianity: their name (derived from Greek) means 'pure ones'. Their beliefs are often classified as Gnostic: they taught a dualism of good (spirit) and evil (matter).

65 The Sicilian Vespers was a successful rebellion on the island of Sicily that broke out at Easter 1282 against the rule of the French-born King Charles I, who had ruled the Kingdom of

Sicily since 1266. Within six weeks, approximately 13,000 French men and women were slain by the rebels, and the government of King Charles lost control of the island. It was the beginning of the War of the Sicilian Vespers.

66 Pascal Paoli (1725–1807) was a Corsican patriot and leader of the resistance against the Genoese and the French on the island.

67 See note 49.

68 Raised as a Huguenot, Théophile de Viau participated in the Protestant wars in Guyenne from 1615–16 before becoming a poet. Jean François Paul de Gondi, the Cardinal de Retz, was the first archbishop of Paris. In addition to being a man of the church he was a leader in the aristocratic rebellion known as the Fronde (1648–53) and wrote his memoirs that became a classic of seventeenth-century French literature. In 'The Great Beast' Weil discusses Aubigné, Théophile, and Retz in a list of French writers who were 'neither servants nor adorers of force'. See 'Quelques réflexions sur les origines de l'hitlérisme' OC II 3, p. 213. See 'The Great Beast: Reflections on the Origins of Hitlerism' in *Selected Essays: 1934–1943*, trans. Richard Rees, Oxford: Oxford University Press, 1962.

69 Charles-Maurice de Talleyrand-Périgord (1754–1838) was a controversial French statesman and diplomat. His political survival throughout, and during the transitions between, the regimes of the French Revolution, Napoleon, the restoration of the Bourbon monarchy, and King Louis-Philippe has divided historians as to whether he was a wily opportunist or a true patriot.

70 See note 8.

71 Although Weil does not present it as such, this is almost a direct quotation from Richelieu's *Memoirs*. He writes, 'Le salut des hommes s'opère définitivement en l'autre monde [. . .]; mais les États n'ont point de subsistence après ce monde, leur salut est present ou nul' (*Mémoires*, Société d'Histoire de la France, 1927–1931, vol. IX, p. 34). See also Weil's discussion of the role of Richelieu in French history in 'The Great Beast'.

72 Charles-Marie-Photius Maurras (1868–1952) was a French writer and politician who founded *Action Française*, a far-right monarchist movement with an associated journal of the same name. Like the movement, which he created in 1894 in the context of the Dreyfus affair, Maurras is known for being anti-Semitic, anti-parliamentarist, and counter-revolutionary.

73 Matthew 4:8–10; Luke 4:5–8.

74 Pierre Corneille (1606–84), author of poetry and drama known for his French classical tragedy. During his lifetime, under Richelieu, patronage of the arts increasingly came under monarchy control.

75 See note 68.

76 Henri de Saint-Simon (1760–1825) was a political and economic theorist and founder of Saint-Simonianism. Jean de la Bruyère (1645–96) was a philosopher and moralist remembered especially for his satire. Liselotte (otherwise known as Elisabeth-Charlotte Duchess of Orleans (1676–1744)) was a prolific correspondent from the Court of Versailles. Weil takes the testimony of all of these writers as 'a testament to the life human beings actually lived'.

77 Reference to Roland's horse in the epic poem, 'La Chanson de Roland'. It was an excellent horse in every way, but its only defect was that it was dead.

78 George Sand (1804–76) was the pen name of socialist novelist and memoirist Amantine Lucile Aurore Dupin. Here Weil is referring to the work Promenade dans le Berry: Mœurs, coutumes, légendes.

79 Joseph Fouché (1759–1820), the Duke of Otranto, was a French statesman remembered particularly for the harsh suppression of the Lyon insurrection of 1793, his role in the 18th Brumaire, and for serving as Minister of the Police from 1799 through the transitions the Directory, the Consulate, and the Empire.

80 Guignol is a form of puppet theatre dating from the eighteenth century. It was created by a worker in the silk trade after that industry was disrupted by the Revolution, and named after its protagonist, Guignol, a silkweaver. It is widely considered children's entertainment but contains satire and social commentary that amuses adults.

81 Weil may have in mind here a passage from article 427 of the Treaty of Versailles: 'that labour should not be regarded merely as a commodity or article of commerce'.

82 Lucien Lévy-Bruhl (1857–1939), was a French anthropologist who believed he had discovered a 'primitive' or 'pre-logical' mentality in his study of the psychology of 'primitive' peoples. He published several books on this topic, including The Primitive Mentality (La Mentalité primitive, 1922).

83 Encyclopaedists is the name given to the group of French Enlightenment philosophers and men of letters who collaborated in the production of the famous Encyclopédie. The work was planned

by Denis Diderot and was announced as a *Dictionnaire raisonné des sciences, des arts, et des métiers* – it was intended to provide a comprehensive alphabetical resource covering all human knowledge from an Enlightenment point of view.

84 'Let him be anathema' or, in the conciliar period, 'excommunicated'. It is found in Greek in the writings of Paul (Galatians 1:8–9), and was used subsequently in the councils of the Early Church.

85 In the French text Weil inverts Stephen Decatur's saying, often cited out of context, as: 'right or wrong my country'.

86 Matthew 6:19–21.

87 This is likely to be a reference to the Pastoral Letter of German Bishops drafted at the Fulda Conference on 26 June 1941 in response to the 'restrictions and limitations' the Nazi government imposed on the practices and teaching of the Church. It was a plea to be read in all pulpits on 6 July of that year: 'Dear Members of the dioceses: We Bishops [...] feel great sorrow about the existence of powers working to dissolve the blessed union between Christ and the German people [...] [T]he existence of Christianity in Germany is at stake.'

88 Luke 14:26.

89 Luke 18:19.

90 Charles Eugène de Foucauld (1858–1916) was a French officer, explorer, and priest who was killed in a failed kidnapping attempt in Algeria in 1916. The Second Bureau of the General Staff was the French military intelligence agency founded in 1871; it was dissolved after the armistice in 1940.

91 Luke 4:6.

92 See Adolf Hitler, *Mein Kampf,* translated by Ralph Manheim, Boston: Houghton Mifflin, 1943, chapter 6.

93 See note 71.

94 Plato, *Republic*, VI, 493.

95 *The Book of the Dead*, chapter 125.

96 The French runs together two verses. The first is Philippians 2:6; the second from Hebrews 5:8.

97 Herodotus, *Histories*, IV, 93–4.

98 See p. 89, n. 74.

99 The eponymous protagonist of this tragedy is a Christian convert who would rather be martyred than renounce his faith.

100 Weil paraphrases a line from the socialist Catholic Charles Péguy's (1873–1914) poem 'Eve', a Christian epic containing over 7,600 verses. In French these lines read: '*Heureux ceux qui*

sont morts pour la terre charnelle, / Mais pourvu que ce fût dans une guerre juste.'

101 Vercingetorix (82–46 BCE) was king and chief of the Arverni, a Gallic tribe of the Arverni who rebelled unsuccessfully against Roman rule under Julius Caesar.

102 Alphonse de Lamartine (1790–1869) was a renowned Romantic poet, historian and statesman. Here Weil cites 'La Marseillaise de la paix', an 1841 response Lamartine wrote to 'Rhin allemand' a poem dedicated to him by M. Becker, in which Lamartine denounces militaristic nationalism.

103 John 14:6.

104 See Book III of Rousseau's *Émile*.

105 I John: 4:20.

106 See Pascal's account of *l'esprit géometrique* and its limitations in 'Of the Geometrical Spirit'.

107 See note 35.

108 See note 37.

109 Matthew 23:37 [annotated French text gives the Lucan version: Luke 13:34].

110 See Appian, *Roman History* VIII, 12.81.

111 *Le Rouge et le Noir* (1830) is a psychological novel by Stendhal.

112 *Grandes Écoles* are elite institutions of higher education.

113 See *The Spirit of the Laws*.

114 François Villon (1431–63) is among the best-known French poets of the Middle Ages. Here Weil cites his work 'Le testament'.

115 This is the starting point of 'Part III' in tripartite editions of *The Need for Roots*.

116 See the parable of the ten virgins, Matthew 25:1–13.

117 2 Corinthians 12:9.

118 Charles VI was crowned King at the age of eleven; France was ruled by his uncles as regents until he terminated the regency at the age of twenty-one.

119 The Ems telegram (or Ems dispatch), dated 13 July 1870, reported an encounter between William I of Prussia and the French ambassador to then-chancellor Otto von Bismarck. The next day – Bastille Day – newspapers published a version edited by Bismarck which led to the declaration of the Franco-Prussian War.

120 The National Revolution was the Vichy government's name for its national regeneration programme.

121 Attempts to justify French colonial expansion under the Third
     Republic appealed to the idea that France was undertaking a
     '*mission civilisatrice*' (civilizing mission).

122 Matthew 7:16–18 and 12:33; Luke 6:43–4.

123 Matthew 6:19–21.

124 Matthew 5:48.

125 See Matthew 7:3–5; Luke 6:41–2.

126 Jérôme Carcopino (1881–1970) was a historian known for his
     work on politics, religion, and early Christianity. He was secre-
     tary of State for Education and Youth from February 1941 to
     April 1942.

127 Camille Jullian (1859–1933) taught at the Collège de France and
     was the author of a significant history of Gaul (*Histoire de la
     Gaule*, Paris: Hachette, 1908–1926).

128 In this fable the Beasts suffered a plague. A tribunal was con-
     vened by the Lion, who claimed that the plague was punishment
     from the Gods and that they should judge among them which
     beast was the most evil, and therefore to be sacrificed to appease
     the gods. The Ass, who did little wrong, was condemned and
     eaten.

129 The Institut Catholique is a Catholic centre of higher education
     in Paris.

130 Lucius Cornelius Sulla (138–79 BCE) was a Roman general
     who won the civil war of 88–82 BCE, after which he became
     dictator. He was the first man of the Republic to take power by
     force.

131 See Marcus Aurelius, *Meditations*, IX, 29.

132 Ludovico Ariosto (1474–1533), Italian Renaissance poet known
     for his epic poem *Orlando furioso* (1516).

133 Étienne de La Boétie (1530–63) was a French jurist and
     political philosopher whose works include the *Discourse on
     Voluntary Servitude*. Weil discusses him in the 'Meditation on
     Obedience and Liberty' fragment in *Oppression and Liberty*,
     p. 133ff.

134 Matthew 7:17. This is the second time Weil cites this verse (see
     note 122).

135 The Palais de la Découverte is a science museum in the Grand
     Palais, built in 1937 for the international exhibition on Art and
     Technology in Modern Life. See p. 183.

136 Félix-Alexandre Le Dantec (1869–1917), biologist and philoso-
     pher of science whose views were atheist, materialist, and
     determinist.

137 The Bonnot Gang was a criminal anarchist group operating in France and Belgium in the Belle Époque (1911 to 1912). 'Raymond la Science' was the nickname given to one of its members, Raymond Callemin.

138 Adolf Hitler, *Mein Kampf*, trans. James Murphy, 1939, p. 205 at https://greatwar.nl/books/meinkampf/meinkampf.pdf

139 Fyodor Dostoevsky, letter of 1854 to Natalya Fonvizina, *Pol'noe sobranie sochinenii*, 30 vols., Leningrad: Nauka, 1972–1990, 28.2: 176. The text is often quoted in English, e.g. in Rowan Williams, *Dostoevsky*, London: Continuum, 2008, p. 15.

140 John 14:6; 6:31 and 53–6.

141 The term *élan vital* is a significant concept in the work of Henri Bergson, who coined it in *Creative Evolution* (1907). It also features in his later work on religion, *The Two Sources of Morality and Religion* (1932), where he outlines the conception of mysticism with which Weil disagrees here.

142 Pascal's wager is the name given to an argument by Blaise Pascal in the *Pensées* (L418). In it, Pascal does not seek to provide a demonstration of God's existence – it is not a proof – but rather offers prudential reasons, on the balance of possible gains and losses, that belief in the existence of God is 'the best bet'.

143 Harpagon is the miser in Molière's *The Miser*; Grandet is the miser in Balzac's *Eugénie Grandet*.

144 *Dr Williams' Pink Pills for Pale People* were marketed in the late nineteenth and early twentieth centuries as treatments for fatigue and anaemia.

145 Johann Carl Friedrich Gauss (1777–1855) was an influential German mathematician and physicist.

146 Jean Racine, *Athaliah*, Act I Scene 2, trans. J. Donkersley, A. Gombert's Edition 1825, reprinted Espros Classics, 2023.

147 Lao Tzu, ancient Chinese philosopher and poet, was the founder of Taoism and the author of best *Tao Te Ching* (here Weil refers to chapter 73 of that work).

148 Weil's works often employ the term '*attente*' instead of '*patience*'. In *Waiting for God*, she discusses her preference for '*attente*' as an 'attitude that operates salvation'. See Simone Weil, *Attente de Dieu*, Paris: Fayard, 1966, p. 193. And in English, see especially the essays 'Reflections on the Right Use of School Studies with a View to the Love of God' and 'Forms of the Implicit Love of God' in *Waiting for God*, trans. Emma Craufurd, London: Harper Perennial, 2009.

149 John 12:47–8.

150 Matthew 20:1–16.

151 1 Corinthians 13:12.

152 Luke 14:11.

153 Possibly an allusion to the sixth-century hymn *Vexilla Regis prodeunt*.

154 Weil's text contains an erroneous citation here to Matthew 3:22; the correct verse has been inserted in her parentheses.

155 See Lucian, *Philopseudes*, 14.26.

156 John 15:24, 22.

157 John 10:32. The French biblical quote is different from the English 'good works'. In French it is 'belles actions' (beautiful actions), echoed below in Weil's assertion that 'there can be no other proof than beauty'.

158 John 20:29.

159 Matthew 6:26, 28; 10:29.

160 The eleventh-century Castilian knight El Cid is a celebrated national hero of Spain and the subject of the Medieval epic poem *El Cantar de mio Cid*.

161 Lope de Vega, *The Star of Seville,* trans. Philip M. Hayden, in *The Chief European Dramatists*, ed. Brander Matthews, Boston: Houghton Mifflin, 1916, p. 191.

162 Thomas Edward Lawrence (1888–1935), called Lawrence of Arabia, was a British archaeologist, military officer, and writer of *The Seven Pillars of Wisdom*, a work Weil admired.

163 Revelation 13:10.

164 See Maritain, *Les Droits de l'homme et la loi naturelle,* 1942, in *Christianisme et démocratie* followed by *Droits de l'homme*, Paris: Desclée de Brouwer, 2005, p. 171.

165 Jacques-Henri Bernardin de Saint-Pierre (1737–1814) was a botanist and writer best known for his 1788 novel *Paul et Virginie*. He believed that nature was anthropocentrically designed. Here Weil is likely to be referring to this passage from his *Études de la nature*: 'Il n'y a pas moins de convenance dans les formes et les grosseurs des fruits. Il y en a beaucoup qui sont taillés pour la bouche de l'homme, comme les cerises et les prunes; d'autres pour sa main, comme les poires et les pommes; d'autres beaucoup plus gros comme les melons, sont divisés par côtes et semblent destinés à être mangés en famille: il y en a même aux Indes, comme le jacq, et chez nous, la citrouille qu'on pourrait partager avec ses voisins. La nature paraît avoir suivi les mêmes proportions dans les diverses grosseurs des fruits destinés à nourrir l'homme, que dans la grandeur des feuilles qui devaient lui

donner de l'ombre dans les pays chauds; car elle y en a taillé pour abriter une seule personne, une famille entière, et tous les habitants du même hameau.' See *Études de la nature*, ch. XI, sec. *Harmonies végétales des plantes avec l'homme*, 1784.

166 Jacques-Bénigne Lignel Bossuet (1627–1704) was a renowned bishop and theologian. He was preacher to Louis XIV, a skilful orator and stylist, and an advocate of the divine right of kings.

167 *Explication française* is an exercise in textual analysis placed on the *lycée* curriculum in France by Victor Cousin's educational reforms in 1840. It involves analysis of the text's language, meaning, derivation, and relation to other texts.

168 Genesis 21:19.

169 Hitler, *Mein Kampf*, quoted by Alain Supiot, *Homo Juridicus*, Verso, 2007, p. 56. No reference in the French.

170 Weil has freely adapted the text of the *Bṛhad āraṇyaka Upaniṣad* I, 4, 11–14, translated by Émile Sénart (Paris: Les Belles Lettres, 1934). She replaces 'Brahma' with God and 'dharma' with justice.

171 *Bṛhad āraṇyaka Upaniṣad* I, 5, 23.

172 Anaximander (610 BC–*c.*546 BC) was a pre-Socratic philosopher who succeeded Thales as the head of the Milesian school. He was interested in investigating the origin or establishing principle of things and was the first philosopher to use the term ἀρχή (arche) to refer to the object of this search. Here Weil cites the *Fragments*. See *Les Présocratiques*, Paris: Gallimard, 'Bibliothèque de la Pléiade', 1988, p. 39.

173 Genesis 9:14,15.

174 Psalm 104 : 9. 'They' – the waters. English Bible translations not the same as French.

175 Plato, *Timaeus*, 48 a.

176 Cleanthes, *Hymn to Zeus*, verses 7–10. Cleanthes succeeded Zeno of Citium as the head of the Stoic school in Athens, trans. Stephen Hanselman, dailystoic.com/cleanthespoem/.

177 Penicillin was discovered by Alexander Fleming in 1928. The purified compound was isolated at the University of Oxford in 1940 and it was produced in sufficient quantities to begin human trials in 1941. They were successful enough that the British War Cabinet established a Penicillin Committee in early 1943, leading to mass production.

178 Antoine Lavoisier was the first to observe the Law of Conservation of Mass (or principle of mass) in 1789.

179 See Genesis 3:17–19.
180 See Machiavelli, *Florentine Histories*, Book III, 12–17.
181 Peter Abelard (1079–1142) was a Scholastic condemned at the council of Soissons in 1121 and again under the influence of Bernard of Clairvaux at the Council of Sens in 1140. He was a pre-eminent philosopher and logician who was first to use the term 'theology' in its modern sense and argued that reason should be used in matters of faith.
182 Hebrews 5:8–9 (slightly longer quote needed in English to make sense, as the word order is different in French).
183 This incomplete sentence is in Weil's MS and in ELN, but not in other editions.

Index